CHELSEA HOUSE PUBLISHERS

Modern Critical Views

Further titles in preparation.

Modern Critical Views

ROBERT PENN WARREN

Modern Critical Views

ROBERT PENN WARREN

Edited with an introduction by

Harold Bloom

Sterling Professor of the Humanities
Yale University

1986
CHELSEA HOUSE PUBLISHERS
New York
New Haven   Philadelphia

PROJECT EDITORS: Emily Bestler, James Uebbing
ASSOCIATE EDITOR: Maria Behan
EDITORIAL COORDINATOR: Karyn Gullen Browne
EDITORIAL STAFF: Laura Ludwig, Linda Grossman, Perry King
DESIGN: Susan Lusk

Cover illustration by Paul Henry

Library of Congress Cataloging in Publication Data

Robert Penn Warren.
    (Modern critical views)
    Bibliography: p.
    Includes index.
    1. Warren, Robert Penn, 1905–   —Criticism and interpretation—Addresses, essays, lectures.
I. Bloom, Harold. II. Series.
PS3545.A748Z858 1986   813'.52   85–21324
ISBN 0–87754–662–2

Chelsea House Publishers
Harold Steinberg, Chairman and Publisher
Susan Lusk, Vice President
A Division of Chelsea House Educational Communications, Inc.
133 Christopher Street, New York, NY 10014

Contents

Editor's Note

This volume brings together a representative selection of the best criticism so far devoted to the varied literary achievements of Robert Penn Warren, arranged in the chronological order of publication. The "Introduction" centers upon Warren's most recent poetry, in his fifth *Selected Poems*, while reflecting also upon his demanding moral stance.

I have begun the chronological sequence by juxtaposing three very varied overviews of Warren's work. W. M. Frohock emphasizes what he considers fundamental limitations in Warren's fiction, a view totally rejected by Cleanth Brooks in his passionate analysis. In some sense, the essay by Joseph Frank can be judged to mediate between these oppositions, as Frank attempts to balance Warren's own antithetical drives towards romanticism and realism.

The next sequence centers upon Warren's major novels, starting with two contrasting readings of *All the King's Men* by Jonathan Baumbach and Arthur Mizener. These are followed by Walter Sullivan on *Band of Angels*, Allen Shepherd on *At Heaven's Gate*, and Richard Law on *Night Rider*, a touch later in the chronological sequence of published criticism. Since all of these essays consider Warren's relation to history, I have accompanied them by Daniel Aaron's sensitive account of Warren's meditations upon history.

The final sequence of essays concentrates upon Warren's major achievement, his later poetry, with some related consideration of his criticism and fiction. Richard Howard, perhaps our most prescient critical reviewer of contemporary poetry, introduces Warren's characteristic mode. This is followed by the editor's brief account of the revised *Brother to Dragons*, and by David Wyatt's overview of Warren's work, with an emphasis upon the critic as artist. After T. R. Hummer's reading of the poetic sequence *Audubon*, the main body of Warren's later poetry receives three very different analyses by Calvin Bedient, the editor and Paul Mariani. Now in 1985, Warren's poetry remains ongoing, and we can hope that our criticism of him will learn increasingly the true mode of response that his authentic aesthetic dignity deserves. John Burt's profound essay on *World Enough and Time*, which concludes this volume, can be regarded as a prelude to that criticism of the future.

Introduction

I

Robert Penn Warren, born April 24, 1905, in Guthrie, Kentucky, at the age of eighty is our most eminent man of letters. That truism is vitalized by his extraordinary persistence of development into a great poet. A reader thinks of the handful of poets triumphant in their later or last phases: Browning, Hardy, Yeats, Stevens, Warren. Indeed, "Myth of Mountain Sunrise," the final poem among the new work in the fifth Warren *Selected Poems*, will remind some readers of Browning's marvelous "Prologue" to *Asolando*, written when the poet was seventy-seven. Thinking back fifty years to the first time he saw Asolo (a village near Venice), Browning burns through every sense of loss into a final transcendence:

> How many a year, my Asolo,
> Since—one step just from sea to land—
> I found you, loved yet feared you so—
> For natural objects seemed to stand
> Palpably fire-clothed! No—

"God is it who transcends," Browning ends by asserting. Warren, older even than Browning, ruggedly remains the poet of immanence, of something indwelling and pervasive, though not necessarily sustaining, that can be sensed in a mountain sunrise:

> The curdling agony of interred dark strives dayward, in stone
>   strives though
> No light here enters, has ever entered but
> In ageless age of primal flame. But look! All mountains want slow-
> ly to bulge outward extremely. The leaf, whetted on light, will cut
> Air like butter. Leaf cries: "I feel my deepest filament in dark rejoice.
> I know the density of basalt has a voice."

Two primal flames, Browning's and Warren's, but at the close of "Myth of Mountain Sunrise" we receive not "God is it who transcends," but: "The sun blazes over the peak. That will be the old tale told." The epigraph to the new section of this *Selected Poems* is from Warren's favorite theologian, St. Augustine: "Will ye not now after that life is descended down to you, will not you ascend up to it and live?" One remembers another epigraph Warren took from the *Confessions,* for the book of poems *Being Here* (1980): "I thirst to know the power and nature of time." Warren now has that knowledge, and his recent poems show him ascending up to living in the present, in the real presence of time's cumulative power. Perhaps no single new poem here quite matches the extraordinary group of visions and meditations by Warren that includes "Red-Tail Hawk and Pyre of Youth," "Heart of Autumn," "Evening Hawk," "Birth of Love," "The Leaf," "Mortmain," "To a Little Girl, One Year Old, in a Ruined Fortress" and so many more. But the combined strength of the eighty-five pages of new poems that Warren aptly calls *Altitudes and Extensions* is remarkable, and indeed extends the altitudes at which our last poet of the Sublime continues to live, move and have his being.

II

Warren's first book was *John Brown: The Making of a Martyr* (1929). I have just read it, for the first time, and discovered, without surprise, that it made me very unhappy. The book purports to be history, but is Southern fiction of Allen Tate's ideology, and portrays Brown as a murderous nihilist, fit hero for Ralph Waldo Emerson. Indeed I find it difficult to decide, after suffering the book, whether the young Warren loathed Brown or Emerson more. Evidently, both Brown and his intellectual supporter seemed, to Warren, instances of an emptiness making ruthless and passionate attempts to prove itself a fullness. But *John Brown,* if read as a first fiction, does presage the Warren of *Night Rider* (1939), his first published novel, which I have just re-read with great pleasure.

Night Rider is an exciting and remorseless narrative, wholly characteristic of what were to be Warren's prime virtues as a novelist: good story-telling and intensely dramatic unfolding of the moral character of his doom-eager men and women. Mr. Munn, upon whom *Night Rider* centers, is as splendidly unsympathetic as the true Warren heroes continued to be: Jerry Calhoun and Slim Sarrett in *At Heaven's Gate* (1943), Jack Burden and Willie Stark in *All the King's Men* (1946), Jeremiah Beaumont and Cassius Fort in *World Enough and Time* (1950). When Warren's crucial personages turned more amiable, starting with poor Amanda Starr in *Band of Angels* (1955), the books alas turned much less interesting. This unfortunate phenomenon culminated in Warren's last novel (so far), *A Place to Come To* (1977), which Warren himself ranks with *All the King's Men* and *World Enough and Time.* I wish I could agree, but re-reading *A Place to*

Come To confirms an earlier impression that Warren likes his hero, Jed Tewksbury, rather too much. Without some real moral distaste to goad him, Warren tends to lose his narrative drive. I find myself wishing that Tewksbury had in him a touch of what might be called Original John Brown.

Warren's true precursor, as a novelist, was not Faulkner but Conrad, the dominant influence upon so many of the significant American novelists of Warren's generation. In one of his best critical essays, written in 1951 on Conrad's *Nostromo*, Warren gave an unknowing clue as to why all his own best work, as a novelist, already was over:

> There is another discrepancy, or apparent discrepancy, that we must confront in any serious consideration of Conrad—that between his professions of skepticism and his professions of faith . . .
>
> Cold unconcern, an "attitude of perfect indifference" is, as he says in the letter to Galsworthy, "the part of creative power." But this is the same Conrad who speaks of Fidelity and the human communion, and who makes Kurtz cry out in the last horror and Heyst come to his vision of meaning in life. And this is the same Conrad who makes Marlow of "Heart of Darkness" say that what redeems is the "idea only" . . .
>
> It is not some, but all, men who must serve the "idea." The lowest and the most vile creature must, in some way, idealize his existence in order to exist, and must find sanctions outside himself . . .

Warren calls this a reading of Conrad's dual temperament, skepticism struggling with a last-ditch idealism, and remarks, much in T.S. Eliot's spirit:

> We must sometimes force ourselves to remember that the act of creation is not simply a projection of temperament, but a criticism and a purging of temperament.

This New Critical shibboleth becomes wholly Eliotic if we substitute the word "personality" for the word "temperament." As an analysis of Conrad's dramatism in his best novels, and in *Nostromo* in particular, this has distinction, but Warren is not Conrad, and like his poetic and critical precursor, Eliot, Warren creates by projecting temperament, not by purging it. There is no "cold unconcern," no "attitude of perfect indifference," no escape from personality in Eliot, and even more nakedly Warren's novels and poems continually reveal his passions, prejudices, convictions. Conrad is majestically enigmatic, beyond ideology; Warren, like Eliot, is an ideologue, and his temperament is far more ferocious than Eliot's.

What Warren accurately praises in Conrad is not to be found in Warren's own novels, with the single exception of *All the King's Men*, which does balance skepticism against belief just adroitly enough to ward off Warren's moralism. *World Enough and Time*, Warren's last stand as a major novelist, is an exuberant work marred finally by the author's singular fury at his own creatures. As a person who forgives himself nothing, Warren abandons the Conradian skepticism and proceeds to forgive his hero and heroine nothing. Re-reading *World Enough and Time*, I wince repeatedly at what the novelist inflicts upon Jeremiah Beaumont and Rachel Jordan. Warren, rather like the Gnostics' parody of Jehovah, punishes *his* Adam and Eve by denying them honorable or romantic deaths. Their joint suicide drug turns into an emetic, and every kind of degradation subsequently is heaped upon them. Warren, a superb ironist, nevertheless so loves the world that he will forgive it nothing, a stance more pragmatically available to a poet than to a novelist.

III

Warren's poetry began in the Modernist revival of the Metaphysical mode, as a kind of blend of Eliot's *The Waste Land* with the gentler ironies of Warren's own teacher at Vanderbilt, John Crowe Ransom. This phase of the poetry took Warren up to 1943, and then came to an impasse and, for a decade, an absolute stop. *At Heaven's Gate, All the King's Men* and *World Enough and Time* belong to that silent poetic decade, and perhaps the major sequence of his fiction usurped Warren's greater gift. But he was certainly unhappy in the later stages of his first marriage, which ended in divorce in 1950, and it cannot be accidental that his poetry fully resumed in the late summer of 1954, two years after his marriage to the writer Eleanor Clark, and a year after the birth of his daughter, the accomplished poet Rosanna Warren.

The book-length poem, *Brother to Dragons* (1953, revised version 1979), formally began Warren's return to verse, and is undoubtedly a work of considerable dramatic power. I confess to admiring it only reluctantly and dubiously, ever since 1953, because its ideological ferocity is unsurpassed even elsewhere in Warren. Much improved in revision, it remains unnerving, particularly if the reader, like myself, longs to follow Emerson in forgiving himself, if not everything, then at least as much as possible. But Warren—unlike Emerson, Nietzsche, Yeats—does not wish us to cast out remorse. Like his then master Eliot, though in a more secular way, Warren was by no means reluctant to remind us that we *are* Original Sin. *Brother to Dragons* is rendered no weaker by its extraordinary tendentiousness, but is not necessarily persuasive, if you happen not to share its moral convictions.

Warren's shorter poems, his lyrics and meditations, evolved impressively through three subsequent volumes: *Promises* (1957), *You, Emperors and Others* (1960) and a *Selected Poems* (1966), where the new work was grouped as *Tale of Time*. I recall purchasing these volumes, reading them with grudging respect, and concluding that Warren was turning into a poet rather like Melville (whom he was to edit in a *Selected Poems of Herman Melville*, in 1970) or the earlier Hardy. Warren's poems of 1934 through 1966 seemed interestingly ungainly in form, highly individual in genre and rhetoric, and not fundamentally a departure from Eliot's High Modernist mode. A poetry of belief, I would have judged, rather dismissively, and not of overwhelming concern if a reader was devoted to Hart Crane and Wallace Stevens, and to contemporary volumes such as Elizabeth Bishop's *Questions of Travel* (1965) and John Ashbery's *Rivers and Mountains* (1967). I could not foresee the astonishing breakthrough that Warren, already past the age of sixty, was about to accomplish with *Incarnations* (1968) and *Audubon: A Vision* (1969). Other critics of Warren's poetry see more continuity in its development than I do. But in 1968 I was a belated convert, transported against my will by reading *Incarnations*, and able at least to offer the testimony of a very reluctant believer in a poetic greatness now become indisputable and maintained by Warren throughout these nearly two decades since he began to write the poems of *Incarnations* in 1966.

IV

Incarnations opens with a closely connected sequence of fifteen poems called *Island of Summer*, which is the volume's glory. Unfortunately, Warren has included only five of these in his new *Selected Poems*, but they are the best of a strong group, and I will discuss only those five here, since Warren subtly has created a new sequence or a condensed *Island of Summer*. Like the original work, the sequence is a drama of poetic incarnation, or the death and rebirth of Warren's poethood. In what is now the opening meditation, "Where the Slow Fig's Purple Sloth," Warren associates the fig with fallen human consciousness and so with an awareness of mortality:

> When you
> Split the fig, you will see
> Lifting from the coarse and purple seed, its
> Flesh like flame, purer
> Than blood.

It fills
The darkening room with light.

This hard, substantive riddling style is now pure Warren, and has very little in common with the Eliotic evocations of his earlier verse. "Riddle in the Garden" even more oddly associates fruits, peach and plum, with negative human yearnings, suicidal and painful, and with a horror of inwardness. A violent confrontation, "The Red Mullet," juxtaposes the swimming poet and the great fish, eye to eye, in a scene where "vision is armor, he sees and does not/Forgive." In a subsequent vision of "Masts of Dawn," the optical effect of how "The masts go white slow, as light, like dew, from darkness/Condensed on them" leads to what in some other poet might be an epiphany, but here becomes a rather desperate self-admonition, less ironic than it sounds: "We must try/To love so well the world that we may believe, in the end, in God." This reversed Augustinianism preludes an overwhelming conflagration of Warren's poetic powers in the most ambitious poem he has yet written, "The Leaf."

When he was fifteen, Warren was blinded in one eye by a sharp stone playfully thrown by a younger brother, who did not see that Warren was lying down on the other side of a hedge. Only after graduating from Vanderbilt, did Warren get round to having the ruined eye removed and replaced by a glass eye. Until then, the young poet suffered the constant fear of sympathetic blindness in his good eye. There may be some complex relation between that past fear and Warren's most remarkable and prevalent metaphor of redemption, which is to associate poetic vision both with a hawk's vision and with a sunset hawk's flight. This trope has appeared with increasing frequency in Warren's poetry for more than half a century and even invades the novels. So, in A Place to Come To, Jed Tewksbury endures the same vision as he loses consciousness after being stabbed:

> I remember thinking how beautiful, how redemptive, all seemed. It was as though I loved him. I thought how beautifully he had moved, like Ephraim, like a hawk in sunset flight. I thought how all the world was justified in that moment.

"The Leaf" centers itself upon the image of a hawk's redemptive flight, with the difference from earlier Warren being in the nature of the redemption. Opening with a renewed vision of the fig as emblem of human mortality and guilt, and of "the flaming mullet" as an encounter in the depths, the poem proceeds to an episode of shamanistic force:

> Near the nesting place of the hawk, among
> Snag-rock, high on the cliff, I have seen
> The clutter of annual bones, of hare, vole, bird, white

As chalk from sun and season, frail
As the dry grass stem. On that

High place of stone I have lain down, the sun
Beat, the small exacerbation
Of dry bones was what my back, shirtless and bare, knew. I saw

The hawk shudder in the high sky, he shudders
To hold position in the blazing wind, in relation to
The firmament, he shudders and the world is a metaphor, his eye
Sees, white, the flicker of hare-scut, the movement of vole.

Distance is nothing, there is no solution, I
Have opened my mouth to the wind of the world like wine, I wanted
To taste what the world is, wind dried up

The live saliva of my tongue, my tongue
Was like a dry leaf in my mouth.

Nothing in Warren's earlier poetry matches this in dramatic intensity, or in the accents of inevitability, as the poetic character is reincar-
nated in him by his sacrificial self-offering "near the nesting place of the
hawk." Much of Warren's earlier guilt and sorrow comes together here,
with beautiful implicitness: the fear of blindness, the decade of poetic
silence, the failure of the first marriage, and most mysteriously, a personal
guilt at poetic origins. The mystery is partly clarified in the poem's next
movement:

The world is fruitful, In this heat
The plum, black yet bough-bound, bursts, and the gold ooze is,
Of bees, joy, the gold ooze has striven
Outward, it wants again to be of
The goldness of air and—blessedly—innocent. The grape
Weakens at the juncture of the stem. The world

Is fruitful, and I, too,
In that I am the father
Of my father's father's father. I,
Of my father, have set the teeth on edge. But
By what grape? I have cried out in the night.

From a further garden, from the shade of another tree,
My father's voice, in the moment when the cicada ceases, has called to me.

Warren's father had died in 1955, at the age of eighty-six. Robert
Franklin Warren, who wanted above everything to be a poet, became a
banker instead, solely to support not only his own children, but also a
family of young children bequeathed to him by his own father, who had
married again and then died. Reflecting upon all this, Warren has said:

"It's as if I've stolen my father's life," somberly adding: "If he had had the opportunity I did, with his intelligence and energy, he'd have done a lot better than I did."

This is probably part of the sorrow heard in: "I,/Of my father, have set the teeth on edge." Experientially, it would be the larger part, but imaginatively it may yield to the burden of a more strictly poetic inheritance, the Eliotic influence, which Warren almost involuntarily here disavows and surmounts. Eliot's "not the cicada" from *The Waste Land* becomes here the moment when Eliot's presence in Warren's voice ceases, to be replaced by the poetic voice that Robert Franklin Warren had to abandon. The return of the father's voice becomes the blessing of Warren's new style, the gift given by Warren in his father's name. By reversing the Biblical trope from Jeremiah 31: 29–30, in which the children's teeth are set on edge, Warren ironically celebrates the harshness of his new style:

> The voice blesses me for the only
> Gift I have given: *teeth set on edge.*
>
> In the momentary silence of the cicada,
> I can hear the appalling speed,
> In space beyond stars, of
> Light. It is
>
> A sound like wind.

From this poem on, Warren rarely falters, whether in *Audubon: A Vision* or in the half dozen books of shorter poems (or new sections in selected volumes) that have followed. The achievement throughout these books necessarily is mixed, but there are several scores of poems that manifest all the stigmata of permanence.

V

I want to look at just one of these poems, because it raises again, for me and for others, the ancient problem of poetry and belief. The poem is "A Way to Love God" from *Can I See Arcturus From Where I Stand?*, the sheaf of new poems in the *Selected Poems* before the one under review. I quote only the poem's final vision, which is no grislier than the ones preceding it:

> But I had forgotten to mention an upland
> Of wind-tortured stone white in darkness, and tall, but when
> No wind, mist gathers, and once on the Sarré at midnight,
> I watched the sheep huddling. Their eyes

Stared into nothingness. In that mist-diffused light their eyes
Were stupid and round like the eyes of fat fish in muddy water,
Or of a scholar who has lost faith in his calling.

Their jaws did not move. Shreds
Of dry grass, gray in gray mist-light, hung
From the side of a jaw, unmoving.

You would think that nothing would ever again happen.

That may be a way to love God.

By loving God, Warren always appears to mean loving the truth, in all its dreadfulness. This is an ancient polemic in all his work, poetry and prose, and does not beg the questions of truth but rather asserts a necessarily personal conviction as to the truth. Warren, despite the critical efforts of his more pious exegetes, is a skeptic and not a believer, but a Bible-soaked skeptic. His way of loving God is to forgive himself nothing, and to forgive God nothing. The aesthetic consequences of this stance, in a poetry written since 1966, seem to me wholly admirable, while the spiritual grimness involved remains a formidable challenge for many readers, myself among them. Missing from this new *Selected Poems* is a notorious sequence, "Homage to Emerson, On Night Flight to New York," to be found in the *Tale of Time* section of *Selected Poems: 1923–1975*. I don't regret its deletion, but it has a cognitive value in clarifying Warren's lifelong distaste for Emerson. Here is its first part, "His Smile":

Over Peoria we lost the sun:
The earth, by snow like sputum smeared, slides
Westward. Those fields in the last light gleam. Emerson—

The essays, on my lap, lie. A finger
Of light, in our pressurized gloom, strikes down,
Like God, to poke the page, the page glows. There is
No sin. Not even error. Night,

On the glass at my right shoulder, hisses
Like sand from a sand-blast, but
The hiss is a sound that only a dog's
Ear could catch, or the human heart. My heart

Is as abstract as an empty
Coca-Cola bottle. It whistles with speed.
It whines in that ammoniac blast caused by
The passages of stars, for
At 38,000 feet Emerson

Is dead right. His smile
Was sweet as he walked in the greenwood.

> He walked lightly, his toes out, his body
> Swaying in the dappled shade, and
> His smile never withered a violet. He
>
> Did not even know the violet's name, not having
> Been introduced, but he bowed, smiling,
> For he had forgiven God everything, even the violet.
>
> When I was a boy I had a wart on the right forefinger.

The final line is perhaps redundant, since the entire poem vigorously thrashes Emerson for his supposedly deficient sense of fact. Accusing Emerson of an abstract heart is not original with Warren, but I wince properly at the effective anti-transcendentalism of: "At 38,000 feet Emerson/Is dead right." At ground level, I believe Emerson to be dead right also. "His Smile" is a good polemic, and should be admired as such. The vexed issue of poetry and belief rises rather when I re-read a poem like "A Way to Love God," which is a sublime nightmare from my perspective, but a truth from Warren's. A secularized conviction of sin, guilt, and error is an obsessive strand in all of Warren's work, and for him it helps constitute a stance which is more than rhetorical. However, the effect is only to increase his *otherness*, the rich strangeness of a kind of poetic strength wholly different from the best living poets of my own generation: Ashbery, Merrill, Ammons and others, and from their precursor, Stevens.

Ideological ferocity never abandons Warren, but he passionately dramatizes it, and he has developed an idiom for it that is now entirely his own. He would appear to be, as I have intimated elsewhere, a sunset hawk at the end of a great tradition. I doubt that we will ever again have a poet who can authenticate so heroic a stance. He has earned, many times over, his series of self-identifications with aspects of the truth. The second new poem in the *Selected Poems*, "Mortal Limit," is a sonnet celebrating again his great image of the hawk:

> I saw the hawk ride updraft in the sunset over Wyoming.
> It rose from coniferous darkness, past gray jags
> Of mercilessness, past whiteness, into the gloaming
> Of dream-spectral light above the last purity of snow-snags.
>
> There—west—were the Tetons. Snow-peaks would soon be
> In dark profile to break constellations. Beyond what height
> Hangs now the black speck? Beyond what range will gold eyes see
> New ranges rise to mark a last scrawl of light?
>
> Or, having tasted that atmosphere's thinness, does it
> Hang motionless in dying vision before

It knows it will accept the mortal limit.
And swing into the great circular downwardness that will restore

The breath of earth? Of rock? Of rot? Of other such
Items, and the darkness of whatever dream we clutch?

So long as he abides, there will be someone capable of asking that grand and unanswerable question: "Beyond what range will gold eyes see/New ranges rise to mark a last scrawl of light?"

W. M. FROHOCK

Mr. Warren's Albatross

Robert Penn Warren has written four novels, all of which teem with violent action: *Night Rider* (1938), *At Heaven's Gate* (1941), *All the King's Men* (1945), and *World Enough and Time* (1950). On the four he has built an impressive reputation. It is saying nothing new to remark that he is one of the few first-rate novelists to emerge in the United States recently.

The novels are only a fraction of his literary work. He began as one of the Nashville Fugitive poets, and has written poetry which is eminently respectable—although quite possibly more respected than read. Since the early thirties he has been an active critic, publishing frequently in the since defunct *American Review* and later in such literate little quarterlies as the *Sewanee Review* and the *Kenyon Review*. Accordingly he is identified both with the professional Southerners and the "new" (i.e., close-to-the-text, remote-from-all-else) critics, and in this latter connection has received the accolade of wrath from traditionalist literary scholars such as Professor E. E. Stoll. As a teacher he has confected, in collaboration with Cleanth Brooks, what is unquestionably the most useful manual extant for teaching the young to read poetry. And between times he has also held a Rhodes scholarship, written a strange biography of John Brown (1929), published a collection of short fictions, *The Circus in the Attic* (1948), and one narrative poem, *Brother to Dragons* (1953), taught in several colleges, and helped edit several magazines.

Warren, therefore, is that very rare phenomenon among American writers, a successful novelist who is also a sophisticated, self-conscious, all-round man of letters. Many American novelists can and should be read as if they were lyric poets: the critic can go straight to the central issue of sensibility, define the dominant emotion in his subject's work, seek out the manner in which emotion is related to, and maybe dominates, the technique—and come out with a reasonably trustworthy account of the novelists' meaning and worth. But such a method won't work with Warren. He is too learned. He has studied Proust, James, Gide, and Dostoevski, not to speak of worthies like Percy Lubbock, and he knows how to contrive such a degree of dramatization that it is hard to catch him attributing his own emotions to the people in his books. This ability to disappear behind his characters does not, of course, necessarily make him a better novelist, but it certainly does make him different from most of those whom we have come to think of in recent years as our best.

But Warren, for all his qualities, falls considerably short of greatness. Here is a man whose talent leaps out at the reader from every page that he writes, who truly commands the Engligh language, who has mastered the novelist's craft, and who can create characters. And yet we come to the end of his books with a feeling that somehow we have just missed having that superlative reading experience which a genuinely superior novel provides. Why?

Surely the answer does not lie in Warren's material—the kind of people and the kind of life he writes about—for great novels have been made of material of all kinds. Nor does it lie in a simple failure of technique. I suspect, rather, that the difficulty comes from Warren's basic attitude toward his material, which forces him to put more strain on his technical ability than it can bear without giving off, at inopportune moments, a very audible creak. The test of any technique is whether or not it gives the illusion of life. Creaking dissipates this illusion.

Warren's novel—meaning now the fundamental novel which Bernard DeVoto, in *The World of Fiction,* says that every novelist writes again and again under various forms—grows out of a dynamic background provided by the clash of cultures which has plagued the South for more than a century, in which the old poverty-ridden, agrarian culture defends itself against a progressive, aggressive, basically urban one. The conflict is internecine, for even though the new culture is allied with northern and eastern money, there are southerners on both sides. Money is always involved, but so many emotional and moral stresses are also present that the cleavage is more than economic. The agrarian remnant are most often the poor and the victims of exploitation. They are also the decent, the genuine, the simple-hearted, with whom the reader's sentiment is easily enlisted.

What is at issue is quite distinct from the old theme of the disappearance of the plantations; more often than not in Warren's novels, the descendants of the plantation owners have joined forces with the new, urban culture, while the agrarians are the red-necks, the wool-caps, the ten-acres-and-a-mule people. Their plight commands the sympathy of the hero even when, as in the cases of Jack Burden and Jeremiah Beaumont, his personal interests and loyalties are oriented toward the other camp. And as the reward of his allegiance, the hero finds himself caught between several sets of millstones.

In *Night Rider* the small tobacco farmers are being squeezed so hard by the eastern buyers that they form an association which begins as a bargaining agency and ends by dedicating itself completely to lawless terrorism, arson, and murder. Men like Perse Munn join it to defend themselves and their kind, and find eventually that they have had to sacrifice their own social integrity.

In *At Heaven's Gate* Bogan Murdoch, the central figure, subverts the best of the hill people and drives the rest off their farms into his mines and industries. His henchmen, like Jerry Calhoun and Private Porsum, discover that they can be faithful to Murdoch only at the expense of betraying their own agrarian people.

Willie Stark, in *All the King's Men*, is the champion of the red-necks, the protector of the poor men from the back parishes, the scrub farms, the sand-hill country. But to work for Willie, Jack Burden has to turn against the people of Burden's Landing and against the kind of social decency which, in spite of their alliance with the new culture, they represent.

And even *World Enough and Time*, romantic tale of the Kentucky frontier that it is, places its hero in the same uncomfortable situation. The bankrupt farmers want replevin to tide them over hard times and are virtually at war against the landowning men behind whom stand the eastern bankers. Jeremiah Beaumont casts his lot with the "replevin men," even though he has married the heiress to the remains of a good plantation and has few interests in common with the people he joins. Like Burden, like Perse Munn, like Jerry Calhoun and Private Porsum, his choice starts him on the road to misery.

For the hero is not only trapped between conflicting loyalties. When he casts his lot with the agrarians he turns out also to be accepting a criminal career. Perse Munn stays with the association when it is forced underground, commits one murder with impunity but is accused and convicted of one he does not commit, becomes a fugitive, and is at length hunted down and killed. Jeremiah Beaumont serves as the unwitting tool of the replevin men in killing his old benefactor Cassius Fort, is jailed, takes flight, and is eventually murdered for the reward on his head. Jack Burden survives Willie Stark's disaster and is never technically outside the law, but it is also true that he has been able to serve Stark only at the cost of his own and the world's moral reprobation. He knows that he has been a criminal even though he has not been behind bars; and while he has not been a fugitive in the literal sense that the other heroes were, his hell-for-leather drive to California, when he learns that Anne Stanton has become Stark's mistress, is an enactment of the ritual of flight. Like the other heroes he is running away from the horrid consequences of his choice. Thus in *Night Rider*, *World Enough and Time*, and *All the King's Men*, the career of the hero follows the same almost mythic pattern: he assumes the sufferings of a group (i.e., the agrarians), descends into criminality, incurs condemnation, becomes a fugitive, and, in two or three cases, dies.

And what happens to the hero who makes the opposite choice? Well, "Bulls-Eye" Jerry Calhoun, the ex-All-American forward passer who comes from his father's farm via the state university to a vice-presidency of one of Murdoch's banks, realizes too late that he has sold his birthright and criminally cheated those who trusted him. He, too, has a taste of jail (on suspicion of having murdered Murdoch's daughter), and ends up back on his father's farm, a dispirited moral ruin. Obviously there is little comfort in being the hero of a Warren novel. Whichever choice the hero makes, he is trapped.

He is also helpless. Symbolic of his general frustration is his inability to establish a satisfactory sexual relationship. Perse Munn becomes so absorbed in the affairs of his association that he first neglects, then brutalizes his wife, who thereupon abandons him; he subsequently takes as mistress Lucille, the daughter of his friend Christian, but is unable to overcome the emotional paralysis which afflicts her. Jerry Calhoun becomes engaged to Bogan Murdoch's daughter, after she has already been his mistress, but she becomes aware of his moral nullity long even before he does and leaves him for the succession of men which includes her eventual murderer. Anne Stanton, at eighteen, senses a similar weakness in Jack Burden. His later marriage to the voluptuous Lois is an immense physical success, but such an emotional failure that in no time he is running after common prostitutes; and although at the end of the novel he has married Anne Stanton and is living with her, the union is surrounded by an unmistakable atmosphere of middle age and spent passion. It should also be noted that in all four novels the first sexual episode between hero and heroine takes place clandestinely under a parent's roof and in such circumstances that the danger of interruption is very real. The hero is thus not only unsuccessful in his sexual relationships; these also shadow forth the tragic atmosphere of betrayal, voluntary and involuntary, in which his life is lived.

For in the world where Mr. Warren's people live, treachery is the rule. Perse Munn's association is sold out to the buyers by men like Senator Tolliver, who perhaps formed it only so that they could betray it when the time was ripe. Munn in his turn betrays Christian, who is laid low by a stroke when he discovers that the man he has befriended has been sleeping with Lucille. And this happens after a more complex episode of betrayal in which Munn (who is a lawyer as well as a farmer) defends a fellow-member charged with murder and then learns that the wretch is in fact guilty and has allowed an innocent Negro to be hanged in his place. Jack Burden first becomes attached to Stark when Stark learns that he has been a cat's-paw for his original backers, and is present when at last Stark is murdered by the long-range machination of his lieutenant, Tiny Duffy; and Burden himself succeeds in driving to suicide the venerable—and only once venal—Judge Irwin. Jerry Calhoun finally comes to realize that his own usefulness to Murdoch, as vice-president of Southern Fidelity, is that he makes a fine front for swindle. Thus while it is true that only in *World Enough and Time* is a deftly wielded knife the actual instrument of treachery, in all the novels a bared and secret blade could stand as a central, basic, and essential symbol.

We note also that in these novels of the embattled agrarians, the pattern of betrayal is also a pattern of patricide—and its reverse. In *All the King's Men* the fact is literal: Jack Burden presents Judge Irwin with irrefutable evidence of the judge's guilt, the old man quietly shoots himself, and that same afternoon Burden learns from his mother that he is really Irwin's son. In the other instances, the relationship is the familiar one so dear to psychologists: the older man stands to the younger in the status of a father substitute. This is not something we merely read into the texts. Mr. Warren's criticism shows him to be thoroughly familiar with the literature of psychoanalysis; he can hardly be unaware of the psychoanalytical implications of his novels. They must be intentional. The number of such father-son relationships in his novels is amazing. Willie Stark, for instance, is surrounded not only by parasites but also by a swarm of more or less disabled persons (e.g., Sadie Burke, Jack Burden himself) who need him as a staff to lean on. He is as much in the position of the Universal Father as was the late President Roosevelt. The people who cheer him from the State House lawn certainly see in him much more than a mere political advocate. Each of Mr. Warren's heroes is involved in some such system of personal relations. Perse Munn attaches himself to one father figure after another: Tolliver, who betrays him; Christian, whom he betrays; and Professor Ball, who allows him to take the blame for the shooting which has been Ball's own handiwork. Jerry Calhoun abandons his father, whose simple, clumsy goodness embarrasses him in comparison with the silkiness of Bogan Murdoch. The man whom Jeremiah Beaumont lures to the door and stabs twice, quickly, in the darkness is the same Colonel Cassius Fort who picked him up when he was a penniless border orphan, persuaded him to go to Bowling Green to learn what law a man could learn in those parts, and started him on what could have been a most excellent career. "We have all wanted to kill our fathers," says one of the Karamazovs. Indeed! In comparison with the life of a Warren hero in the conflict between agrarian and urban cultures, Dostoevski's men are mild. Warren's fathers are just as hot after killing the sons.

Obviously the world of Warren's novels is an extremely horrid one. It is dominated by the agrarian conflict. The conflict forces upon the hero a choice between alternatives either of which must bring him ill. He faces a gamut of crime, imprisonment, reprobation, flight, and probable destruction. He finds himself impotent and surrounded by treachery. He also finds himself both betrayer and betrayed; and furthermore, those whom he betrays and who betray him are those who have turned to him in need and whom he has needed.

But a dark and repulsive world is not necessarily the cause of a novel's weakness—as the works of William Faulkner, with which Warren's have inevitably to be compared, testify with great eloquence. Thus we have to look elsewhere for the answer to our question, and it is here that a recurrent characteristic of Warren's people which has no direct and immediately visible connection with the agrarian conflict acquires a certain importance. This characteristic is that frequently they are psychological enigmas.

At Bowling Green, Jeremiah Beaumont takes a room at a Mrs. Barron's and falls in with her son Wilkie, a gay blade and replevin man who initiates Jeremiah into the political brawling of the time. He also tells Jeremiah about the misfortunes of Miss Rachel Jordan, the planter's daughter who has borne a stillborn child out of wedlock to Cassius Fort. A feeling of destiny and a strange thirst for justice draw Beaumont to the girl. He makes her marry him and forces her—we never know quite how—to set as a condition of their marriage that he kill Fort. For a while they are relatively happy and Jeremiah keeps putting off his end of the bargain. Then one day a political broadside, extremely insulting to Rachel and purportedly inspired by the enemies of replevin, reaches Beaumont's hands. He murders Fort. Beaumont is apprehended, as he knows he will be, but he is confident that he has arranged affairs so that if his friends speak only what they believe to be the truth, the crime cannot possibly be attached to him. But his friends have been corrupted and even Wilkie Barron, although with a show of reluctance, testifies damagingly. Jeremiah is found guilty and sentenced to hang.

Of all who have combined to put Jeremiah in this fix, the only one to make amends is Wilkie. One night as Rachel and Jeremiah sit in jail, masked men overpower the guards. The leader is Wilkie. He arranges an escape down river to the canebrake kingdom of a degenerate French river pirate. Here Rachel goes insane, and Jeremiah contrives to escape only to be killed for money by his guards. But before he dies, Jeremiah learns that the one cause of all his misfortune, the man who sent him to Rachel Jordan, gave him the idea of murdering Fort, issued the broadside which recalled him to his flagging purpose, and in fact engineered the whole catastrophe *was no other than this same Wilkie Barron.*

Now Beaumont has always thought of himself as a free moral agent. He has even thought of the murder as a "gratuitous act"—the expression is an anachronism, of course, but the words are there. He has also been obsessed by the idea that his life is a drama of which he is both creator and protagonist. He, Jeremiah Beaumont, will arrange his own destiny. And at the end it turns out that all along he has been the helpless puppet of this backwoods Smerdyakov!

This may not be the kind of novel Dostoevski would have written if he had taken it into his head to write a story about Daniel Boone. But at this point *World Enough and Time* begins to sound a little like the celebrated *Adventures of Lafcadio,* whose author, André Gide, was one of Dostoevski's fervent admirers. In Gide's story the hero unpleasantly pushes a casual but unattractive traveling companion off a moving train, for no other reason than that he wants to commit a perfect crime, that is, one which will show no motive of the kind that the police understand. Success would constitute proof of his own freedom of conduct. But afterward he learns that he owes his safety to a skulking character named Protos. In pushing his victim the hero loses his hat, with very recognizable initials on the sweatband, as well as one of his cuff links. When the police find the hat the initials have been snipped out of it, and Protos himself later returns the cuff link to its owner. In both Gide's story and Warren's, a character who feels himself entirely free finds that someone else has arranged his destiny for him.

Yet although the freedom of Beaumont's acts is revealed to be an illusion, Wilkie Barron's acts are presented to us as entirely gratuitous.

Through what motive did he come to his diabolical role? We do not have the least idea. Barron remains an enigma to the end of his life. We learn that after the close of the main story he makes a brilliant marriage, starts on a promising political career, goes to Washington, and there commits suicide. Remorse? The reader may think so if he likes, but there is little in the story to point to such a conclusion.

There used to be a time when we understood what made the characters of a novel act as they did. Their motives were in the open. Julien Sorel behaved like the abominable little bounder he was because he had an ingrained, if perverted, notion of his duty to himself. Becky Sharp expected certain things of life and directed her conduct so as to help life provide them. Old Goriot died in his garret because his love for his daughters ran away with his sanity. Steinbeck's Joads took to the highway because ignorance and cupidity had driven them off their Oklahoma land. One can say *why* the action took place in every case. Clarity of motive was one of the things that made art preferable to life: these people might be knaves and fools, but one felt a certain security in their company because their knavery and foolishness made sense. That kind of fiction offered us an avenue into a world more reasonably and intelligently ordered than the one we live in.

But not any longer! Clarity of motive is another dispelled illusion. The new psychologists have shown us our ignorance and taught us that if we want to understand our motives we have to buy the comprehension. Seeing how complicated human behavior really is, we prefer to read about the incompletely comprehensible heroes of Hawthorne, Melville, Kafka, and Dostoevski. It is not enough that Huck Finn should fail to understand the tumult in his own heart when it looks as if he will have to surrender poor Jim; if Mark Twain had known what we know about writing novels, he would have contrived his book so that the reader would not understand the conflict either. Then critics could have wallowed and reveled in the murk of Huck's subconscious and emerged finally with an explanation which would have connected Huck's discomfort with his creator's ambivalent feelings about the conflict between North and South. In brief, the enigmatic hero is having his day.

Doubtless the case of Wilkie Barron should not be taken too seriously. He appears in a "romantic" novel, and what is romantic had better be kept thoroughly so. But it is to be noted that Warren scatters his enigmas all over the place, both in this book and in the earlier ones. We hardly understand the feeling of drama and destiny that drives the hero, and Rachel Jordan's conduct can scarcely be explained by the fact that she has had an illegitimate child. Willie Stark is also a puzzle. No one watches Stark more closely than Jack Burden, or knows him better; but Burden is never quite able to decide what he thinks of his boss. At the end of the book he has still to convince himself, if he can, that "Willie was a great man." Now, judged by his life, Willie was a political plug-ugly, a public plunderer, an adulterer, and a number of other unattractive things. If he is to be taken as great, we can only take him as such on the strength of his motives. And since not even Burden can penetrate these motives, we are in the presence of one real enigma and possibly two—for Burden's motives also are somewhat in shadow.

Bogan Murdoch's case is rather like Stark's: after his empire has collapsed and his associates have discovered the extent of his malefactions, there stands Murdoch, boasting to the newspapermen with dignified if tarnished heroism of how much he can still do to bring a new structure out of the debris, pleading with the public to trust him. This man has not been broken by the loss of his business, the alienation of his wife, or the murder of his daughter, although he has a clear though indirect responsibility in all three events. And what explains his behavior? Inhuman callousness? Self-delusion? Hypocrisy? One explanation is as good as another in the absence of any definite indication from the author.

The same sort of mystery surrounds the character of Perse Munn; but even without his evidence it is possible to affirm that in at least three novels out of four, the motives of one or more of the leading characters are highly secret. Of the two options open to the novelist—to explain the characters by speaking in his own person, or to allow us to understand them through their action—Warren exercises neither.

An examination of one aspect of his technique suggests that he consciously intends not to exercise either option. I mean the aspect which, since Henry James, we have been calling point of view, which has to do with the kind of mediate position the author takes between the action of his novel and the reader. The manuals of fiction catalogue the various possibilities: the omniscient narrator, the nonparticipating observer, the first-person participant, and so forth. In the course of four novels Warren has tried four different stances.

The action of *Night Rider* is seen mostly as the central actor would have seen it, and is narrated in the third person by the novelist. But the action is seen always from a considerable distance. We are never permitted any intimacy with the hero, and are prevented from identifying our fate with his and thus forming that sympathy which is so essential. We are *told* how he feels, but we can hardly say that we *feel with* him. As a matter of fact, we never get on first-name terms with him: other characters in the story call him Perse, but in the summaries of the action, where the novelist speaks directly to the reader, he refers always to Mister Munn. This may be only a symptom, but it is a richly suggestive one and cannot fail to have its effect on the reader: few of us can work up much interest in the fate of a man we know so distantly. There is a similar feeling of remoteness in the formality of the language in which the scenes of emotion are handled. For example, when Munn is contemplating his wife—whom he loves and will shortly lose—we are rather chilled by such descriptive touches as: "What light there was the woman's hair caught." And where we should probably be given the most intensely emotional scene of all, when Munn goes to Captain Todd's house to tell the old man that young Benton Todd has been killed in the raid, we get absolutely nothing at all. Such remoteness seems to me a major defect of the book.

At Heaven's Gate, a much more complicated novel than its predecessor, is mainly about the people who gravitate toward Bogan Murdoch. Again the story is told by a third-person narrator, but this time with the action seen through the eyes of various characters according to what opportunity offers. Meanwhile, a parallel narrative, told as a first-person confession in chapters alternating with those of the main action, narrates the life of a simple, virtuous hill man named Ashby Porsum Wyndham. Wyndham fights with his brother and leaves their farm for a woman, goes to work in Murdoch's mine, is fired for fighting, sees his wife and child die, and gets religion. He takes to the road, preaching salvation; is at last jailed because followers shoots a policeman; and then, refusing to leave the jail because convicted by his crazy conscience, he stands at the end of the book as a symbol of simple, agrarian honesty. Here the two strands of the novel come together. Wyndham's example inspires his cousin Private Porsum (the local war hero) to tell the truth and thus bring the Murdoch empire down about Murdoch's ears. Paradoxically, the secondary story is much more of a success than is the main one. We see and know Ashby Wyndham because we see through his eyes and know how life looks to him. But although we see Bogan Murdoch through the eyes of a variety of characters, we do not quite see what his wife hates so in him, or quite why his daughter leaves home, or how he so completely takes in young Jerry Calhoun. We are never permitted to look directly into Murdoch or to look at the action as he sees it. One man seems more clear-eyed than the rest, but he, the accountant Duckfoot Blake, is characterized as eccentric, and we never know what authority to attribute to his vision. As a result, Murdoch remains enigmatic.

A similar condition obtains in *All the King's Men,* and explains why this otherwise excellent novel is not completely successful. Jack Burden stands near the center of the story and does the narrating. We know what Burden knows about Stark, understand when he understands, are baffled when he is baffled. Unfortunately, Burden is a frequently baffled young man as well as a tortured, maladjusted one, and he never comes to see his boss plain. The political-moral ambiguity which has annoyed so many critics of *All the King's Men* rises out of this technical difficulty. If the action of this novel were seen by any eye unbeclouded by its owner's neuroses, the illusion of reality might be less intense; but the ambivalence of feelings about Willie Stark would certainly disappear without delay.

It is significant that the novel in which Warren succeeds best in handling the point of view is also the one in which—because the characters are not our contemporaries, because the issues involved are not issues which confront the ordinary reader, and because the nature of the story is frankly romantic—the enigmatic character as such is most easily acceptable. In *World Enough and Time* the story falls in the third person and the narrator, anonymous, unseen, and only occasionally felt, is a historian reconstructing from the available documents the tragedy of Jeremiah Beaumont. (The real-life Jeroboam Beauchamp left a confession which, together with the transcript of his trial, has been used by a number of writers including William Gilmore Simms, Thomas Holley Chivers, and Edgar Allan Poe.) Under the persona of the historian, for one thing, Warren is free to write as he likes. He was not free in this sense in *All the King's Men*, where the narrator had to stay in character. Jack Burden's characteristic expression was slangy, painful-ironic understatement, whereas Warren has a penchant for intense, powerful formal prose. There are places where Jack Burden, without much warning, suddenly develops a strikingly formal literary style, so that the reader gets the feeling that Burden is resting for a moment and has turned over the narrator's job to Warren. In *World Enough and Time,* on the other hand, Warren can appropriately luxuriate in his rich prose:

> She stood there in her black dress, panting, in the powerful humming July afternoon. Beyond the garden where the yellow roses hung in the heat, the cornfield stretched away on one side, and the corn at that season would be waist-high, savagely green, swelling in stalk and blade from the fat soil and the sun. In the trees behind her the July flies would make their grinding, remorseless, barbaric sound like a nerve twitching in her head. From the stone gateposts the rutted red-clay lane, dusty now, fell away, leading to cabins and houses she could not see, to faces she would never know, to forests, to the wilderness itself, but not to Virginia.

One is always justifiably suspicious of critics who proclaim that certain qualities of prose can take the place of other desiderata in a novel.

But one actually is swept along by the flow of words in *World Enough and Time*. It is a vast advantage to the novelist to have found a device which makes large quantities of writing like the above appropriate.

In his other books, Warren has found no such device. He has renounced his natural eloquence in order more freely to manipulate the point of view. In such a self-conscious writer who knows so well what he is about, this sacrifice clearly indicates how important it is (to him) to keep the motives of the main characters obscure.

Actually, their motives *have* to be kept secret. Just imagine for a moment that the reader of *Night Rider* had been allowed to become intimate with Perse Munn and developed a certain sympathy for him. Certainly a much more rigorous treatment of Munn's motives would have been required. For a man like old Captain Todd, represented in the book as the incarnation of integrity, does not have Munn's trouble. He joins the association and as long as it remains more or less legal and above ground he stays with it; but when it departs on its career of desperate, underground action, he withdraws, decently and with dignity, taking the respect of his fellow-members with him. His course is the course of wisdom, prudence, and morality. The first question a reasonably moral reader wants answered is: Why should not Munn have behaved in the same way instead of holding to his hell-bent course?

Warren's kind of novel *requires* an enigmatic character in its center because the frustrated, criminal, fugitive hero, moving through a world where no man including himself can be trusted, cannot be conceived as completely purposeful and completely aware of the meaning of his acts. If he were, the whole structure of his fictional world would fly apart. Ask Jack Burden to wipe his eyes and see Willie Stark clearly for the thug he is, and he will have to decide either to reject the man permanently or else accept him with overt cynicism. For him to do either, of course, would be to destroy the fiction. Thus the final burden falls upon the technique. It is a testimony to the excellence of Warren's craftsmanship that the creaking of the machinery is not more frequently audible.

In a sense Warren's trouble stems from the fact that he is a "southern regionalist." The particularly exacerbated form of regionalism which developed among southern intellectuals during the depression was as curiously unrealistic a resistance to events as American cultural history has seen in a long time. It resolutely turned its back upon the problems which confronted the country as a whole and tried to make a separate peace. Critics have tried now and then to align the mentality behind it with the varieties of extreme conservatism prevalent at the moment in Europe. The parallel does not hold, because these southerners were not, as the Europeans were, engaged in protecting economic and social privilege. Instead, they were protecting a dream.

Now dreams, heaven knows, are full of psychological significance, especially those daydreams we call fantasies. The agrarian daydream of the early thirties was just such a fantasy as a man creates when, because he is unable to cope with reality otherwise, he fashions a fiction which settles his problem effectively enough to let him go on living.

One would have to be highly unobservant not to recognize this fantasy as it appears in Warren's novels. The essential pattern of his stories repeats itself with a regularity which is almost obsessive: a young man assimilates his fortunes to those of the culture which produced him, and is destroyed by the same forces which are destroying the culture.

Agrarian regionalism as literal fact is on its way out. Fast transportation, mass production, and other such blessings are finishing it off. The radio, the movie, the syndicated editorial, the chain store, the large central factory with long lines of distribution, all conspire to kill out the differences between people of various regions. Rochester dresses us, Hollywood entertains us, Detroit flashes us around the country. What is left of the old regional differences is the psychological reality; the region is a state of mind. And the state of mind that Warren's novels reflect is a singularly unchanging one.

J. Saunders Redding, as keen an observer of the South as one could want, once told an interviewer for the *New York Times Book Review* that he deeply regretted Warren's leaving the South. I doubt whether he has anything to regret. True, Warren now eats and sleeps in the North, but his imagination has stayed behind him in his old country. The novels testify loudly that it has stayed agrarian.

Now there is nothing illegitimate about being a regionalist or an agrarian. But apparently the imagination of the artist can become so thoroughly dominated by his agrarianism that his work loses a certain actuality. We live in a world menaced by more devastating things than the disappearance of the agrarian culture, and the agrarian fantasy is remote from our concerns. To the red-necks Willie Stark may have appeared as a protector and savior—that would be his meaning to an extremist agrarian; to the rest of us, in other words to Warren's readers, Willie was a monster who threatened to destroy us. In general, the same turning away from the actual is the essential source of the weakness of Warren's novels.

He and his colleagues had earlier developed a type of literary criticism which is exposed to the same stricture. These people were some of the most gifted critics we have had. We needed badly the lesson they gave us in close reading of the texts, and their contribution includes not only the criticism they have written but also the general advance in the quality of American criticism which has come about largely through their example. But these critics went so far in their particular direction that much effort has since had to be spent in getting criticism back on center. The members of the circle that grew up around John Crowe Ransom were so devoted to literature that they attributed to it values which transcended the values of life. Anyone who compares the critical work of Allen Tate or of Warren with that of a critic like Lionel Trilling, who has learned much from them without losing his sense of actuality, must realize what a towering advantage it is to be aware of the relations between a book and the life of the man who reads it. The "new" criticism lacks a certain desirable relevance.

So do Warren's novels. Had he wanted to, Henry Nash Smith could have added to his *Virgin Land* a neat little appendix on Warren's books as belated treatments of the "Myth of the Yeoman." As *Virgin Land* makes clear, the Myth of the Yeoman lost its relevance, except as a historical item, many years ago.

There are southerners who wear the South about their necks like the albatross. They assume all the "weaknesses" and "faults" and "guilt" of the South that we hear so much about. They brood and worry. There are two figures in Warren's books who have great significance in this connection. One is Jack Burden, turning at the end of his own story to devote his life to studying the story of Cass Mastern. The other is the anonymous historian studying, laboring to understand (without ever quite reaching its ultimate meaning) the story of Jeremiah Beaumont—a character who was like Cass Mastern in many ways. They seem to me to bear a certain resemblance to the novelist himself. They are devoting themselves, as he is, to the contemplation of the unactual.

Warren will cease to be merely very good, and become excellent, when and if he decides to get rid of the carcass of a dead bird.

CLEANTH BROOKS

R. P. Warren:
Experience
Redeemed in Knowledge

The poetry, the fiction, and even the critical essays of Robert Penn Warren form a highly unified and consistent body of work. But it would be impossible to reduce it, without distorting simplifications, to some thesis about human life. The work is not tailored to fit a thesis. In the best sense, it is inductive: it explores the human situation and tests against the fullness of human experience our various abstract statements about it. But Warren has his characteristic themes. He is constantly concerned with the meaning of the past and the need for one to accept the past if he is to live meaningfully in the present. In this concern there are resemblances to Faulkner, though Warren's treatment is his own. Again, there are resemblances to W. B. Yeats in Warren's almost obsessive concern to grasp the truth so that "all is redeemed/In knowledge." Again, as with Yeats, there is a tough-minded insistence upon the facts, including the realistic and ugly facts—a fierce refusal to shield one's eyes from what is there.

This commitment to the truth, and the deep sense that the truth is rarely simple, account for Warren's sharp scrutiny of the claims of rationality. He never glorifies irrationality: he is not the poet of the dark subliminal urges or the novelist with a mystique to exploit. But he does subject the claims of twentieth-century man to the sternest testing and he is suspicious of the doctrine of progress and of the blandishments of utopianism.

Faulkner's effective, though perhaps unwitting and unconscious, belief in original sin constitutes a bulwark against this heresy. Yeats' vigilant and unflagging resistance to what he calls "Whiggery" constitutes a similar safeguard. One could argue that, in general, the artist's commitment to the concrete situation and his need to focus upon the dramatic exigencies of the human predicament make it easier for him to reject this form of abstraction. Dedication to his art, then, would not necessarily bring the artist to Christianity. It would be foolish to claim *that*. But dedication to his art may well protect the artist from some of the deceptions endemic to our time. On the positive side, dedication to his art will probably help him at least to *see* the problems of the human spirit to which Christianity—and any other serious philosophy—addresses itself.

The work in which Robert Penn Warren challenges most directly some of the liberal secular ideas of our time is his long poem *Brother to Dragons*, published in 1953. It is about Thomas Jefferson, or rather about Jefferson's nephews, Lilburn and Isham Lewis, the sons of Jefferson's sister, Lucy Jefferson Lewis. The Lewises removed from Virginia to western Kentucky. There, after the death of their mother and after their father, Dr. Charles Lewis, had returned to Virginia, the two young men, Lilburn and Isham, murdered one of their slaves. On the night of December 15, 1811, the night when the New Madrid earthquake shook the Mississippi Valley, Lilburn, having called the other slaves together into the meathouse to witness what he was going to do, butchered on the meatblock a slave named George. George's offense had been to break a water pitcher on his way back from the spring to which he had been sent to fetch fresh water.

After some months, hints of the crime leaked out. Lilburn and Isham were indicted for murder, but before they could be arrested and put in jail, Lilburn was dead. Apparently the brothers had planned to stand, each on one side of their mother's grave, and shoot each other. When the sheriff's posse came up, Lilburn had been shot and was dying, Isham was captured, but while awaiting trial, broke jail and disappeared—to turn up, of all places, at the battle of New Orleans in 1815, one of the two Americans killed in that engagement. This, at least, was the story that the Kentucky riflemen brought back with them from New Orleans. In any case, the indictment naming Isham bears under the date March 20, 1815, the docket: "Ordered that this suit abate by the death of the defendant."

It is a fantastic story, a terrible and blood-chilling story. It is, however, a true story, with the documents on record. Thomas Jefferson must have been aware of the depths of wanton cruelty to which his nephews had sunk, but nowhere among the Jefferson Papers is there any reference to it. It is hard to imagine what the great Virginian who thought so much of man's possibilities, who penned the Declaration of Independence with its confident claims for man, who knew and was sympathetic to the French eighteenth-century rationalists—it is difficult and exciting to try to imagine what Jefferson's reaction must have been. This is the task that Warren takes upon himself. To my mind his effort of imaginative reconstruction results in a great and moving poem. That has been also the opinion of some of the most discerning critical minds here and in Great Britain. But not of all, I should add. For a great many Americans, Jefferson comes close to being a sacred figure, and to dare to portray a Jefferson troubled and in doubt, a Jefferson embittered and cynical, even though only temporarily, was to lay profane hands upon the idol. In fairness to Warren's conception of Jefferson, I should say that *Brother to Dragons* is not written in any spirit of debunking. It is a great Jefferson who emerges at the end of Warren's poem, a Jefferson who has, in giving up his more callow hopes in man, actually strengthened his basic belief in man's potentialities. At the end of the poem Jefferson is a chastened though not a disillusioned man.

A book-length poem does not adequately reveal itself in brief quotations. If I confine myself to quotations of reasonable length, I can hope to do no more than suggest something of the flavor of the poem. The impassioned dialectic and the stages of the drama through which the action works to its final resolution must be taken on faith unless one has read the poem. Yet I do want to quote two or three excerpts. Here is the way in which Warren imagines Jefferson's hopes for man as he sat down to write the Declaration of Independence:

> We knew we were only men
> Caught in our errors and interests. But I, a man,
> Suddenly saw in every face, face after face,
> The bleared, the puffed, the lank, the lean, all,
> On all saw the brightness blaze, and I knew my own days,
> Times, hopes, books, horsemanship, the praise of peers,
> Delight, desire, and even my love, but straw
> Fit for the flame, and in that fierce combustion I—
> Why, I was dead, I was nothing, nothing but joy,
> And my heart cried out, "Oh, this is Man!"

> And thus my minotaur. There at the blind
> Blank labyrinthine turn of my personal time,
> I met the beast. . . .
>   . . . But no beast then: the towering

Definition, angelic, arrogant, abstract,
Greaved in glory, thewed with light, the bright
Brow tall as dawn. I could not see the eyes.

So seized the pen, and in the upper room,
With the excited consciousness that I was somehow
Purged, rectified, and annealed, and my past annulled
And fate confirmed, wrote. And the bell struck
Far off in darkness, and the watch called out.
Time came, we signed the document, went home.
Slept, and I woke to the new self, and new doom.
I had not seen the eyes of that bright apparition.
I had been blind with light. That was my doom.
I did not know its eyes were blind.

I would like to quote also the poet's own commentary on man seen against the background of nature—man who is not "adjusted" to nature and can never be adjusted—who must live in an agony of will, and who finally in his need projects upon nature itself the struggle with circumstance that engages his own heart. The scene is winter, as it descends upon the Lewis brothers after their mother's death and burial:

And the year drove on. Winter. And from the Dakotas
The wind veers, gathers itself in ice-glitter
And star-gleam of dark, and finds the long sweep of the valley.
A thousand miles and the fabulous river is ice in the starlight.
The ice is a foot thick, and beneath, the water slides black like a dream,
And in the interior of that unpulsing blackness and thrilled zero
The big channel-cat sleeps with eye lidless, and the brute face
Is the face of the last torturer, and the white belly
Brushes the delicious and icy blackness of mud.
But there is no sensation. How can there be
Sensation when there is perfect adjustment? The blood
Of the creature is but the temperature of the sustaining flow:
The catfish is in the Mississippi and
The Mississippi is in the catfish and
Under the ice both are at one with God.
Would that we were!

By the end of the poem Jefferson can accept the past with its violence and evil; he is willing to acknowledge the fact of his kinship with his black-browed butcher of a nephew, and he exults that

            . . . nothing we had,
            Nothing we were,
            Is lost.
            All is redeemed,
            In knowledge.

Jefferson tells his sister that "without the fact of the past we cannot dream the future," and he remembers that he had once written to Adams, his old political rival and friend,

> To Adams, my old enemy and friend, that gnarled greatness, long ago.
> I wrote to him, and said
> That the dream of the future is better than the dream of the past.
> Now I should hope to find the courage to say
> That the dream of the future is not
> Better than the fact of the past, no matter how terrible.
> For without the fact of the past we cannot dream the future.

The necessity for accepting the past is the dominant theme of what is probably the best known of Warren's novels, *All the King's Men*. The task of making sense of history is the specific problem of its hero. Jack Burden is a young man who is trying to write his dissertation for a Ph.D. in history. His chosen topic is the life of an ancestor of his who died during the Civil War. The papers and documents have come down through the family to Jack. He has all the facts about this ancestor, Cass Mastern, but somehow the facts do not make sense to him. Cass Mastern as a young man was sent away to school at Transylvania College in Kentucky. While he was there he seduced—or perhaps it may be more accurate to say that he was seduced by—the wife of his friend, whose house he has frequently visited as a guest.

Later something occurred to make Mastern realize that his friend's death by gunshot was not the accident that the world had supposed. His friend had somehow learned of the betrayal and had shot himself. Cass Mastern in his remorse tries in various ways to expiate his sin. When the Civil War breaks out, he refuses a commission, marches in the ranks, never firing a shot himself but courting the bullet that he hopes will find him. Finally, in 1864, the bullet does find him, and he dies in hospital of the infected wound. Jack Burden knows the facts, and even possesses Mastern's carefully kept and intimate journal, but he cannot understand why Mastern did what he did. This is the way in which Jack, speaking of himself in the third person, was able to put the matter some years later:

> I have said that Jack Burden could not put down the facts about Cass Mastern's world because he did not know Cass Mastern. Jack Burden did not say definitely to himself why he did not know Cass Mastern. But I (who am what Jack Burden became) look back now, years later, and try to say why.
> Cass Mastern lived for a few years and in that time he learned that the world is all of one piece. He learned that the world is like an enormous spider web and if you touch it, however lightly, at any point,

the vibration ripples to the remotest perimeter and the drowsy spider feels the tingle and is drowsy no more but springs out to fling the gossamer coils about you who have touched the web and then inject the black, numbing poison under your hide. It does not matter whether or not you meant to brush the web of things. Your happy foot or your gay wing may have brushed it ever so lightly, but what happens always happens and there is the spider, bearded black and with his great faceted eyes glittering like mirrors in the sun, or like God's eye, and the fangs dripping.

But how could Jack Burden, being what he was, understand that?

What Jack Burden was then, and how he later became something different constitute the matter of the novel. The knowledge that Jack's earlier life and his years at the university failed to give him, he learns painfully as a cynical newspaper reporter, watching, among other things, the meteoric career of Willie Stark as Stark rises to dictatorial power in this southern state. Through much of the course of the novel Jack Burden is acting as Stark's man Friday, advising him, doing various jobs for him, and, among these, applying his talents for historical research to the past lives of the governor's political opponents. What he is able to dig up usually disposes of that particular opponent. And, Jack cannot help noticing, there is usually something to dig up—no matter what the subject's reputation for probity. Once, when Jack demurs that there can be nothing to find in the past of the respectable Judge Irwin, Willie Stark assures Jack that there is always something: "Man is conceived in sin and born in corruption and he passeth from the stink of the didie to the stench of the shroud. There is always something."

There is not time, and for my purposes there is no need, to treat in detail the involved plot of this rich, violent, even melodramatic novel. Warren's novels are written with a kind of Elizabethan gusto. Though the school of criticism with which he is sometimes associated is charged with being overintellectual, formal, and even Alexandrian, Warren's own creative work, in its color and strident action, calls in question that oversimple account. Neither his poetry nor his fiction wear a prim and chilly formalism.

All the King's Men has been often described as a novel that depicts under a thin disguise the career of the late Huey P. Long. When the novel first appeared, a number of critics who should have known better disgraced themselves by their inability to make a distinction between the character of Willie Stark and that of the late senator from Louisiana. Certainly many things in the novel remind one of Louisiana under the Long regime; but this is a novel, not a biography, and finally—despite the importance of Willie Stark—the novel tells *Jack Burden's* story. The story of Willie Stark finally has its importance because of the way in which it affects the story of Jack. For as I said a few minutes ago, this novel is an account of how Jack Burden came to be a man capable of understanding the story of Cass Mastern—which means, of course, ultimately capable of understanding his own life and his relation to his parents, his friends, and the world.

Before Jack reaches this stage of knowledge, however, he has to be carried even further toward disillusionment and despair. For a time he comes to believe that man is a thing, a mere mechanism. He believes in what he calls "the Great Twitch." Men simply react to stimuli. Their actions are only more complicated versions of what happens when one runs an electric current through the severed legs of a frog. Given the stimulus, there is the automatic response.

The violence latent in the situation depicted in the novel finally comes to a head. Willie Stark is shot and killed by the young doctor Adam Stanton, who is Jack's boyhood friend; and Stanton himself is cut down by a fusillade fired by Stark's bodyguard. Moreoever, Jack not only observes the death of his friends, he finds himself directly involved in violence, for he learns that he has been the unwitting cause of the death of his own father. For a time, as Jack tells us, his belief in the Great Twitch was a comfort, for if there was no God but the Great Twitch, then no man had any responsibility for anything, and he was somehow absolved from having caused his father's death. But later Jack tells us

> he woke up one morning to discover that he did not believe in the Great Twitch any more. He did not believe in it because he had seen too many people live and die. He had seen Lucy Stark and Sugar-Boy and the Scholarly Attorney and Sadie Burke and Anne Stanton live and the ways of their living had nothing to do with the Great Twitch. He had seen his father die. He had seen his friend Adam Stanton die. He had seen his friend Willie Stark die, and had heard him say with his last breath, "It might have been all different, Jack. You got to believe that."
>
> He had seen his two friends, Willie Stark and Adam Stanton, live and die. Each had killed the other. Each had been the doom of the other. As a student of history, Jack Burden could see that Adam Stanton, whom he came to call the man of idea, and Willie Stark, whom he came to call the man of fact, were doomed to destroy each other, just as each was doomed to try to use the other and to yearn toward and try to become the other, because each was incomplete with the terrible division of their age. But at the same time [that] Jack Burden came to see that his friends had been doomed, he saw that though doomed they had nothing to do with any doom under the godhead of the Great Twitch. They were doomed, but they lived in the agony of will.

The sobered and chastened Jack Burden, in his new knowledge and sympathy, is now actually able to understand and accept the man whom he had been brought up to believe was his father but whom from boyhood he had secretly despised because he felt that he lacked force and manhood. Now, long divorced from Jack's mother, the supposed father has become something of a religious fanatic—in the cynical young newspaperman's eyes, at least—writing religious tracts and doing good works in the slums of the city. But as the novel closes, Jack has brought him home to live out under Jack's protection the few months remaining to him. Jack even helps him with some of his tracts, since the old man, too feeble to write, can still dictate. One of the passages he dictates claims Jack's special attention:

> "The creation of man whom God in His foreknowledge knew doomed to sin was the awful index of God's omnipotence. For it would have been a thing of trifling and contemptible ease for Perfection to create mere perfection. To do so would, to speak truth, be not creation but exten-sion. Separateness is identity and the only way for God to create, truly create, man was to make him separate from God Himself, and to be separate from God is to be sinful. The creation of evil is therefore the index of God's glory and His power. That had to *be* so that the creation of good might be the index of man's glory and power. But by God's help. By His help and in His wisdom."
>
> He turned to me when he had spoken the last word, stared at me, and then said, "Did you put that down?"
>
> "Yes," I replied.
>
> Staring at me, he said with sudden violence, "It is true. I know it is true. Do you know it?"
>
> I nodded my head and said yes. (I did so to keep his mind untroubled, but later I was not certain but that in my own way I did believe what he had said.)

The elder Mr. Burden's notion that man is "doomed to evil" veers toward the Manichaean heresy, but the truth that he is trying to render is evidently close to that to which Milton testified in *Paradise Lost*. Milton, of course, was careful to point out that man's fall was not *decreed* by God; yet God clearly did create the potentiality of evil as the necessary price to be paid for making man a free agent. Moreover, in His perfect fore-knowledge, God knew that man would misuse his power to choose and that he would fall into sin. As God sums the doctrine up in Book III:

> I made [man] just and right,
> Sufficient to have stood, though free to fall.
> Such I created all th' Ethereal Powers
> And Spirits, both them who stood and them who faild;

Freely they stood who stood, and fell who fell.
Not free, what proof could they have givn sincere
Of True allegiance, constant Faith or Love. . . .

Mr. Burden would evidently gloss the last three lines as follows: man *not* created free to fall would be merely an extension of God—no true creation.

Warren touches upon the problem of evil in a number of his poems. A very brilliant treatment is given in the momentarily bewildering poem entitled "Dragon Country." The country in question is, as the allusions in the poem make plain, Warren's native Kentucky. But as the dedication of the poem ("To Jacob Boehme") hints, the country in question is a country of the mind in which men encounter not human forces merely but principalities and powers. There is no reason, of course, why the two countries should not be one and the same, and in the poem they do coalesce. Indeed the brilliance of the poem comes in large part from the sense of the earthy and commonplace—"fence rails . . . splintered," "Mules torn from trace chains," the salesman traveling over the Kentucky hills "for Swift, or Armour"—and from the tone, colloquial, racy, and dry with a countryman's wit—both of which elements contrast with the preternatural horrors that are recounted, and thus give substance and solidity to them.

The reader of the poem may still ask "But why Kentucky?" And the answer would have to be: Kentucky, or any other Southern state. For the poem reflects the Southern experience, in which evil has an immediacy and reality that cannot be evaded or explained away. In that experience man is still confronted with the hard choice. He cannot simply call in the marriage counselor or the police or the psychiatrist. It is with this aspect of the Southern experience that "Dragon Country" deals.

We know, of course, that dragons simply do not exist. Yet what could have done the damage to Jack Simms' hogpen? And how account for some of the things that have happened since?

So what, in God's name, could men think, when they couldn't bring to bay
That belly-dragging earth-evil, but found that it took to air?
Thirty-thirty or buckshot might fail, but then at least you could say
You had faced it—assuming, of course, that you had survived the affair.

We were promised troops, the Guard, but the Governor's skin got thin
When up in New York the papers called him Saint George of Kentucky.
Yes, even the Louisville reporters who came to Todd County would grin.
Reporters, though rarely, still come. No one talks. They think it
    unlucky. . . .

Turned tongue-tied by the metropolitan press, not able to admit that the evil has reality, even the friends and relatives of the victims explain the facts away. When a man disappears, his family reports that he has gone to work in Akron, "or up to Ford, in Detroit." When Jebb Johnson's boot was found with a piece of his leg inside it, his mother refused to identify it as her son's.

Now land values are falling; lovers do not walk by moonlight. Certain fields are going back to brush and undergrowth. The coon "dips his little black paw" undisturbed each night in the stream.

> Yes, other sections have problems somewhat different from ours.
> Their crops may fail, bank rates rise, on rumor of war loans be called,
> But we feel removed from maneuvers of Russia, or other great powers,
> And from much ordinary hope are now disenthralled.
>
> The Catholics have sent in a mission, Baptists report new attendance.
> But that's not the point. We are human, and the human heart
> Demands language for reality that has no slightest dependence
> On desire, or need. Now in church they pray only that evil depart.
>
> But if the Beast were withdrawn now, life might dwindle again
> To the ennui, the pleasure, and night sweat, known in the time before
> Necessity of truth had trodden the land, and heart, to pain,
> And left, in darkness, the fearful glimmer of joy, like a spoor.

But this last difficult stanza is no Manichaean celebration of evil. The poem is not simply saying how much better off are the Kentuckians who inhabit the dragon's country, because they have to live so dangerously. The "fearful glimmer of joy" that the last line hints of comes not from evil as such but from the "necessity of truth." Admitting the element of horror in life, conceding the element of mystery, facing the terrifying truth—these are the only actions that can promise the glimmer of ultimate joy.

It is almost a misnomer to say that Warren's poem "Original Sin" is about the problem of evil at all. In the context of this poem "evil" is too specific a term, but, as we shall see, the poem does deal with a related problem.

ORIGINAL SIN: A SHORT STORY

> Nodding, its great head rattling like a gourd,
> And locks like seaweed strung on the stinking stone,
> The nightmare stumbles past, and you have heard
> It fumble your door before it whimpers and is gone:
> It acts like the old hound that used to snuffle your door and moan.

You thought you had lost it when you left Omaha,
For it seemed connected then with your grandpa, who
Had a wen on his forehead and sat on the veranda
To finger the precious protuberance, as was his habit to do,
Which glinted in sun like rough garnet or the rich old brain bulging
    through.

But you met it in Harvard Yard as the historic steeple
Was confirming the midnight with its hideous racket,
And you wondered how it had come, for it stood so imbecile,
With empty hands, humble, and surely nothing in pocket:
Riding the rods, perhaps—or grandpa's will paid the ticket.

You were almost kindly then, in your first homesickness,
As it tortured its stiff face to speak, but scarcely mewed;
Since then you have outlived all your homesickness,
But have met it in many another distempered latitude:
Oh, nothing is lost, ever lost! at last you understood.

But it never came in the quantum glare of sun
To shame you before your friends, and had nothing to do
With your public experience or private reformation:
But it thought no bed too narrow—it stood with lips askew
And shook its great head sadly like the abstract Jew.

Never met you in the lyric arsenical meadows
When children call and your heart goes stone in the bosom;
At the orchard anguish never, nor ovoid horror,
Which is furred like a peach or avid like the delicious plum.
It takes no part in your classic prudence or fondled axiom.

Not there when you exclaimed: "Hope is betrayed by
Disastrous glory of sea-capes, sun-torment of whitecaps
—There must be a new innocence for us to be stayed by."
But there it stood, after all the timetables, all the maps,
In the crepuscular clutter of *always, always,* or *perhaps.*

You have moved often and rarely left an address,
And hear of the deaths of friends with a sly pleasure,
A sense of cleansing and hope, which blooms from distress;
But it has not died, it comes, its hand childish, unsure,
Clutching the bribe of chocolate or a toy you used to treasure.

It tries the lock; you hear, but simply drowse:
There is nothing remarkable in that sound at the door.
Later you may hear it wander the dark house
Like a mother who rises at night to seek a childhood picture;
Or it goes to the backyard and stands like an old horse cold in the pasture.

The subtitle is "A short story." The poem is a kind of narrative, the account of a man haunted by a nightmare. The words "Original Sin" may be thought to tell us what the nightmare is, and they certainly give a clue, but they can be a distraction if we take our conception of original sin too rigidly from either Aquinas or Calvin, or even tailor it to meet the requirements of Sigmund Freud. The meaning of the nightmare rests upon a reading of the poem itself.

There is another clue worth mentioning at the outset: like many another Warren poem, in "Original Sin" the protagonist is referred to quite casually as "you." The implication is that the nightmare belongs to everyman. The nightmare's great head is an empty head: it rattles "like a gourd." But its nodding, it becomes plain, is not a gesture of intelligence—a sign of recognition or assent—it is merely the bobbing, the awkwardly carried, too-heavy head; for the nightmare is as witless as a hydrocephalic child. It cannot form words; it whimpers or mews: its hand is childish and unsure as it clutches the bribe of chocolate or the "toy you used to treasure."

In the poem the nightmare is associated with childhood; you had thought of it as being a part of your childhood world, a world that included grandpa with the curious wen on his head, sitting on the veranda in Omaha. It shocked you, therefore, when the nightmare turned up, of all places, in Harvard Yard, but after the first shock, you in your first homesickness were almost glad to see it. Hideous though it was, you felt almost kindly toward it. But whether you feel kindly toward it or loathe it, you cannot shake it off. This is presumably what "at last you understood": that nothing is ever lost—that the past can never be escaped. If the poem ended here, we might be tempted to think that the nightmare stood merely for the past—the monstrous and irrational world of the child's nightmare. But the poem does not end there. The stanzas that follow show that the nightmare is much more than the ghost of the past.

Those stanzas describe the occasion on which the nightmare appears and the kind of occasion in which it remains decently absent. For imbecilic though it is, the nightmare observes what amounts to a gentlemanly code. It forbears to shame you before your friends. It also remains hidden at the moments of apparent intellectual vision and at moments of emotional crisis. It has nothing to do with the experience of poignant beauty— the "lyric arsenical meadows when children call," nor with the pang of Gethsemane agony—the "orchard anguish," nor with the moment of terror, when horror has come to fruition and hangs like a ripened fruit, asking to be tasted, to be gorged.

The nightmare also absents itself from those occasions of calculation in which you fondle the axioms by which you live. It was absent, for example, when you made the brave resolution to begin over again and to found yourself upon a "new innocence." At that moment of insight it became clear to you that what betrays us is the multiplicity of experience. Therefore we must resolve not to allow ourselves to be distracted by that multiplicity, even though it may seem at times rich and glorious. We must demand better charts: we must strictly adhere to the charts, and thus keep ourselves from being swallowed up in the welter of our multiform world. Yet, after all the "time tables, all the maps," there you suddenly saw the nightmare, standing in the twilight clutter of *"always, always, or perhaps."*

This crepuscular clutter may at first seem a different sort from that of the "sun-torment of whitecaps" by which the speaker says that "Hope is betrayed." Yet both are multiplicity, even though one is sunlit and the other twilit. The best predictions somehow go awry; calculation miscalculates. The confidently voiced proposition has to be revised downward from an assertion of truth to a claim for probability—the confident *always* gives way to the lame *perhaps*.

The nightmare is much more than the ghost of the past: it is associated with the contingent element in the universe, that factor which renders the best timetables inaccurate, the most carefully surveyed maps, defective. In a world which aspires to a certain neat precision, contingency is indeed a nightmare, subhuman in its lack of conscious purpose, slovenly with its unkempt locks "like seaweed strung on the stinking stone." For the nightmare inhabits a world which defies the logical ordering of our daylight, working world. Since it is irrational, it is therefore monstrous: the timetable can find no place for it.

As we have seen, the nightmare avoids the glare of full day and the glare of full consciousness. Most often it comes to you in the twilight fringe of consciousness. Half asleep, you hear it fumble at the lock. You sense that it is in the house. Later, you may hear it wander from room to room. It moves about "Like a mother who rises at night to seek a childhood picture" or it stands outside "like an old horse cold in the pasture." To what do these comparisons point? They occur in the climactic position in the poem; they are surely more than casual analogies.

If we look back through the poem, we find that "it" has been compared to a child, to an imbecile, to an animal (though a faithful domestic animal like the old hound or the old horse), and now, to the mother. All of these are types of subrationality or irrationality, for even the mother acts in disregard of—or in excess of—the claims of rationality. The picture will keep until daylight; it will be the easier found by daylight. But, obsessed with her need, she rises at night to fumble patiently through the darkened rooms. It is a childhood picture. The child has presumably left the house—has perhaps long since become a man, and put away childish things. But the mother yearns toward the child that was. There is no use in reasoning with her, for her claim transcends reason; and, anyway, she will be happier left to her search.

But the things to which the nightmare is compared have something else in common; none of them has anything to do with the realm of practical affairs. The child and the idiot obviously do not have, but neither does the mother, the hound, or the horse. They are all superannuated: the old hound snuffling at the door, and the old horse turned out to pasture, and the mother living in the past. The reference to the timetables and the maps is relevant after all, for maps and timetables are the instruments of action, abstract descriptions of our world in which the world is stripped down to be acted upon; and all action has a future reference. Yet the future grows out of the past, and is, we may say if we think in terms of pure efficiency, always contaminated by the past. Our experiments never work out perfectly because we can never control all the conditions: we never have chemically pure ingredients, a perfectly clean test tube, absolutely measured quantities. Most of all, we ourselves are not clean test tubes.

Indeed, as the next-to-the-last stanza makes clear, the nightmare is the irrational being who lies at the depths of your own being, for it comes "Clutching a toy you used to treasure." It is the you that cannot be disowned, even though as you grow older you hear "of the deaths of friends with a sly pleasure," feeling in spite of yourself "A sense of cleansing and hope," knowing that one more tie with the past and with that irrational you has been broken.

The new innocence, for which the speaker, bewildered by the sun-torment of whitecaps, cries out, would be aseptic, chemically pure; but we ourselves are never that. Animal man, instinctive man, passionate man—these represent deeper layers of our nature than does rational man. Considered from the standpoint of pure rationality, these subrational layers are, as we have seen, a contamination, something animal—or actually worse than animal, imbecilic, an affront to our pride in reason. But it is in these subrational layers that our higher values, loyalty, patience, sympathy, love are ultimately rooted. These virtues are not the constructions of pure rationality, and so the comparison with which the poem ends—to the mother, yearning past reason for the childhood picture, and to the old horse, patient in the cold pasture—are once more relevant.

I have interpreted the poem as a critique of secularizing rationality, and by doing so have risked oversimplifying it. We must not simplify the poem into a tract or a sermon. It is a poem, which means that it has its own drama. Its meaning cannot, without essential loss, be detached from the drama. Dramatic tension is maintained throughout the poem: the revulsion of horror, the necessary association of the horror with the past, and specifically with one's own past; the false confidence that one has escaped it; the sick realization that one cannot escape it—these are dynamically related to each other. Not least important, one should add, is the speaker's final attitude as the poem closes: I should not describe it as mere passive acceptance; it is certainly more than cynical bitterness. It may even contain a wry kind of ironic comfort: the listener drowses off in the consciousness that, moving about or merely patiently waiting, "it" is there, and can be counted upon to remain.

But any paraphrase blurs the richness and complexity of the final attitude. The poet is not telling us *about* the experience; he is *giving* us the experience. For the full meaning the reader has to be referred to the poem itself. The poem is hard to summarize, not because of its vagueness but because of its precision. "What it says"—the total experience, which includes the speaker's attitude as a part of it—the total experience can be conveyed by no document less precise than the poem itself. The full experience—the coming to terms with reality, or with God, or with one's deepest self, cannot be stated directly, for it is never an abstract description. It can be given to us only dramatically, which means indirectly.

In a sense, then, the poem constitutes a kind of concrete instance of our problem as well as a statement of it. This poem—and any poem, I should say—makes use of a method of indirection. The truth of a poem does not reside in a formula. It cannot be got at by mere logic. Poetry itself is incommensurable with charts and timetables. It is a piece of—perhaps I should say an "imitation" of—our fluid and multiform world. That is why fewer and fewer people can read such poems as this. Perhaps if we could read poetry, we might understand our plight better: not merely because we could hear what our poets have to tell us about our world but because the very fact that we could read the poems would itself testify to an enlargement of our powers of apprehension—would testify to a transcendence of a world abstracted to formula and chart. A growing inability to read poetry may conversely point to a narrowing of apprehension, to a hardening of the intellectual arteries which will leave us blind to all but that world of inflexible processes and arid formulas which may be our doom.

Warren's characteristic theme—man's obligation to find the truth by which he lives—comes in for a fine restatement in a recent poem and a recent novel. Both put a young soldier's idealism to the test; both have a Civil War setting. The poem is entitled "Harvard '61: Battle Fatigue." The young Harvard man of the class of 1861 has died in the fight to free the slaves, but in death he is puzzled—even nettled—by the fact that others have died bravely for a bad cause—or perhaps, for no cause at all.

> I didn't mind dying—it wasn't that at all.
> It behooves a man to prove manhood by dying for Right.
> If you die for Right that fact is your dearest requital,
> But you find it disturbing when others die who simply haven't the right.

The way in which certain "unprincipled wastrels of blood and profligates of breath" have flung themselves into death has confused the issues. There was, for example, the middle-aged Confederate soldier whom he shot and killed just before he received his own death wound. The man was, he exclaimed to himself, "old as my father" and the dying Confederate soldier, observing the boy's blanched face, had even given him a bit of fatherly advice, saying to him: "Buck up! If it hadn't been you,/Some other young squirt would a-done it."

But even as the young Harvard idealist heard these words,

> The tumult of battle went soundless, like gesture in dream. And I was
>   dead, too.

> Dead, and had died for the Right, as I had a right to,
> And glad to be dead, and hold my residence
> Beyond life's awful illogic, and the world's stew,
> Where people who haven't the right just die, with ghastly impertinence.

The young idealist has a case: he had indeed tried to slay "without rancor" and had striven to keep his heart pure "though hand took stain." In a sense, then, he has earned a certain right to his squeamishness. In any case, such squeamishness touches some answering chord in the hearts of all of us nowadays who regard war as the ultimate horror and justify, if at all, our participation in it only in terms of its necessity and our own purity of purpose. As for the poet's attitude toward the idealistic young fighter for the right, "Harvard '61" is only one half of a double poem, the other member of which has to do with the gnarled and bewhiskered Confederate whom the young man killed. The inclusive title for this double poem is, significantly, "Two Studies in Idealism: Short Survey of American, and Human, History." The poet is not condemning idealism but extending our conventional notions of it and in the process showing how deeply it is rooted in human nature. If the member of the class of '61 is being chided, it is not for his dedication or his bravery but for a too-simple view of reality and a certain pharisaical self-righteousness.

In his latest novel, *Wilderness*, Warren addresses himself once more to the problem of the idealist caught up in the Civil War. His criticism of idealism has not changed, but in this instance his treatment of the idealist is not glancing and ironic but direct, serious, and fully and obviously sympathetic.

The hero of the novel is a young Bavarian Jew, Adam Rosenzweig. He has a club foot, but in spite of this deformity and in spite of the bitter opposition of his uncle—his only close relative, for Adam's parents are dead—he makes his way to America in order to take part in the War to help free the slaves.

What Adam finds, of course, is the mixture of good and evil, the contradictions and cross purposes, that one always encounters in a great war. He finds, for example, that the inhabitants of New York City are not unanimous in regarding the conflict as a holy war for freedom. Some of them even resent the Negroes as being the indirect cause of their being conscripted to fight. Adam finds himself caught up in such a conscription riot on the very day that he lands. The mob is killing such Negroes as it can find.

The general situation in which Adam finds himself has an aspect more troubling still. As he makes his way toward the battlefields, his immediate companions turn out to be men who are vicious or cowardly or callous. Though he is sorry for the Negro Mose Talbutt and tries to teach him to read, he finds it hard to accept him fully or even to come to a genuine liking of him. Though he applauds Jed Hawksworth for having displayed the sense of justice and integrity that forced him to leave his native South, Adam cannot find in Hawksworth a brother idealist or even a warm human being. In sum, Adam's persistent difficulty is that of accepting man with all of his imperfections and believing that the ideal can have any place in a creature so faulty.

In the stinking mud of the army's winter quarters in northern Virginia, the sensitive young man is almost overwhelmed with the ugliness and cruelty and crassness of human life. A soldier celebrated for heroic exploits in battle turns out to be in the camp a drunken bully. An ignorant washerwoman who hangs around the camp is sentenced to the lash for prostitution and Adam hears her shrieks as the whip falls. The state of affairs seems to call in question everything that he has lived for up to this time and the whole meaning of his quest.

The last two chapters of this short novel bring to a head this crisis in Adam's affairs. He has slipped away from the wagon train and driven his sutler's vehicle into the Wilderness where the confused and bloody battle will be fought. He is at last alone. The battle will eventually reach into the glade where his team is tethered. There he will face an ultimate testing of his conception of human kind and of reality.

Few authors would have dared to compress so many successive states of mind into so short a time span, as Adam's mood shifts from dejected loneliness to tender affection, or from obsessive guilt to pride in his new-found masculine power, or from cynicism to human sympathy, before he finally attains to self-knowledge and through that knowledge to a way of accepting humankind. Certainly few authors could have brought it off. But Warren has earlier set forth very skillfully the circumstances which have made Adam what he is and the psychological pattern through which Adam will be forced to move. Moreover, the battlefield itself so eagerly sought by Adam, and won to with such difficulty, provides the necessary forcing bed for Adam's development. There he finds himself detached from and yet a part of the battle, in the "cold center of stillness in the storm which was the world." There is opportunity for thought, yet involvement is imminent. Finally, after the skirmishers strike into his hidden glade, fight over Adam's almost passive body, and then rush away, the burning forest, which has been set afire by the guns, forces Adam toward decision and action.

But unless the reader already possesses the supporting context, including Adam's earlier history, there is little point in trying here to lead him step by step through the drama of Adam's development. No summary, in any case, can preserve the drama. But it will do no harm to mention some of the elements at work in Adam's Wilderness experience.

The day begins with a pang of loneliness as Adam wakes from a dream of his mother, the mother who, he feels, had at the end come to hate him because he sided with his father in believing that it was right to sacrifice one's family in the fight for liberty. Though his mother had not forgiven him, he yearns for forgiveness. In the dream she had seemed to proffer tenderness and love.

There is Adam's sense of guilt. In particular, he feels remorse for the exasperation which allowed him to lash out at Mose Crawford, the freedman, the night before Mose murdered his tormentor, Jed Hawksworth. Adam believes that his bitter words may have actually triggered the deed. In the silence of the forest, Adam wonders about something else: why did not Mose kill *him,* the man who had actually uttered the harsh words, rather than Jed, and he reflects that the reason must be that Mose had once saved his life: "he thought, *you cannot strike down what you have lifted up.* So Jed, he decided, had had to die in his place." In a curious way, Jed's life has been sacrificed for his own, and he wonders whether "every man is, in the end, a sacrifice for every other man."

Adam's reveries are interrupted when the battle bursts in upon him. A handful of ragged Confederate soldiers overrun the glade, knock Adam down, and, while one of them, a mere boy, sits on Adam's almost passive body, these half-starved men stuff themselves from the supplies in Adam's sutler's wagon. But their hunger humanizes them for Adam: he "felt a sweet sadness fill his heart. He loved the boy because the boy had been very hungry and now had food." The psychology here is sound enough: it is always easier for the Adams of our world to accept the fact that they share a basic humanity with the enemy than to accept the evident bestiality within their allies or the latent bestiality within themselves. For Adam, that more difficult acceptance is late in coming.

First, a detachment of Federal troops surprises the Confederates; then in the ensuing fight Adam manages to reach a rifle and kills one of the Confederate soldiers. The Federal troops rush away in pursuit of the enemy, and Adam once more finds himself alone. He experiences a moment of pride in the proof that, though crippled, he is man enough to act and kill. But his momentary pride flickers out into dejection and bitterness. He is lost in the forest and barefoot—one of the retreating Confederates has taken Adam's boots, including the one carefully fashioned by a Bavarian cobbler especially for his deformed foot. Adam has lost his team: one horse has been killed; the other has run away. He finds himself again questioning his motives for having come to America. Perhaps he had come simply to justify himself. He weighs too the consequences of this coming: besides being responsible for the death of the Confederate soldier, is he not responsible also for the death of Jed Hawksworth?

In his bitterness he feels that the world has betrayed him—even his father, who bequeathed him the idealism that forced him toward the conflict for freedom but who also bequeathed the deformed foot that renders him unable to become freedom's soldier—even his father has betrayed him. For a moment he decides to accept the betrayal. Henceforth he will be tough-minded and hard-boiled. As he walks over to strip the boots from the dead soldier, he feels that he has at last discovered the nature of the world. All that he had previously believed was false. The bitter discovery actually gives him a sense of release and of power. Now at last he knows the truth about reality.

Hardened by this new and devastating knowledge, he tells himself, as he stares at the face of the soldier whom he has killed: "I killed him because his foot was not like mine." This remark is, of course, a fantastic oversimplification, but it does at least testify to Adam's having peered into the depths of himself and having glimpsed the dark side of his own motivation: specifically, the fact that his crippled foot has indeed had its part in his desire to engage in this war. But as he tries to put on the dead soldier's boots, his glance happens to fall upon the phylactery and the talith which he has brought from Bavaria and which, though he had given up his religion, he had never been quite able to bring himself to throw away. In the looting of the wagon, they have been tossed aside. Seeing them, he is suddenly smitten with a sense of desolation. He takes off the dead man's boots and sets them down tidily near the corpse. "In a numb, quiet way he thought how foolish this was." And yet he has to do it. He peers again into the dead man's face and tries to see whether it shows any mark of the young man's life. He wonders how his own dead face will look and asks himself the question: "Am I different from other men?"

The redness in the sky tells him that the forest is now on fire, set aflame by the guns, and he realizes that he ought to go and drag the wounded away from the flames. He strains his ears to hear the cries of the wounded, but he can hear only the imagined cries within his own head. Suddenly, he finds himself praying the prayers that he had learned as a boy: "Have mercy upon the remnant of the flock of Thy hand, and say unto the Destroying Angel, Stay thy hand."

As the book ends, Adam is ready to rise and try to make his rescue. In a sense it will be what he has to do, just as his coming across the sea and joining in the fight for freedom was what he has had to do. But he has broken "the compulsion of the dream" which has held him up to this time. It is not his action in seeking to fight for freedom, because it was a compulsive action, has been wrong. He knows that he would do it again, but now he cries, "in his inwardness: *But, oh, with a different heart!*" He prepares to pick up the dead man's boots (with a different heart he can now accept them), put them on, and hobble out of the forest glade.

What has happened, of course, is that Adam has discovered himself and, now understanding himself, can forgive, and ask forgiveness of, his parents; can accept the past; and can enter into communion with mankind. His experience parallels in general terms the experience of several of Warren's other characters—it is like that of Jack Burden at the end of *All the King's Men*, or that of the heroine of *Band of Angels*, who hates her father for what he has done to her and only at the end finds herself able to forgive him, to accept her past, and thus to find freedom.

This matter of man's relation to the ideal runs through the fiction and the poetry of Warren. A Christian may be tempted to transpose the problem into that of conversion or redemption. But if he yields to the temptation, he must take the responsibility for the transposition and not assume that it formed part of the author's intention. Still, there is no doubt that one can learn from Warren's fiction and poetry a great deal about the psychology of conversion and the cost of redemption even though Warren himself poses his problems in non-Christian terms—often in terms of the movement from ignorance to knowledge or from bafflement and confusion to order and insight.

Warren's poem "Walk by Moonlight in a Small Town" is a beautiful instance. The speaker returns to his boyhood home and finds the little town, in spite of all its tawdry "matter of fact," filled to the brim with mystery.

> And pitiful was the moon-bare ground.
> Dead grass, the gravel, earth ruined and raw—
> It had not changed. And then I saw
> That children were playing, with no sound.
> They ceased their play, then quiet as moonlight, drew, slow, around.
>
> Their eyes were fixed on me, and I
> Now tried, face by pale face, to find
> The names that haunted in my mind.
> Each small, upgazing face would lie
> Sweet as a puddle, and silver-calm, to the night sky.
>
> But something grew in their pale stare:
> Nor reprobation or surprise,
> Nor even forgiveness in their eyes,
> But a humble question dawning there,
> From face to face, like beseechment dawning on empty air.

Here the children remembered from his boyhood put the question to him, not he to them. It is a question that he would answer, but obviously no man can answer:

> Might a man but know his Truth, and might
> He live so that life, by moon or sun,
> In dusk or dawn, would be all one,
> Then never on a summer night
> Need he stand and shake in that cold blaze of Platonic light.

But what the poet says here is humanly impossible. Man can never know his truth so thoroughly that he will not need to shake in the cold blaze of the light of the ideal. It is a beautiful poem and the Christian may perhaps be forgiven for boldly appropriating it as a tender though completely unsentimental statement of the way in which the whole human creation yearns toward the truth that would give it significance and thus redeem it from its all-too-evident mutability into eternity. But how honest the poem is! For the desiderated truth is a judgment as well as a revelation.

JOSEPH FRANK

Romanticism and Reality in Robert Penn Warren

"The philosophical novelist, or poet, is one for whom the documentation of the world is constantly striving to rise to the level of generalizations about value, for whom the image strives to rise to the symbol, for whom images always fall into a dialectical configuration, for whom the urgency of experience, no matter how vividly and strongly experience may enchant, is the urgency to know the meaning of experience." Robert Penn Warren wrote these words in a first-rate critical study of Conrad's *Nostromo*; but, like all creators who also write criticism, Mr. Warren can hardly approach the work of others except in terms of his own preoccupations. Mr. Warren himself is a novelist for whom the image is always striving to rise to the level of symbol, and for whom—to vary his phrase a bit—the meaning of experience always takes on a dialectical configuration. And the excitement of reading his work derives precisely from its combination of spontaneous creative vitality with an artistic ambition continually striving to rise above the level of a banal naturalism.

I

Mr. Warren's first novel, *Night Rider*, appeared in 1939 and his second, *At Heaven's Gate*, in 1943—just at the moment, that is, when the

American intelligentsia were emerging from their flirtation with Marxism. As a member of the Southern Agrarian group Mr. Warren had fought the Marxists all through the thirties, in a battle which involved not only social ideas but aesthetic and philosophical ones as well. The politico-economic program of the Agrarians was, to be sure, an amorphous hodge-podge of states' rights, English Distributism, and belated American Populism; it is hard to believe that the leading Agrarians themselves, who were primarily men of letters, ever took it very seriously. In any case, this aspect of Agrarianism quickly faded from the scene after the mid-thirties and never influenced the work of the Agrarian writers in any significant fashion. Far more important were the Agrarian objections to the sociological naturalism and economic determinism which then formed the dominating atmosphere of American liberal thought; and equally noteworthy was their protest against the reflection of this atmosphere in the literature of the period.

One of the best of Mr. Warren's early essays, for example, was devoted to a demolition of the muckraking novels of T. S. Stribling, who might be described as an inferior Southern Sinclair Lewis. Mr. Warren objected to the facile panaceas for Southern issues implied by Stribling's books, and he compared them unfavorably with the sense of the tragic complexity of life in Faulkner's *Light in August* (this was in 1934, considerably in advance of the Faulkner boom of the fifties). Not all human problems, Mr. Warren argued, were susceptible of sociopolitical solutions; to pretend that they were was simply to falsify experience. And this general position, which forms the valid core of the Agrarian attack on liberalism as a metaphysic, also finds expression in Mr. Warren's first two novels.

Irene Hendry, in the best article on these early books, acutely remarked that Mr. Warren wrote proletarian novels which included what the orthodox examples of the genre left out. At the center of each book is a plot machinery motivated by a political or economic conflict—the uprising of small tobacco farmers against price-controlling cartels in the first, the collapse of a big business tycoon who also controls state politics in the second. In both books, however, Mr. Warren represents his characters' involvement in economic-political action as an escape from moral self-scrutiny.

Percy Munn, the protagonist of *Night Rider*, tries to define himself by his participation in the illegal movement of the night riders growing out of the organization of small farmers. And though Mr. Warren, as an Agrarian, would presumably sympathize with such a movement as an expression of regional independence, he impartially depicts Munn's human disintegration as a result of his increasing absorption in a world of illegality, violence, and murder. Exactly the same theme appears in a poem first published in 1941 ("Terror"), set in the context of the violent political events of the late thirties:

> So some, whose passionate emptiness and tidal
> Lust swayed toward the debris of Madrid,
> And left New York to loll in their fierce idyll
> Among the olives, where the snipers hid;
> And now the North, to seek that visioned face
> And polarize their iron of despair,
> Who praise no beauty like the boreal grace
> Which greens the dead eye under the rocket's flare.
> They fight old friends, for their obsession knows
> Only the immaculate itch, not human friends or foes.

On a wider canvas, and with a much richer range of social types, Mr. Warren continues to explore the implications of this theme in *At Heaven's Gate*. The chief characters in this novel all seek to escape their own inner vacuity, their lack of any true sense of human values, by some external surrogate—economic power or politics whether of the right or the left (the business tycoon and the labor organizer are both equally inhuman), sex, drink, mythomania, the cynicism of despair. All these are efforts to escape from the inner reality of moral decision and moral choice—a reality represented in the book by the itinerant hillbilly preacher Ashby Wyndham. Mr. Warren has never been given enough credit for Wyndham's remarkable monologue in backwoods dialect, which winds through the book in a series of chapters alternating with the main action, and which manages to achieve a moving effect of genuine pathos and almost biblical gravity while constantly skirting the border of the bathetic. It is the example of Wyndham, who refuses to compromise with the iniquities of the world, that brings about the resolution of the action—the collapse of the crooked financial empire of the business tycoon, Bogan Murdock, and the at least partial conversion of a number of the other figures to a sense of moral responsibility.

II

Both of these early novels of Mr. Warren's may thus be labeled antinaturalist in theme; each represents a conscious inversion of the naturalist emphasis on the manner in which human lives are shaped by amoral instinctual drives and social pressures. To live at the mercy of such drives and pressures, from Mr. Warren's point of view, is a fundamental betrayal of the human self; and the intention of both books is to portray the futility of a world in which the only aims of life are a reflection of such forces. In *All the King's Men* (1946), however, Mr. Warren's third and most famous novel, we find a distinct shift in thematic emphasis. It is not so much that the fundamental theme changes as that it is approached from a new angle. The two earlier books had merely portrayed the dichotomy of the moral self and the world, with the latter always presented as the realm of self-alienation. But *All the King's Men* starts from the premise that the self and the world are necessarily interrelated; and it tackles the far more complex theme of the tragic ambiguities arising from their inescapable involvement.

Although *All the King's Men* was originally conceived as a play entitled *Proud Flesh*, there can be little doubt that, as a narrative work, it owes its origin to the sudden metamorphosis of Duckfoot Blake at the end of *At Heaven's Gate*. This character, like the later Jack Burden, is a lucidly cynical participant in Murdock's political and financial skulduggery out of a Manichaean resignation to the world's irremediable evil. But he finally finds the courage to realize that "everything matters," and that it is impossible to evade moral commitment by intellectual detachment. Blake's richly figurative and eruditely obscene dialogue is a first draft for the brilliant rhetoric of *All the King's Men*; and Blake himself foreshadows the intellectual bravado, wise-guy cockiness, and searching self-despair that make up the character of Jack Burden. But while *All the King's Men* is essentially the story of Jack Burden, it also includes at least two other important involvements of the self and the world.

One is that of Dr. Adam Stanton, who is explicitly called a "Romantic." For "he has a picture of the world in his head, and when the world doesn't conform in any respect to this picture, he wants to throw the world away." It is the bitter and worldly-wise Jack Burden who makes this comment, but, in his own hard-boiled fashion, Jack Burden is just as much of a Romantic as Adam Stanton. For even though Jack is neck-deep in the off-color politics of Willie Stark, he is a Romantic by virtue of his purely imaginary ironical detachment from the events in which he takes part; neither he nor Adam Stanton can accept the "impure" reality of the world that confronts them. But while Adam Stanton avenges himself on the world by committing murder and being killed in turn, Jack Burden succeeds in forming "a new picture of the world." This new picture not only leads him to negate his own earlier negation and accept the guilt for his actions but also simultaneously inspires him to forgive the guilt of others. Jack Burden thus transcends his Romanticism, with its impossible demand for an inhuman "purity," and in this way he "earns" the faith and ideals that once more permit him to affront "the convulsions of the world . . . and the awful responsibility of Time."

The character of Willie Stark, in the same novel, poses the problem of Romanticism—not, we can see, as a literary or historical but as an ethical and ultimately metaphysical category—in still other terms. Willie Stark is of course the domineering "man of fact," who manipulates the "impure" reality of the world with a fine unconcern for the moral involutions of both Jack Burden and Adam Stanton. But Willie, it should be noted, becomes this man of fact only after he finds that he has been played for a sucker—only after the backroom boys have shown him that high ideals are no match for a corrupt and well-greased political machine. This causes Willie to abandon his wide-eyed innocence about politics— another variety of Romanticism—and motivates his decision to beat the politicians at their own game. Willie also undergoes a "conversion to the real," with all the latter's impurities; there is a parallel between what happens to Willie at the beginning of the novel and what happens to Jack Burden at the end. But Willie's "conversion" is not made out of guilt and humility; it springs from bafflement, frustration, and a raging sense of power. Willie accepts too much of the world, just as Adam Stanton accepts too little—or, to be exact, not any at all.

All the King's Men thus presents us with three types of dialectical interaction springing from the dichotomy of Romanticism and reality. There is the total rejection of the world in Adam Stanton, who clings desperately to his "idea" of purity; there is the total acceptance of Willie Stark, who abandons *his* "idea" of honest and able government (in fact, if not completely in aspiration) for the fleshpots of power; and there is the transcendence of this dualism in the moral evolution of Jack Burden, who passes from self-hatred, caused by his disillusionment with the "idea" of purity, to a recognition of his responsibility for realizing the "idea" in however imperfect a form. The theme of Romanticism and reality had thus become central for Mr. Warren by the time he composed *All the King's Men;* but, except for the character of Adam Stanton, it could be discerned only in the background of the central action. With *World Enough and Time* (1950), Mr. Warren's fourth novel, this theme now comes forward and occupies the very center of the canvas.

III

World Enough and Time is Mr. Warren's first historical novel (*Night Rider*, set in the early part of the present century, can hardly be considered "historical," and is not so considered by Mr. Warren himself). Like all of Mr. Warren's work, it encountered considerable misunderstanding on publication. Critics took it to be a book about life on the Kentucky frontier in the 1820's; and its merits or demerits were assessed according to the somewhat amorphous standards for this type of historical reportage. In reality, *World Enough and Time* is no more a stock historical novel, whose purpose is merely to re-create the past, than *All the King's Men* was a fictionalized biography of Huey Long. To be sure, Mr. Warren subtitled the book "A Romantic Novel"; and this was taken as confirmation that he intended to compete with *Gone With the Wind.* But what the subtitle conveys, of course, is that Mr. Warren has chosen a narrative mode appropriate to his theme. The historical novel is the creation of the Romantic movement in literature; and by locating his story in the early nineteenth century, when the names of Byron and Scott could appear in the text as appropriate period props, Mr. Warren is able to dramatize a world in which the high decorum of the Romantic image of the self forms the natural ambience of his figures.

Something of this stately decorousness, along with its mocking antithesis of worldliness, is contained in Mr. Warren's very choice of title. *World Enough and Time*—the source is obviously Marvell's famous poem, "To His Coy Mistress," which begins: "Had we but world enough, and time." This is the complaint of a lover to his recalcitrant belle, who dallies with him as if both were living in eternity. Were it possible, he tells her, he would indeed devote a more-than-human leisureliness to his courtship:

> An hundred years should go to praise
> Thine eyes, and on thy forehead gaze;
> Two hundred to adore each breast;
> But thirty thousand to the rest.

He argues quite cogently, however, that death would intervene before such a flattering program could be carried out; and he urges his mistress to awaken to the facts of life: "Now let us sport us while we may."

The poem, then, is based on the antinomy between the desire for an impossible ideal of courtly love, which we can recognize as the essence of Romanticism, and an awareness of the impossible barriers in our poor human lot that make such an ideal self-defeating. It reveals the contradiction, the necessary conflict, between the world and the idea; and this, of course, is Mr. Warren's fundamental theme. The love story of *World Enough and Time* duplicates the conflict of opposites in the poem, although not on the literal level; the "idea" pitted against the limiting conditions of life is not that of coy flirtatiousness but of perfect justice. And this accounts for the epigraph to the book, drawn from Spenser's *Faerie Queene*—an epigraph which alludes to the long-distant time

> When good was onely for itselfe desyred
> And all men sought their owne, and none no more;
> When Justice was not for most meed outhyred,
> But simple Truth did rayne, and was of all admyred.

Jeremiah Beaumont, the hero of *World Enough and Time*, embarks on the quest for perfect Justice influenced by this ideal; and he ends by destroying not only everything he loves but also himself. Yet the tragic irony of his fate, Mr. Warren implies, may nonetheless have a positive lesson to teach the modern world.

Like all of Mr. Warren's novels, *World Enough and Time* was suggested by an actual occurrence. This was a famous Kentucky murder trial in 1826—so famous, indeed, that it was immediately taken up and used by such American writers as Poe and William Gilmore Simms, not to mention others now forgotten. The murderer was a young man named Jeroboam O. Beauchamp, who left his own account of the events. Eventually, through the agency of Katherine Anne Porter, this account came into Robert Penn Warren's hands. Scholars have already hastened to compare the original with Mr. Warren's treatment; but from the very first pages it is clear that Mr. Warren is creating his own world and not transcribing that of history. For even in sketching the atmosphere of the period and the place he immediately evokes the antitheses that will be dramatized in his account of Jeremiah Beaumont's career: "The dirk (of Spanish steel or made from a hunting knife or a Revolutionary sword) and the Bible might lie side by side on the table, or Plato and the dueling pistols on the mantel shelf."

The extremes of murderous violence, on the one hand, and religious or philosophical idealism, on the other, are the poles between which Jeremiah Beaumont will oscillate with the sightless solemnity of a sleepwalker; and each pole is represented by a different narrative voice. The groundwork of the book is the (presumed) journal of Jeremiah Beaumont himself, whose style mingles the pulpit rhetoric of the period with the pompous gravity and Johnsonian orotundity of eighteenth-century moral self-assurance. It evokes a time in which men "took their world greatly and were not embarrassed by the accents of greatness, and knew that in study, field or forum they bore the destiny of man and the judgment of history." Mr. Warren does a superb job of rhetorical pastiche in these sections of the book, and they do more than anything else to make

Beaumont come alive; one finds it hard to think of any other American novelist capable of such effects. But set against this voice from the past is that of the modern narrator, who might be described as a Jack Burden reluctantly being impressed despite himself. For this voice is that of our modern disillusioned naturalism, looking behind the grand gestures and the noble motives for the sordid "truths" of passion or self-interest; but acknowledging, in this very impulse, our own need for self-abasement and self-pity, our own search for rationalizations, excuses, and evasions.

IV

We have said that in *World Enough and Time* Mr. Warren places the theme of Romanticism and reality at the center of his canvas. This is true not only of the external action and the narrative mode but also of the spiritual evolution of his chief character. For the history of Beaumont is constructed to reproduce the various dialectics of Romanticism and reality adumbrated in *All the King's Men*.

The first of these dialectics is that of Adam Stanton, who refused to accept the "impurities" of the world out of self-righteousness. As a young man, Jeremiah Beaumont's education imbues him with the same spirit; he nourishes his dreams of glory on the Latin classics, with their "patterns of human greatness . . . and love of the good beyond flesh or suffering." Later, during a religious phase, he had tried to experience "what truth might be beyond the bustle of the hour and the empty lusts of time." And when he learns that his friend and protector, Colonel Cassius Fort, has seduced a young lady of good family, he sets himself up as her self-appointed champion and attempts to provoke Fort into a duel. Beaumont is impervious both to the stifled anguish of Rachel Jordan, his future wife, and to Fort's sorrowful repentance, which causes the latter to refuse to fight despite extreme provocation. In pursuit of his "idea" Beaumont completely ignores the inner complexities of human reality; but Fort's refusal shows Beaumont that he cannot impose his will on the world and maintain his "purity" (to kill in an honorable duel) at the same time.

The second dialectic is that of Willie Stark—the attempt to play the game of the world for the sake of the idea. Beaumont is tricked into believing that Fort publicly denied his old affair and has accused his ex-inamorata, now Beaumont's wife, of having had relations with a mulatto slave. He thereupon forgets his scruples and decides on murder; now "the world must redeem the idea." Like Stark, however, Beaumont discovers that one cannot accept the terms of the world without becoming its victim. For he is caught and sentenced, not on solid evidence but because the murder has become a political *cause célèbre* and because of the handsome reward attached to solving the crime. "All the lies and false witness against me told truth," he later writes ruefully in his journal. Beaumont had thought to defend "justice" by trickery, deceit, and murder; and what he had desired consciously is achieved unwittingly by those who convict him on corrupt and perjured evidence. There is no essential moral difference between the two deeds, both of which display the ironic disparity between means and ends.

The final dialectic is that of Jack Burden, who clings to his "innocence" in the midst of degradation, but finally realizes his complicity and his guilt. The setting for this concluding phase, which symbolically reflects Beaumont's spiritual condition, is an outlaw settlement in the backwater swamps of the lower Mississippi barely emerging from the primeval slime. Like Jack Burden trying to forget himself in the Great Sleep, or in sex, or in the archetypal flight west to the innocence of nature and a new start, Jeremiah Beaumont gradually descends into the drunkenness, debauchery, and animal-like existence of the other inhabitants of the place. It is only now that he begins to find his communion with mankind—a negative communion in shame and debasement. Here at last is "innocence," for nature knows no guilt; "but that innocence is what man cannot endure and be man." And Beaumont becomes man again when he finally learns that he had been betrayed into murder and hears the bitter truth about himself from his wife.

"You made me hate Fort and you used me," she says, just before committing suicide. "Oh, I didn't hate him, I loved him, and you used me, you used me to kill him, you used me, you ruined me . . ." At last Beaumont sees himself clearly for the first time; and he sets out on the homeward journey to "shake the hangman's hand . . . and call him my brother at last." There can be no pardon for his crime because he is guilty not of an isolated deed but of "the crime of self, the crime of life. The crime is I." His crime is the deadly arrogance and self-sufficiency of the Romantic ego; and whatever the external provocation for his action, there is no way of expiating the "crime of self" except by the assumption of guilt. But Beaumont never succeeds in clasping his guilt and shaking the hangman's hand; he is murdered on the road back by those who, having used him as a tool, fear the political effect of his disclosures.

Interwoven with Beaumont's story is a lively and vivid account of the political conflicts of the day, which is admirably integrated with the main theme and serves Mr. Warren for far more than external motivation. For the chief issue of that period was a law providing relief to the debt-ridden, which had run into opposition from the Kentucky Supreme Court as unconstitutional. Immediately the cry went up to pack the court or to threaten it with violence—to impugn the source and fount of law itself for the immediate end of social justice. There is a clear parallel between this political subplot and Jeremiah Beaumont's willingness to take justice into his own hands. Indeed, as we have noted, Beaumont is eventually tricked into the murder by Fort's political enemies, who desire to get the latter out of their way. The purity of Romantic idealism does not prevent it from being an easy prey to the unscrupulousness of the political fanatic.

The meaning of Beaumont's career is illuminated not only by this political subplot but also by a number of other characters who act as Jamesian "reflectors" to highlight one or another aspect of Beaumont's adventures. Two in particular serve to modulate our sense of Beaumont's culpability. One is the spidery, skeletal, tubercular Percival Skrogg, the living image of the bodiless "idea," who illustrates the murderous potential lurking in Beaumont's lofty exaltations but whose icy and inhuman zealotry also serves to bring out Beaumont's relative warmth and human involvement. Another is Wilkie Barron, Beaumont's "friend" as a young man and the Mephistopheles who, with Skrogg's connivance, ultimately sends him to his doom and is responsible for his murder. Barron's pliant opportunism is used as a foil to underline Beaumont's idealistic obsessiveness, which, no matter how misguided, still represents a search for moral values. And while Barron ends up a wealthy and respected senator in Washington, he inexplicably shoots himself one fine morning, leaving Beaumont's journal, which he could never bring himself to destroy, moldering among his papers.

A different pair of characters are used to point up Beaumont's blindness and self-infatuation. The old backwoodsman Munn Short, Beaumont's jailer, had once been guilty of the same crime as Fort (and even worse); his tale of pardon and repentance lights up the path that Beaumont might have followed but could not until it was too late. Finally, there is the figure of Colonel Fort himself, who is a development of the Willie Stark type from *All the King's Men*—but a Willie Stark who has faced the question of the final meaning of human life and who, despite his power, is chastened by a melancholy wisdom. "I loved him," writes Beaumont, "because I thought I saw the goodness of strength which could give strength to others, and was sad for the weakness of others." Fort, who has attained the wisdom of humility and hence of goodness, is the major analogue against which to measure Beaumont; and he is killed by the latter, symbolically, at the very moment he had worked out a plan for reconciling the competing political factions that were tearing the state apart.

All these figures give us various perspectives on Beaumont; but the final perspective is that of the narrator himself, who, on the very last page, inserts a passage of nonstop prose in the breathless style that John Dos Passos took over from Molly Bloom's soliloquy in *Ulysses*. "Things went on their way, and the Commonwealth of Kentucky has, by the latest estimate, 2,819,000 inhabitants and the only Shawnee in the country is on a WPA mural on a post-office wall"—and so forth, in a parody of a complacent Chamber of Commerce brochure. Juxtaposed against this is Jeremiah Beaumont's anguished query: "I had longed to do justice in the world, and what was worthy of praise. . . . And in my crime and vainglory of self is there no worth lost? . . .Was all for naught?" The answer to this question is contained all through the book, in the grudging recognition of Beaumont's essential nobility forced on the skeptical modern narrator. Or, as Mr. Warren put it more abstractly in his Conrad essay, a year after publishing *World Enough and Time*: "To surrender to the incorrigible and ironical necessity of the 'idea,' that is man's fate and his only triumph."

V

World Enough and Time does not represent any radical new departure for Mr. Warren from the point of view of theme; but it does show him reaching out for more and more subtle and complex ways of dramatizing his moral vision. Once again he centers on the acquirement of self-knowledge—the discovery of moral responsibility and the attainment of the moral life itself through the recognition of a community of guilt. Up to *World Enough and Time*, however, this theme had always been approached in terms of a central conflict between evasion and amorality, on the one hand, and, on the other, some positive image of moral certainty. But now Mr. Warren is attempting to hold a far more delicate balance; the poles are no longer simply morality and its opposite but much subtler discriminations *within* the realm of morality itself—between innocence and wisdom, let us say, or between callow Romantic idealism and sobered moral realism. The multiple perspectives of *World Enough and Time*—with its moving counterpoint of narrative voices and the constant ironic ambiguities of its plot—are themselves a palpable image of the quicksand complexities of the moral life. And the more one reads the book the more it reveals a brooding richness and a perplexed tenderness that make it perhaps the purest and most eloquent expression (in the novel form) of Mr. Warren's sense of life. But to say this is not the equivalent of asserting that the book is an unqualified success; and it seems to me less so, as a fully realized work, than *All the King's Men.*

One of the first problems that confronts a reader of *World Enough and Time* is the melodramatic nature of the action and the uneasy sense that certain scenes would go very well in Technicolor. Take, for example, the following fateful exchange between Beaumont and Rachel Jordan:

> "Love," she said bitterly. "How should I know what love is?"
>
> "I know what it is," he declared. "It is that for which a man would do anything."
>
> "Too late—too late!" she cried. "For all the world is ruined."
>
> He gripped her hand more strongly, and leaned at her speaking rapidly and in a low voice. "One world is ruined," he said, "but we will make another. Do you hear? And to make another we must throw the first away. . . . We must crush it. Destroy it. Do you hear?" etc.

Mr. Warren, of course, consciously courted the risk of such scenes by his whole conception of Jeremiah Beaumont as a Romantic idealist; he was not—as some of his critics were only too happy to assume—tailoring a novel to Hollywood specifications. But the fact remains that Mr. Warren does not always succeed in rescuing certain pages from reading like unconscious parodies of *East Lynne;* and these pages detract from the seriousness with which Beaumont should be taken.

A more important defect arises not so much from the theme itself as from the very nature of Mr. Warren's narrative talent. All his novels show that Mr. Warren has enormous verbal, mimetic, and dramatic gifts; he knows, as the French say, how to "camp" a character before the reader in a few strokes and instantly to bring it to life. But if we survey his work as a whole we become aware that he has always avoided attempting to portray a character from the "inside," that is, to engage directly with a severe inner conflict. Perhaps the reason is that Mr. Warren is a moralist, who believes in the inscrutability of free will; and he has an instinctive mistrust of "psychology." But whatever the explantion, Mr. Warren's characters are always either "flat" and unchanging, or, when they do change, the motivation is invariably given by some external arrangement of the plot that serves as a substitute for a direct grasp of consciousness.

Ordinarily Mr. Warren meets this problem by the use of first-person narrative monologue, in which the character tells his own story. This device seems to place the reader in the heart of the character's consciousness, but Mr. Warren's characters usually confine themselves to a recital of events. Nonetheless, by the proper use of style to indicate feeling and attitude, and particularly by introducing the perspective of the future into the narrative account, the recital can be colored sufficiently to prepare for the psychological shift. This is one reason why Mr. Warren's most satisfactory novel is *All the King's Men,* where such a use of narrative monologue dominates the total perspective. For from the very first pages the reader feels both the disabused irony and cynicism of Jack Burden—his corroding scorn for the hypocrisies of hand-me-down morality—and at the same time his equally savage scorn for himself. It is the emotional tension between these two extremes, as conveyed by the style, that succeeds in carrying the positive affirmation of values at the end.

To a certain extent, somewhat the same technique is used in *World Enough and Time* in Jeremiah Beaumont's diary. Much of the narrative, however, is not direct quotation but résumé and summary; in these parts the style tends to be neutral, and hence to give only an indistinct and muffled access to Beaumont's state of mind. Moreover, while Jack Burden has to undergo only *one* moral transition, Jeremiah Beaumont has to undergo *three*—each representing another phase of the dialectic of Romanticism and reality. For while different phases of this dialectic were given to different characters in *All the King's Men,* the experience of Beaumont encompasses all the phases at one or another stage of his career. It is therefore of the utmost importance to make the shift from one phase to another as vivid and forceful as possible; but Mr. Warren's inability (or unwillingness) to portray a conscience struggling with itself deprives Beaumont of the necessary inner stature to support his role.

As an example, we may cite the following crucial passage, which describes Beaumont's first disillusionment with Fort:

> He thought how little he had in the world. His labor at the law was suddenly a dreary and childish routine. How had he ever thought that the law answered the deep cry of the heart? And his glowing prospects, what were they? A few dollars, a few acres, the envious servility of men. And if he should realize those prospects, his success would have been poisoned at the root. For he would owe all to Fort. To Fort, the villain. Ah, where was the greatness of life? Was it only a dream? Could a man not come to some moment when, all dross and meanness of life consumed, he could live in the pure idea?

One cannot help feeling something perfunctory about this description, a decisive failure on Mr. Warren's part really to project himself into Beaumont's state of mind. The transition to abstract explanation is too hasty, too quick and easy, to convince us that Beaumont's entire life will be unalterably changed from this moment onward.

One thinks of what Dostoevsky might have done with such a scene; and the comparison is not totally unfair because the theme of *World Enough and Time* is very similar to that of *Crime and Punishment*—innocence murdering out of idealism, and learning the truth about the self as the deed develops its own sinister logic. But nowhere do we feel about Beaumont, as we do about Raskolnikov, that the deed springs forth irresistibly from some deep psychic pressure; nowhere are we touched by any inner torment, any agony of conscience or sensibility compelling first the murder and then the final assumption of guilt. Nowhere, in short, does Jeremiah Beaumont seem anything but an automaton, despite the wealth of symbolic incident lavished on him by Mr. Warren to convey the meaning of his history.

This impression of lifelessness given by Beaumont is reinforced by the manner in which Mr. Warren has plotted the action. Every crucial decision of Beaumont's is a result of treachery and deceit; this is true even of his first disenchantment with Fort, for he hears the rumor about Rachel Jordan from Wilkie Barron, who feigns indignation at the villainous seducer. (No adequate explanation is ever given for this first lie; all the later ones have an obvious political rationale.) The reason for this construction is obvious enough: the idea, thinking itself free and pure, is always implicated in the world and at the service of the world, whether it will or no. Mr. Warren's plotting mirrors his theme; but perhaps he has mirrored it here with a too-rigorous consistency. For in so doing he sacrifices the advantage of making Beaumont fully responsible for his own actions. Indeed, Beaumont ends up by seeming a pitiful puppet at the mercy of all kinds of external influences, not a figure whose character is his fate and who derives dignity from his self-determination. No doubt Beaumont is more sympathetic because he is driven to the murder; but here again one thinks of Raskolnikov, who, though he commits his murder in a hallucinatory trance, induces the trance himself by his brooding over the idea of the crime.

These flaws seem to me to prevent *World Enough and Time* from reaching the very first rank as an independent work; but they by no means cancel out entirely its haunting and poignant impact. Indeed, while *Night Rider* and *At Heaven's Gate* exhibit a similar weakness at the center—a failure to endow the leading characters with any convincing depth of inner life—*World Enough and Time*, despite the elaborateness of Beaumont's imputed evolution, seems to suffer less from this congenital deficiency than either of the earlier books. No doubt because it is so highly stylized and formalized, so much a moral allegory or romance rather than a true novel (it is quite fitting that Spenser should stand godfather at the threshold), one is content here with far less psychological verisimilitude and plausible motivation. The core of the book is only nominally in Beaumont; in reality, it lies in the moral musing of the narrative voices and in the lyrical and poetic pregnancy of the symbolic details. This partial success of *World Enough and Time* in reviving a moribund genre—a genre which also includes *Billy Budd* and *The Scarlet Letter*—is impressive evidence of the brilliance, vivacity, and versatility of Mr. Warren's literary gifts. But one cannot help wishing that he could again manage to get as close to another central figure as interesting as Jack Burden, whose ideological and psychological complexity makes *All the King's Men* the most satisfying of Robert Penn Warren's novels.

JONATHAN BAUMBACH

The Metaphysics of Demagoguery: "All the King's Men"

History is blind but man is not.
—*All the King's Men*

Although Robert Penn Warren is a generation or so older than, with one exception, any of the writers treated in this study, he is technically a post-Second-World-War novelist. That is, the larger body of his fiction, including his major novel *All the King's Men*, has been published since 1945. Though a valuable novelist, Warren is also notably a playwright, poet, teacher, scholar, and critic—a man of letters in the best sense. The problem is, how does a man write a novel unself-consciously, when he is aware just how the critic, created perhaps in his own image, is likely to read it? The answer is, he doesn't. At least Warren doesn't.

Almost all of Warren's fiction suffers somewhat from the determined this-marriage-can-be-saved compatibility between Warren the novelist and Warren the explicator. The harder he tries to fuse the two selves, the farther apart they spring, as if resistant to the meddling of an outsider. As Eric Bentley has actually observed, "The problem lies precisely in his [Warren's] being so two-sidedly gifted; he evidently finds it endlessly difficult to combine his two sorts of awareness." Warren's novels are informed by a fairly complex set of intellectual alternatives, while at the same time they rely for their movement on frenetically charged

From *The Landscape of Nightmare*. Copyright © 1965 by New York University Press.

melodramatic action, often for its own sake, for the sake merely of narrative excitement. Though Warren is a serious novelist, and at his best, a brilliant prose writer, there is a curious separation in his novels between the events of the narrative and the meaning Warren insists they accommodate.

Of Warren's eight novels to date, *All the King's Men* (1946) seems to me the most achieved, the most serious and the most enduring—for all its flaws, one of our near-great novels. For some time *All the King's Men* was misread as a disturbingly sympathetic fictionalized account of the demagogic career of Huey Long. Approached as an historical document, the book was condemned by politically liberal critics as a florid, rhetorical justification for a Napoleonic brand of American neo-fascism. There is no need any longer to point out the irrelevancy of this attack, to explain that Jack Burden is the center of the novel and that Willie Stark, "the man of fact," is not *actually* Huey Long, but a kind of "Mistah Kurtz." In fact, in recent years a critical orthodoxy has clustered about Warren's novels, which is not unlike those contemporary angels headed by C. S. Lewis and Douglas Bush who guard the gates around Milton's *Paradise Lost*, protecting it from profanation by the infernal satanists. In both cases the defense is warranted; there is a real enemy. But in both cases the enemy is already within the gates. Though Warren intends Jack Burden to be the center of the novel, Willie Stark is by virtue of his energy the more realized and interesting character. Burden, as thinly disguised authorial spokesman, is a literary conception, created from other fiction rather than from life, a combination, if you can imagine it, of Nick Carraway and Sam Spade. Whatever Warren's intention, the character of Willie Stark, a colossus of human and inhuman possibilities, inadvertently dominates the novel. Inevitably, a distortion results, the kind of distortion which would permit *All the King's Men* to be read as the story of Willie Stark's rise and fall (a tragedy of over-reaching pride brought low by retributive justice).

For all that, Jack Burden, acquiescent narrator, at once vicarious Willie and vicarious Adam, is the novel's center, the ultimate synthesizer of its polarities. While Willie and Adam die unfulfilled, Jack completes the spiritual voyage; he moves, an exemplary sleepwalker, from sin to recognition and guilt to redemption and rebirth. Jack's ritual search for a true father, or at least a true absolute, leads him into Willie's employ (on the coat-tails of his political ascension). Ironically, there is a certain amount of narcissism in Jack's discipleship because he has, in part, created Willie the "Boss," catalyzed him from the raw materials of "Cousin Willie from the country." At the outset, Willie is an innocent, a do-gooder whose campaign speeches are scrupulously honest and drearily dull. Jack gives him his first taste of the apple:

> Hell, make 'em cry, make 'em laugh, make 'em think you're God-Almighty. Or make 'em mad. Even mad at you. Just stir 'em up, it doesn't matter how or why, and they'll love you and come back for more. Pinch them in the soft place. They aren't alive, most of 'em haven't been alive in twenty years. Hell, their wives have lost their teeth and their shape, and likker won't set on their stomachs, and they don't believe in God, so it's up to you to give 'em something to stir 'em up and make 'em feel again. . . . But for Sweet Jesus' sake don't try to improve their minds.
> (*All the King's Men*. New York; Harcourt, Brace & World, Inc., 1946, p. 72. All quotations are from this edition.)

This is the first and last time that Jack gives Willie a short course in cynical wisdom. Once having learned the lesson, Willie becomes the teacher, the authority on man's fallen nature. As Willie tells Jack later on in his (and Warren's) characteristic evangelical rhetoric: " 'Man is conceived in sin and born in corruption and passeth from the stink of the didie to the stench of the shroud. There is always something' " (p. 157).

It is Jack, however, who has initiated Willie's conversion from the man of idea to the man of fact, from romanticism to pragmatism. By demonstrating to him that his start in politics was made possible by political corruption, Jack destroys Willie's sense of innocence, decreates him into manhood. While Jack, who suffers chronically from paralysis of the will, converts Willie through abstract example, Willie converts the uncommitted Jack through practical demonstration. The "Boss" Willie is Jack as he would like to be, but only if he could watch himself being it. For all his admiration of action, Jack is essentially a spectator, an historian waiting for history to happen. Willie performs history for him, tests the efficacy of Jack's theories, while Jack with clinical dispassion sits on the sidelines taking notes. (Jack's role as spectator is defined symbolically in the scene in which he sits in the hospital amphitheatre watching Adam Stanton perform a lobotomy.) As a dutiful son, Jack Burden participates in and even admires his father's ruthless pragmatism without sensing his own culpability. What you refuse to know can't hurt you, but, as Jack discovers, for only so long as you can remain blind. The longer you avoid self-knowledge, however, the more vulnerable you are to its intrusion.

Aside from Willie, Jack has two other fathers: a nominal one who he thinks is real and whom he has rejected (Ellis Burden) and a real one whom he admires and inadvertently kills (Judge Irwin). When Willie assigns him to get "something on" Judge Irwin, who has been outspoken in his criticism of Stark's administration, Jack is forced for the first time to choose between the prerogatives of opposing fathers. (Though he doesn't know that Irwin is his natural father, he respects, resents, and feel obligated to Irwin as a son to a father because of Irwin's decency and friendship over the years.) Looking for a way out of his predicament, Jack tells Willie that Irwin is "washed in the blood" and that an investigation of Irwin's past will be a waste of time. Willie knows, however, that man is fallen, that "there is always something." In investigating the facts of Irwin's life, Jack puts to the test the last illusion he has permitted himself to retain, that despite the rank and malodorous corruption which underlies so much of contemporary life, a truly good man like Irwin remains incorruptible. Jack has another naive notion which justifies the political dirt-digging he does so that Willie can blackmail his opponents: that the truth, regardless of its immediate effects, is always salutary and that unadulterated fact constitutes truth.

In search of the hidden facts of his real father's past, Jack visits Ellis Burden, the Scholarly Attorney turned Religious Fanatic, his nominal father. It is here that the divergent influences of his trinity of fathers come into focus and are symbolically defined. Once again, Jack rejects the Scholarly Attorney, the weak saint, whose life of squalor, piety, and undiscriminating compassion seems purposeless to him when contrasted with Willie Stark's vigorous usefulness. This dispossessed nominal father has adopted a substitute son, George, a former circus aerialist who has reverted to childhood. George, redeemed through the trauma into helpless innocence, spends his time making angels from masticated bread crusts. He is, in an ironic sense, Jack's brother. George's idiot purity embarrasses Jack and he rejects the image of his opposite (his innocent brother) along with his Scholarly Attorney father, along with the past. But, at the same time, he is again rejected by his father, who refuses to answer his questions about Irwin—who is unable to hear him when Jack calls him "Father." The visit is a failure; Jack learns nothing about Irwin, and he experiences the loss of his father all over again.

The uncovering of Irwin's one dishonorable act has massive, unaccountable ramifications. In consequence of Jack's discovery, Judge Irwin commits suicide. Anne Stanton has a self-destructive affair with Willie Stark, Adam Stanton kills Willie Stark, and Willie Stark's bodyguard kills Adam Stanton. For all his disinterested intentions, Jack must bear the burden of responsibility for this proliferation of tragedy. He has set it in motion as surely and perfectly as if he had consciously planned it. The "facts" that incriminate the Judge also indicate the complicity of Governor Stanton, who deliberately covered up for his friend. This further discovery destroys for both Anne and Adam Stanton the idealized notion of their father that has sustained them in their myth of purity as children of innocence—descendants of innocence. When Anne discovers that the purity of the old governor is tainted, she is able to shed her restrictive moral restraints as a snake sheds its skin. If there is no pure God, a pure Satan is the next best thing—he is at least whole. With the loss of her good father, Anne commits a sort of symbolic incest with the bad father—the new governor—searching for an absolute to replace the one she had lost. The loss of innocence in the novel for Jack, Willie, Anne, and Adam is concomitant with the loss of the good father.

It is Adam, Jack's innocent self, the least convincing of all Warren's characters, who guilelessly gives Jack his first lead in uncovering Irwin's blemished past. Adam answers Jack's cunning, direct question, "Was Judge Irwin ever broke?" because he is too ingenuous not to. However, Adam's innocent volunteering of harmless information about Judge Irwin is, in its effects, irresponsible as only innocence can be. It gives Jack the necessary clue to unearth Irwin's guilty secret, which, in ramification, destroys each of the participants in the central action of the novel. Adam's ingenuousness here anticipates his later, more destructive, act of innocence—his self-righteous assassination of Willie Stark. To say any more about Adam is beside the point. Whereas some of Warren's characters are half-human, half-idea, Adam is pure idea; he is an allegorical personification of *Innocence*. But without life, he is finally nothing, a figment of the author's imagination.

All of Warren's main characters experience at one time or another the loss of innocence and are characterized in terms of their accommodation to their Fall. Judge Irwin, sustained like Adam by the myth of self-purity, has attempted to evade the implications of his one intentionally corrupt act (his Fall) by shutting it out of his memory. Some thirty years later, Jack, the unacknowledged child of his loins, confronts him with the forgotten past. Jack's confrontation has a twofold significance; Jack is the manifestation of Irwin's other sin, his adulterous affair with Jack's mother, so that he becomes for Irwin the symbol of his fallen past, the tale-bearer of one crime and the embodiment of the other. Warren images Jack's information as a barb finding meat, suggesting its lethal nature. The Judge, illuminated by self-knowledge at once destructive and redemptive, bears his pain stoically. For a moment Irwin is tempted to reveal to his son the nature of their relationship in order that Jack withhold his information, but he doesn't—because it is beside the point.

"I wouldn't hurt you," he said. Then, reflectively, added, "But I could stop you."
"By stopping MacMurfee," I said.

"A lot easier than that."

"How?"

"A lot easier than that," he repeated.

"How?"

"I could just. . ." he began, "I could just say to you—I could just tell you something. . . ." He stopped, then suddenly rose to his feet, spilling the papers off his knees. "But I won't," he said cheerfully and smiled directly at me.

(p.347)

The moment of recognition is averted. By not telling Jack—an act of mortal restraint—Irwin accepts full responsibility for his sin. Irwin's withholding of his "truth" is, given the occasion, more honorable than Jack's revelation of his. The next morning Jack is awakened by his mother's "bright, beautiful silvery soprano screams." In her hysteria, she continues to shriek at Jack, "You killed him. You killed him," without identifying the "him": " 'Killed who?' I demanded, shaking her. 'Your father,' she said, 'your father and oh! you killed him' " (p.350).

Without further clarification, Jack realizes what had happened as if he had known all the time, in the secret wisdom of instinct, that Irwin was his father. That the Judge shoots himself through the heart indicates symbolically the implication of Jack's betrayal. Despite the terrible consequences of his act, Jack reflects on his responsibility for Irwin's suicide, as if it were an intellectual abstraction, which does not touch him personally. At first he considers his father's death as the just retribution of Mortimer Littlepaugh, the man whom Irwin's own corrupt act drove to suicide. Then:

Or had it been Mortimer? Perhaps I had done it. That was one way of looking at it. I turned that over and speculated upon my responsibility. It would be quite possible to say that I had none, no more than Mortimer had. Mortimer had killed Judge Irwin because Judge Irwin had killed him and I killed Judge Irwin because Judge Irwin had created me, and looking at matters in that light one could say that Mortimer and I were only the twin instruments of Irwin's protracted and ineluctable self-destruction. For either killing or creating may be a crime punishable by death, and the death always comes by the criminal's own hand and every man is a suicide. If a man knew how to live he would never die.

(p. 353)

It is a characteristically easy rationalization for Jack, one which enables him to avoid for a time the implications of his behavior. Like every man, he too is a suicide (though a moral rather than a physical one) and, ultimately, ineluctably, his sins revisit him like retributive ghosts. As a result of Irwin's death, Jack loses two fathers, the weak but saintly

Scholarly Attorney and the strong but tainted judge. Willie Stark, the evil father, the father who has cuckolded him, is all that is left for Jack in a world of decimated fathers, and finally Jack kills him too. As Jack tells us, " 'I had dug up the truth and the truth always kills the father.' " In a symbolic sense, only after Jack destroys his fathers can he become a man himself. As part of his quest for knowledge (manhood), Jack kills the fathers of his world only to resurrect them finally in himself.

Jack's articulated intellection dissipates the effect of this scene as it does much of the richly rendered experience of the novel. Granted his cleverness, Jack is verbally aware of too much, and also too little; Warren is forever peeking over his shoulder, but withholding from his narrator the whole picture. That Jack as narrator is almost always the deception of an insight ahead of the reader is one of the recurring distractions of the novel. With rare exception, the reader is not permitted to discover meanings; they are discovered for him.

When Willie loses his innocence, he is transformed almost overnight from the son of his world to its father. Willie's spiritual metamorphosis (which resembles Kurtz's in *Heart of Darkness*), though thematically subordinate to Jack's guilt-and-redemption passage, dominates the action of the novel. Willie's career anticipates and parallels Jack's, as a father's anticipates a son's, though it is enlarged where Jack's is diminished, and Willie never successfully makes the spiritual voyage back from hell. Like Kurtz, the "Boss" has gone too far into darkness ever to return into light.

Willie becomes governor. Ostensibly, his ends have not changed, only his means of achieving them. Gradually, however, the ends become inseparable from their means and Willie yields himself to his most voracious interior devils. The thesis is classic and bromidic: power tends to corrupt; absolute power tends to corrupt absolutely. With a difference, however: Warren inverts the cliché; for all his sins, "Willie is a great man." This is the verdict of his wife Lucy, to whom he has been unfaithful, whose son he has destroyed through vanity, and of Jack Burden, whom he has disillusioned and nearly destroyed. Since the redeemed Jack Burden, who has moved from blindness to whole sight represents, one must believe, the point of view of the novel, this must stand as Warren's judgment of Stark. The question remains: Is it a reasonable judgment borne out by the experience of the novel? Or is it a piece of gratuitous iconoclasm, the cliché-anti-cliché?

Warren enlists sympathy for Willie by indicating that the context in which he is forced to operate (southern politics) is unreclaimably corrupt. Whereas Tiny Duffy and Willie's opponent MacMurfee are interested in petty graft as an end, Willie's ego wants nothing less than recognition by posterity. Willie is a real devil at sup among dwarfed, flabby devils; in that he is more real and more potent than the others, he is to that extent more admirable. Once Willie has fallen, he discovers his true voice, the voice of the rabble rouser, the appeal to primordial violence:

> You asked me what my program is. Here it is, you hicks. And don't you forget it. Nail 'em up! Nail up Joe Harrison. Nail up anybody who stands in your way. Nail up MacMurfee if he don't deliver. You hand me the hammer and I'll do it with my own hand. Nail 'em up on the barn door.
>
> (p. 96)

The easier it becomes for Willie to manipulate the crowd, the less respect he has for its common fallen humanity. As he becomes more powerful, he becomes, like Kurtz and like Macbeth, more voracious, more proud, more evil. Willie's palpable moral decline is manifested for us when he covers up for an underling who has taken graft. It is not in the act of covering up but in his justification for it that Willie's inhumanity and presumption are manifested:

> My God, you talk like Byram was human! He's a thing! You don't prosecute an adding machine if a spring goes bust and makes a mistake. You fix it. Well, I fixed Byram. I fixed Byram. I fixed him so his unborn great-grandchildren will wet their pants on this anniversary and not know why. Boy, it will be the shock in the genes. Hell, Byram is just something you use, and he'll sure be useful from now on.
>
> (p. 136)

Willie's self-defining presumption is that he *knows* himself a superior being, aspiring to law, to omnipotence, to God. The machine metaphor he employs reveals his attitude not only toward Byram but toward the populace in general: people are things to be used by him, "the Boss," for *his* purposes. From Willie's "bulging-eyed" point-of-view, everything, all existence, has been set in motion to serve him.

Willie's will to power, his lust for omnipotence, is defeated by what might be called a tragic virtue. Despite Willie's professed thesis that "you have to make the good out of the bad because that's all you have to make it out of," that all men are innately corrupt, that "political graft is the grease that keeps the wheels from squeaking," he wants to build a magnificent, immaculate hospital as his gift to the state, untainted by the usual petty corruption and graft. In pursuing this ideal, Willie refuses a deal with Gummy Larson, the power behind his enemy MacMurfee, whose defection to Willie would leave the "Boss" all but unopposed. Having fallen from Paradise into Hell, Willie wishes—his one romantic illusion—to regain his lost purity, to buy back Paradise. Willie tries to explain his motives to Jack:

"Can't you understand either? I'm building that place, the best in the country, the best in the world, and a bugger like Tiny is not going to mess with it, and I'm going to call it the Willie Stark Hospital and it will be there a long time after I'm dead and gone and you are dead and gone and all those sons-of-bitches are dead and gone and anybody, no matter he hasn't got a dime, can go there . . ."

"And will vote for you," I said.

"I'll be dead," he said, "and you'll be dead, and I don't care whether he votes for me or not, he can go there and . . ."

"And bless your name," I said.

That Willie, so compellingly articulate on other occasions, cannot cogently rationalize his motives suggests that they are contradictory to him as well as to Jack. He wants at once to be noble and to have everyone admire his nobility—selflessness for the sake of self. Yet, and herein lies the contradiction, he also wants redemption.

As part of his obsessive desire to transcend his corruption, his dream of greatness, Willie hires Adam Stanton to run his hospital, hoping through connection, through transfusion of spirit, to inform himself with Adam's innocence. Ironically, Willie has, with almost perfect instinct, chosen his redeemer, his redeemer as executioner. Adam and Willie as ideological polarities must inevitably merge or destroy each other. Jack unites them, he is the means of their collaborative self-destruction.

Willie's brief affair with Adam's sister Anne, is another extension of his specious quest for innocence. What Willie pursues is not innocence, really, but seeming innocence—respectability. His holy search for the false grail is the tragic flaw in his otherwise perfect expediency. Willie's lost innocence resides not with Adam and Anne, but with his wife Lucy and his father; his substitution of Anne for Lucy symbolizes his degeneration, his spiritual blindness. In his obsession with purity, Willie makes an enemy of the spiteful Tiny Duffy and puts too much faith in the erratically naive, the fallen innocent, Adam, thereby predicating his own destruction. Duffy makes an anonymous phone call to Adam, falsifying the implications of Anne's affair with Willie. The inflexibly idealistic Adam, unable to live in an imperfect world, acts as the unwitting tool of vengeful petty corruption and gratuitously murders Willie. Specious innocence and cowardly corruption conspire to destroy the "Boss" at the height of his power and at the threshold of his apparent self-reform.

Willie's deathbed scene is the most potent of the various dramatic climaxes in the novel. In it Warren brings sharply into focus the moral paradox of Willie's ethic—the tragedy of his unachieved, over-reaching ambition; it is rendered as Judge Irwin's death is not, as a profoundly affecting experience. It is the death of Jack's last symbolic father—an extension of all his fathers—leaving him, for a time, alone and uncommitted in the chaos of his ungoverned universe. I quote the scene at length because it is a resonant fusion of idea and action, a moment of illumined truth.

> For a minute he didn't speak but his eyes looked up at me, with the light still flickering in them. Then he spoke: "Why did he do it to me?"
>
> "Oh, God damn it," I burst out, very loud, "I don't know." The nurse looked warningly at me.
>
> "I never did anything to him," he said.
>
> "No, you never did."
>
> He was silent again, and the flicker went down in his eyes. Then, "He was all right, the Doc."
>
> I nodded.
>
> I waited, but it began to seem that he wasn't going to say any more. His eyes were on the ceiling and I could scarcely tell that he was breathing. Finally, the eyes turned toward me again, very slowly, and I almost thought that I could hear the tiny painful creak of the balls in their sockets. But the light flickered up again. He said, "It might have been all different, Jack."
>
> I nodded again.
>
> He roused himself more. He even seemed to be straining to lift his head from the pillow. "You got to believe that," he said hoarsely.
>
> The nurse stepped forward and looked significantly at me.
>
> "Yes," I said to the man on the bed.
>
> "You got to," he said again. "You got to believe that."
>
> "All right."
>
> He looked at me, and for a moment it was the old strong, probing, demanding glance. But when the words came this time, they were very weak. "And it might have been different yet," he whispered. "If it hadn't happened, it might—have been different—even yet."
>
> (p.400)

Willie's deathbed claim is an easy one to make; it is as impossible to prove as to disprove. One is tempted to say to him, as Jake does to Brett at the end of *The Sun Also Rises*, "Isn't it pretty to think so?" though sigificantly Jack does not. However, it is not out of motives of sentiment that Jack withholds his ironic disbelief. He is not fully convinced that Willie's self-justification is unjust. The possibility remains: "It might have been different—even yet." Willie is, after all, a paradox.

In becoming Willie's executioner, Adam, in his blind way, follows the example of Willie's career—he becomes Willie. For the "man of fact" and the "man of idea," as Jack classified them, there has been an alternation of roles. Each incomplete, seeking completeness, has chosen his polar opposite as an exemplary image. In building the hospital without the "grease" of political graft, Willie is operating idealistically—in Adam's image. In brutally shooting down Willie, Adam is acting as disciple of the man whose power-authority is symbolized by the meat axe. From Jack's standpoint, Willie is superior to Adam: "A man's virtue may be but the defect of his desire, as his crime may be but a function of his virtue." If a man has not faced temptation, or, as in Adam's case, has not admitted its existence, his purity is illusory and beside the point.

Willie's relationship to his son Tom is another variation on the novel's father-son conflict, and it serves as an ironic comment both on Jack's relationship to his real father and to Willie. Jack's search into Irwin's discreditable past is continually juxtaposed to scenes of Willie worshipfully watching Tom perform on the football field: " 'He's my boy—and there's not any like him—he'll be All-American. . . .' " Tom Stark is the perfect physical extension of Willie's wishful self-image; he is all man of action—with the bottle, on the gridiron, and in bed—one hundred percent performance, no waste. Burden sees him as "one hundred and eighty pounds of split-second, hair trigger, Swiss-watch beautiful mechanism." Inhuman but perfect, he is the embodiment of Willie's crass values. Willie is willing to overlook Tom's personal decay so long as he continues to function as a perfect mechanism on the football field and so sate Willie's rapacious vanity. Willie's attitude toward Tom is symbolic of his attitude toward the governmental machine—proud, permissive, and blind. Corruption is permissible because it "keeps the wheels from squeaking." His failure with Tom is symptomatic of his potential failure as governor; to satisfy his vanity Willie would have all men, even his own son, made into functioning "things." Inadvertently, Willie destroys Tom, who is, outside of personal power, the "thing" he loves most in his world. When Tom has been barred from playing football for breaking college rules (the boy manages, among his heroics, to cripple one girl in an auto crash and to impregnate another), Willie pressures the coach into reinstating him. Almost immediately after Tom comes into the game, as if in direct consequence of Willie's corrupt use of authority, his spine is snapped by a vicious tackle. As a result, the son of the man of action is left actionless, without the use of his arms and legs. As the emotional paralysis of Jack catalyzes, in a sense, the action of Willie, Willie's action causes the physical paralysis of Tom. The irony is evident: ultimately a machine stops, even a perfect Swiss-made mechanism breaks down if it is dropped too often. The sins of the father are visited on the son. Similarly, the "breaking" of the son anticipates the destruction of the father; it is an intimation of Willie's mortality.

Whereas in Jack's case the son kills the father, in Willie's the father
kills the son. However, Tom is, through the ineluctable chain of cause
and effect, also the instrument of Willie's destruction. As a consequence of
Tom's impregnating the daughter of one of MacMurfee's men, Willie is
forced through blackmail to compromise his principles and give the corrupt Gummy Larson the hospital-construction contract. After Tom's injury, however, the guilt-ridden Willie breaks the contract. Tiny Duffy,
who has been intermediary in the deal, exacts his vengence; he initiates
Willie's murder through Adam's pride.

Before Adam shoots him down, Willie accepts Tom's paralysis as a
judgment for his sins and seeks expiation through good works: "you got to
start somewhere." As Irwin ultimately redeems Jack, Tom almost redeems
Willie, but not quite; after his fall, Humpty-Dumpty cannot be put together
again. Willie, like Tom's paralyzed body, is denied rebirth. Willie's death
does, however, make possible the redemption of Tom's illegitimate son,
whom Lucy decides to adopt and name, of all names, Willie Stark.
Through his son's son, Willie regains his lost innocence.

With the death of Willie, the effective father, Jack has no one left
to whom he can transfer his responsibility. However, before he can
achieve manhood, Jack has one other father with whom he has to come to
terms—Cass Mastern; the subject of his Ph.D. dissertation is Jack's historic
father. The episode of Cass Mastern, a self-contained short story with the
novel, is intended as a gloss (in Warren's term, "the myth") on the larger
action of the main narrative. Though it illuminates certain themes in *All
the King's Men* and is in itself an exceptionally resonant tale, Cass's
tragedy is hardly indispensable to the novel. In any event, at the cost of
temporarily stopping the action, it gives added dimension to Burden's
odyssey into self-knowledge, his passage from innocence to limbo to guilt
to redemption. Though Jack has pieced together all the facts of Cass
Mastern's life, he is unable to complete his dissertation. The significance
of Cass's story eludes him, though he is aware that it has significance.
Neither Jack's early philosophic idealism ("What you don't know won't
hurt you") nor his disillusioned belief in the Great Twitch (that man is an
involuntary mechanism and no one is responsible for anything) is adequate to a comprehension of Cass's sainthood. Cass, though innocent and
virtuous, falls into an affair with Annabelle Trice, his best friend's wife.
As a consequence, three lives are destroyed. Thereafter Cass, suffused
with guilt, makes his existence a continuous penance for his sin. He
finally joins the southern army and gives up his life while refusing to fire a
shot in his own defense. Through martydom he achieves expiation. At
the end, Cass becomes a religious fanatic, and on his deathbed he sends a

strange letter to his successful brother. The passage is typical of the evangelical eloquence of Warren's rhetoric:

> Remember me, but without grief. If one of us is lucky, it is I. I shall have rest and I hope in the mercy of the Everlasting and his blessed election. But you, my dear brother, are condemned to eat bread in bitterness and build on the place where the charred embers and ashes are and to make bricks without straw to suffer in the ruin and guilt of our dear Land and in the common guilt of man.
>
> (p.162)

Cass's martyrdom is exemplary; it is not only his own guilt for which he has suffered and died but the guilt of the land, "the common guilt of man." In the mystery of Cass's life and death resides the meaning of Jack's life, which is to say the essential meaning of all our lives. As Cass has written in his journal, and as Jack finally discovers for himself, " 'It is a human defect—to try to know oneself by the self of another. One can only know oneself in God and His great eye.' " After the recognition of his guilt, it is in God that Cass does find himself; similarly, after Jack accepts his guilt, it is in himself that he finds Cass and, ultimately, God. The recognition of guilt for Cass (and by implication for Jack) is an awesome discovery.

> It was, instead, the fact of all these things—the death of my friend, the betrayal of Phebe, the suffering and rage and great change of the woman I had loved—all had come from my single act of sin and perfidy, as the boughs from the bole and the leaves from the bough. Or to figure the matter differently, it was as though the vibration set up in the whole fabric of the world by my act had spread infinitely and with ever increasing power and no man could know the end. I did not put it into words in such fashion, but I stood there shaken by a tempest of feeling.
>
> (p. 178)

Cass's revelation is existential; that is, since the ramifications of a particular act are for the most part unknowable and the inherent responsibility for its entire chain reaction inescapable, the burden of guilt is endless—and unbearable. So Cass, in search of redemption, tracks down the various consequences of his act of sin only to discover that there is no undoing of the harm he has already caused. What he has done is irrevocable. It is only by "living in God's eye"—a saint's life—that he can hope to achieve expiation and redemption.

Since Duncan Trice, who is considerably older than Cass, initiates him into vice, he is, in effect, the father of Cass's adultery with Annabelle. What Cass has learned from Duncan he had put into practice with Duncan's wife. Therefore, Cass's crime, Warren suggests, is implicitly incestuous, for if Duncan, the man whose death he effects, is his "substitute" father, Annabelle as his wife is a sort of symbolic mother. This is essentially what Cass understands when he proclaims himself "the chief of sinners and a plague spot on the body of the human world."

Cass's experience acts as an anticipatory parallel to Jack's own nightmare passage, though the connections are remote and abstract. When Jack discovers that Duffy "had killed Stark as surely as though his own hand had held the revolver," he feels absolved of responsibility, free at last to act, to vindicate the deaths of Willie and Adam. However, Jack's newborn sense of freedom is illusory. It is for him another evasion of responsibility, in a way the least admirable of all. Convincing himself as Willie had, and as Adam had when he squeezed the trigger, that an act is a self-willed moral entity, Jack assumes for himself the role of avenging angel; he wishes to destroy Duffy in order to justify himself. However, after Jack chastises Duffy, " 'You are the stinkingest louse God ever let live!' " and threatens him with exposure, he realizes that " 'I had tried to make Duffy into a scapegoat for me and to set myself off from Duffy,' " that Duffy is his alter ego, his corrupt brother, and whatever he had said about Duffy was also true of himself. In the power of Warren's prose, we get the visceral horror of Jack's self-revulsion:

> It was as though in the midst of the scene Tiny Duffy had slowly and like a brother winked at me with his oyster eye and I had known he knew some nightmare truth, which was that we were twins bound together more intimately and disastrously than the poor freaks of the midway who are bound by the common stitch of flesh and gristle and the seepage of blood. We are bound together forever and I could never hate him without hating myself or love myself without loving him.
>
> And I heaved and writhed like the ox or the cat, and the acid burned my gullet and that's all there was to it and I hated everybody and myself and Tiny Duffy and Willie Stark and Adam Stanton.
>
> (p.417)

Jack, by evading the responsibility for his own sins, had amid the corruption about him, retained the illusion of innocence. Since he had not acted out of conscious choice, but had merely yielded to the demands of the "Boss," he had been able to slough off the burden of guilt. Once he discovers himself free to act, he becomes aware that the possibility of all acts, the whole spectrum of good and evil, are in him; that he is, as human being, Oedipus and Duffy and Willie and everyone else. Having discovered the magnitude of his guilt—that he is responsible not only for his own sins but for all sins—Jack begins his return from the interior hell in which he has languished so long. He cannot leave hell, of course, until he has discovered its boundaries.

When Jack runs into "Sugar-Boy," Willie's driver and bodyguard (*the* man of action), he is presented with the opportunity of destroying Duffy with no risk to himself. He restrains himself not out of the paralysis ("the defect of desire") which prevented him many years before from making love to Anne when she offered herself to him but because Duffy is his "twin," and if he can sanction Duffy's murder he must sanction his own. (Cass refused to kill in the Civil War because: " 'How can I, who have taken the life of my friend, take the life of an enemy, for I have used up my right to blood?' ") Jack's refusal to take easy vengeance on Duffy is not inaction but a decisive moral act.

For a time, as a projection of his self-hate, Jack has a baleful view of all humanity. When he comes to love his mother, whom he has rejected long ago, he is able as a consequence to stop hating himself, which also means no longer hating the rest of the world. The redemption of his mother through the recognition of her love for Irwin (his real father) is Jack's salvation; it reestablishes for him the existential possibility of love. However, as Jack discovers, the process has been circular, for " 'by killing my father I have saved my mother's soul.' " This discovery leads Jack into a further revelation (which is Warren's thesis) that " 'all knowledge that is worth anything is maybe paid for by blood.' "

For all his belief in the purgative powers of knowledge, Jack lies to his mother when she asks about the motives for Irwin's suicide, telling her that his father killed himself because of failing health. It is, however, a salutary lie, the least he can do for his mother. As his mother's rebirth has resurrected him, Jack's lie resurrects the image of his father for his mother. (Jack's withholding of the truth from his mother closely parallels Marlowe's lie to Kurtz's intended at the end of *Heart of Darkness*. In both cases the lie is noble, and, in a sense, the truth.) His reconciliation with his mother begins his reconciliation with the past. For without the past Jack cannot really participate in the world of the present. By rediscovering the past he is able to recreate the present, to be spiritually reborn into a world in which before his destructive self-awareness he had only acquiescently participated. He moves into his father's house, affirming his linear heritage, accepting for himself at last the role of man and father. He marries his boyhood sweetheart Anne Stanton, to whom he had once in love and innocence committed his life irrevocably. In marrying Anne, Jack saves her in much the same way Pip saves Estella at the end of *Great Expectations*. Anne is the symbol to him of his lost innocence, and in redeeming her he at last redeems himself. Having accepted the past with its hate and love, its guilt and pride, its evil and good, Jack can be regenerated into the world of the present, redeemed through suffering and self-knowledge.

When Stark and Adam destroy each other, Jack emerges from the vicarious experience of their deaths as the synthesis of their alternatives, as a whole man. Through the responsibility his manhood imposes on him, he brings the Scholarly Attorney, old and dying, into his home. Finally, it is the old man, the religious fanatic, the "unreal" father from whom Jack learns the ultimate facts of life, who becomes a "real" father. ("Each of us is the son of a million fathers.") Jack comes to believe in the old man's religious doctrine that " 'The creation of evil is . . . the index of God's glory and His power. That had to be so that the creation of good might be the index of man's glory and power. But by God's help. By His help and in His wisdom' " (p.437).

Through his "father," Jack is able to understand the significance of Cass Mastern's life in the "eye of God." After Jack's nominal father dies and he has completed his study of Cass Mastern, fulfilling at last all of his obligations to the past, he can leave Judge Irwin's house, the womb of his rebirth, and "go into the convulsion of the world, out of history into history and the awful responsibility of time." While Cass has sacrificed his life to redeem himself, Jack achieves redemption somewhat easily and painlessly. For this reason, Jack's ultimate salvation seems externally imposed (redemption as happy ending), abstract and literary rather than real. Yet to object to Warren's fine novel because it falls short of its potentialities seems finally presumption. To have it better than it is would be at the expense of gambling with what it has already achieved—a fool's risk. *All the King's Men* is a great scarred bear of a book whose faults and virtues determine one another. The greatness of this bear devolves upon the magnificence of its faults and the transcendence into art of its palpable mortality.

ARTHUR MIZENER

Robert Penn Warren: "All the King's Men"

Robert Penn Warren has had at least four careers as a writer. He has written six volumes of poems, one of which, *Promises*, won him the Pulitzer Prize in 1957; his *Selected Poems* won the Bollingen award for 1966. He had already received the Pulitzer Prize for Fiction in 1946 with *All the King's Men*, the third of his [ten] novels. He has written a biography of John Brown and two books on segregation. He has been one of the important contributors to the critical renaissance of the Twentieth Century and found (with Cleanth Brooks) a way to make its insights available to students in the most influential textbook of our time, *Understanding Poetry*. There is something symbolic about this last achievement, for the most persistent of Mr. Warren's beliefs is that men must, at whatever cost, carry knowledge into the world, must live their daily lives by its lights and must subject it to the test of experience.

Mr. Warren is usually thought of as a member of the Fugitive Group that gathered in the 1920s at Vanderbilt, where the young Warren studied with John Crowe Ransom and roomed for a time with Allen Tate. It is difficult to imagine a better apprenticeship in the craft of writing than working with Ransom, and to have been exposed to the grace, the wit, and the violence of Allen Tate's mind must have been almost too stimulating. Yet the association of Warren with the Fugitives is misleading, too. There were other important influences in his life, at California and Yale and Oxford, where he did graduate work, and wherever it was that he

From *The Southern Review* 3 (1967). Copyright © 1967 by *The Southern Review*.

acquired the attitude—very different from either Ransom's or Tate's—that he has always had.

The starting point for that attitude—as for the different one taken by Tate—is the problem of self-realization and self-possession. The speaker in Tate's "Ode to the Confederate Dead" can

> praise the vision
> And praise the arrogant circumstance
> Of those who fall
> Rank upon rank, hurried beyond decision,

but they are not real to him; he cannot share their vision or even truly understand it, though for a moment of pious respect for the past he imagines them rising like demons out of the earth. What is real for him is their tombstones, as neatly aligned as their ranks had been, decaying slowly in a neutral air.

> Row after row with strict impunity
> The headstones yield their names to the element,
> The wind whirs without recollection

in a world where impunity is absolute and the idea of meaningful action ("yielding") a pathetic fallacy. The conception of nature that had given the lives of these Confederate dead coherence and value is gone. "Here by the sagging gate, stopped by the wall" of the cemetery, the speaker feels a despair at his situation that is intensified by his recognition of what the world buried there, and long since reduced by time to "verdurous anonymity," had been like. (Tate particularly likes barriers that emphasize the metaphysical impenetrability he is concerned with by their physical insignificance; the mirror of "Last Days of Alice" is even more striking than the sagging gate of the "Ode," in which a version of that mirror in fact also turns up in the passage about the jaguar that "leaps/For his own image in a jungle pool, his victim.") For Tate the cost of losing an endurable vision of nature is the loss of the world; deprived of the vision of a community and its discipline, the individual sinks into the incoherent abyss of impulse where

> You shift your sea-space blindly
> Heaving, turning like the blind crab.

This is the nightmare in which George Posey, the hero of Tate's novel, *The Fathers*, exists. "But," says the narrator of *The Fathers*, "is not civilization the agreement, slowly arrived at, to let the abyss alone?" Tate's image of the civilized man is the narrator's father, Major Buchan, whose feelings have been perfectly disciplined to the expressive social ritual of antebellum life at Pleasant Hill. There is in *The Fathers* an understanding that a civilization is subject to time and change: George Posey destroys the life of Pleasant Hill even before the Civil War destroys the system it is a part of. But for Tate that change is simply an occasion for despair, for the recognition that we can never be Major Buchan, only George Posey.

To Warren the world of our time seems a convulsion quite as terrible as it is for Tate. But for him the world exists beyond any conception of it we may have; and it always has. We cannot know the past—but only some destructive conception of it—until we recognize that Willie Stark of *All the King's Men* is right when he says of it, "I bet things [then] were just like they are now. A lot of folks wrassling around." That knowledge about the past does not make the past meaningless, any more than does the knowledge that for the same reason we will never create a Utopia makes the future meaningless. It only makes the past and future real.

In one of the several poems Mr. Warren has written about the maternal grandfather (he was a cavalry officer under Forrest) who is his Major Buchan, the grandson begins by thinking that

> life is only a story
> And death is only the glory
> Of the telling of the story,
> And the *done* and the *to-be-done*
> In that timelessness were one,
> Beyond the poor *being done.*

Then his grandfather describes how he and his men once hanged a group of bushwackers, and suddenly the boy understands that his grandfather's past life was not a story, not something that exists only as a timeless *done* but something that was once *being done* in the terrible now of time.

> Each face outraged, agape,
> Not yet believing it true—
> The hairy jaw askew,
> Tongue out, out-staring eye,
> And the spittle not yet dry
> That was uttered with the last cry.

> The horseman does not look back.
> Blank-eyed, he continues his track,
> Riding toward me there,
> Through the darkening air.

> The world is real. It is there.

But it is very tempting to deny that the life of the past took place in the real world of time, as life in the present does, and to reject the life of the present as inconceivable in the light of what one imagines the past to have been. That is what Adam Stanton in *All the King's Men* does all his life; it is what Jack Burden, the novel's narrator, does for a long time, so that when, for example, he meets the sheriff and Commissioner Dolph Pillsbury in the Mason City court house, he wants to believe such creatures do not exist. With repudiating irony he tells himself that Dolph Pillsbury is "just another fellow, made in God's image and wearing a white shirt with a ready-tied black bow and jean pants held up with web galluses." But he knows Dolph Pillsbury is real, even if he won't admit it to himself (it is the Jack Burden who tells the story, long afterwards, who does admit it): "*They ain't real,* I thought as I walked down the hall [of the courthouse], *narry one.* But I knew they were."

It is not that man does not need a vision of the ideal possibilities of life or that actual life does not often seem grotesquely horrible in comparison with that vision. It is not even that, for some men, it is not altogether too easy to accept the world as it is and forget its unrealized possibilities (as Willie Stark for a while does). The danger is that men who do not forget these possibilities may, like Jack Burden, refuse to understand that they are possibilities for the world and are real only in the world. The risk of trying to realize these possibilities in the world is destruction, but not to take that risk is never to live. "For if," as Shakespeare's duke says, "our virtues/Did not go forth of us, 'twere all alike/As if we had them not." (There are interesting similarities between *All the King's Men* and Shakespeare's "dark" comedies, *Measure for Measure* and *Troilus and Cressida*). But it is temptingly easy, too, to think that one must not enter the grotesque reality of the world if one has any virtues.

When, in *Flood*, a prison guard refuses to shoot a madman who is murdering another guard for fear of hitting an innocent man, the Warden says, "Jesus Christ, a innocent man! There ain't no innocent man! You are fired." Yet it remains true, as the novel's cultivated lawyer says, that "When I look out the window and see some pore misguided boogers doing the best they can—according to their dim lights . . . what you might call the pathos of the mundane sort of takes the edge off my grim satisfaction." No man can afford not to shoot a murderous madman on the theory that the bystanders who are sure to be hurt are innocent (no man is) or on the theory that, since no man is innocent, men are not worth his trouble. Both theories assume that one is innocent oneself and that this innocence can be preserved by avoiding the infection of a world that is not. But the world is made up of men just like us, guilty men in ready-tied bow ties and jean pants, certainly; and made in God's image, too.

For Mr. Warren the worst is not to go into the convulsion of the world, terrible as it is to do that. No one in fact exists anywhere else. But men can deprive themselves of the responsibility (and the freedom) of being there by refusing to submit their virtues to the test of action, as Jack Burden does, or by acting as if virtue does not exist, as do the host of small-time pursuers of happiness who people Mr. Warren's novels, such as Marvin Frey, "a sporting barber with knife-edge creases in his striped pants, ointment on his thinning hair, hands like inflated rubber gloves. . . . You know how he kids the hotel chippies and tries to talk them out of something, you know how he gets in debt because of his bad hunches on the horses and bad luck with the dice, you know how he wakes up in the morning and sits on the edge of the bed with his bare feet on the cold floor and a taste like brass on the back of his tongue and experiences his nameless despair."

"Mentre che la speranza ha fior del verde," says the epigraph of *All the King's Men* (Per lor maladizione si non si perde/ che non possa tornar l'etterno amore,/ mentre che la speranza ha fior del verde. By their curse none is so lost that the eternal love cannot return while hope keeps any of it green. *Purgatorio*, III, 133–135). In this Canto, Dante sees his shadow and Virgil, confessing he is lost, knows he must consult the penitents. Sinclair observes that Dante's casting a shadow "illustrate[s] the dualism of flesh and spirit . . . which is not to be resolved in theory, only in experience"; and of Virgil consulting the penitents, he says, "In this need penitence is wiser than reason, and reason is then most reasonable when it looks beyond itself. The soul's life is experience, a given thing—a *quia*, in the language of scholasticism—to be known only in living, in the last resort as unsearchable as God." ("State contenti, umana gente, al *quia*," I. 37).

One of Mr. Warren's major objects in *All the King's Men* is to make the world of time in which experience occurs exist for us in all its ordinary, familiar, immediate reality. The novel's story of the typical political struggle in which the country boy, Willie Stark, rose to power and of his exercise of that power, of the career of Judge Irwin of Burden's Landing with its judicial integrity, its marriage for money, its deal with the power company—this story is representative of the public life of our time. It occurs in an American world that is shown in beautifully precise detail, a world of country farmhouses and county court houses and small-town hotels, of pool halls and slum apartments and the "foul, fox-smelling lairs" of cheap rooming houses, of places at Burden's Landing and the Governor's mansion and the state capital, of country fairgrounds and city football stadiums and endless highways. Moreover, this story is told us by Jack Burden who is (among other things) a trained historian and experienced newspaper man and can give us an authoritative account of the immediate meaning of the events, the tangled train of intentions and acts that cause them and flow from them. The world appears overwhelmingly real in *All the King's Men*. It is there. Because there is where experience, which is the life of the soul, occurs.

It is the wisdom of reason in looking beyond itself to experience that Jack Burden refuses—or is unable—to recognize until the very end, when he finally sees that, if knowledge is indeed the end of man as he has always believed, "all knowledge that is worth anything is maybe paid for by blood." Until then he cannot commit his soul to experience because he cannot face what experience will do to the perfection of the story his reason has made up about his life. He struggles to keep his existence a timeless preserve of images of Anne Stanton afloat on the water with her eyes closed (but even then the sky was dark greenish-purple with a coming storm) and of ideas about the world that make it unreal. "I had got hold of [a] principle out of a book when I was in college, and I had hung onto it for grim death. I owed my success in life to that principle. It had put me where I was. What you don't know won't hurt you, for it ain't real. They called that Idealism in my book I had when I was in college, and after I got hold of that principle I became an Idealist. I was a brass-bound Idealist in those days. If you are an Idealist it does not matter what you do or what goes on around you because it isn't real anyway."

This Idealism was merely Jack Burden's excuse for living as if the world of time—where people try to do their best according to their dim lights and fail and grow old—were not real. He clung to this principle "for grim death" (of the soul, at least) and secretly fancied that his failure to do anything was a special kind of success. It was a way of hiding from the knowledge of experience that "was like the second when you come home late at night and see the yellow envelope of the telegram sticking out from under the door. . . . While you stand in the hall, with the envelope in your hand, you feel there's an eye on you . . . [that] sees you huddled up way inside, in the dark which is you, inside yourself, like a clammy, sad little foetus . . . that doesn't want to know what is in that envelope. It wants to lie in the dark and not know, and be warm in its not-knowing." (When Byram White's corruption is exposed he stands before Willie Stark "drawing himself into a hunch as though he wanted to assume the prenatal position and be little and warm and safe in the dark.") Jack Burden wanted to remain forever kissing Anne Stanton in the underwater world into which she took the highest dive of her life (but when they came to the surface she swam straight for the beach). He looked longingly at the May foliage of the trees and thought of himself "inside that hollow inner chamber, in the aqueous green light, inside the great globe of the tree . . . and no chance of seeing anything . . . and no sound except, way off, the faint mumble of traffic, like the ocean chewing its gums." (This lotus-eater's dream was interrupted by Sadie Burke, who told Jack Burden that Anne Stanton had become Willie Stark's mistress.)

Jack's Idealism allows him to reject as absurd caricatures of humanity the beings who fall below his standards, but it also costs him his capacity to feel, so that it is really he who does not exist humanly rather than the imperfect creatures he rejects. Anne Stanton understands this without being able to explain it.

> "Oh, you just think you are sorry. Or glad. You aren't really."
>
> "If you think you are sorry, who in hell can tell you that you aren't?" I demanded, for I was a brass-bound Idealist then, as I have stated, and was not about to call for a plebiscite on whether I was sorry or not. . . .
>
> "Oh, Jack," she said, ". . . can't you love them a little, or forgive them, or just not think about them, or something?"

Yet he can maintain this attitude only by an effort of self-persuasion. He has to keep telling himself that his mother is maddeningly stupid, because he is touched by the bravery of her defiance of age and wants to respond to her love when she smiles at him "with a sudden and innocent happiness, like a girl"; he dwells on the ludicrous horror of Tiny Duffy and the The Boys, only to find in the end that he cannot hate even Tiny. What is worse, he is often driven perilously close to recognizing that what makes him think others subhuman exists in himself. He will not touch Anne Stanton; if he does Anne will cease to be the sleeping beauty of heartbreaking innocence he has wanted her to remain ever since he saw her floating with her eyes closed that day. Instead he marries Lois who, he imagines, is merely a "beautiful, juicy, soft, vibrant, sweet-smelling, sweet-breathed machine for provoking and satisfying the appetite." But Lois "could talk, and when something talks you sooner or later begin to listen to the sound it makes and begin, even in the face of all the other evidence, to regard it as a person . . . and the human element infects your innocent Eden pleasure in the juicy, sweet-breathed machine." When Lois thus turns out to be—honestly and stubbornly—a kind of person intolerable to anyone of even moderate standards, Jack runs away, first into the Great Sleep and then to divorce. Whenever Jack Burden is faced with the dualism of flesh and spirit he runs away. His worst moment is caused by Anne Stanton's affair with Willie Stark, when he has to flee all the way to California and discover an entirely new principle, The Great Twitch, to hide behind.

Just as Jack will not go into the world of experience with Anne Stanton, so he will not give his ideals of personal conduct the reality of action. As long as he can convince himself that he is merely a technician, he can feel he is not responsible for what is done: he is just obeying orders. When he cannot—as when he is asked to put some real feeling into his column for the *Chronicle*—he quits. When he investigates Judge Irwin for Willie Stark, he is just exercising his technique. He had tried that once before, as a Ph.D. student, when he investigated Cass Mastern. But he laid that job aside unfinished because he wanted to keep his belief that "the world was simply an accumulation of items, odds and ends of things like broken and misused and dust-shrouded things gathered in a garret," whereas Cass Mastern had "learned that the world is all of one piece . . . that the world is like an enormous spider web and if you touch it, however lightly, at any point, the vibration ripples to the remotest perimeter." Perhaps, the narrator adds, the Jack Burden of those days "laid aside the journal of Cass Mastern not because he could not understand, but because he was afraid to understand for what might be understood there was a reproach to him."

With Judge Irwin he is again the researcher, with the research man's faith that the past is only a story, that "all times are one time, and all those dead in the past never lived before our definition gives them life, and out of the shadow their eyes implore us. That is what all us historical researchers believe. And we love truth." He does his job on Judge Irwin well: "It was a perfect research job, marred in its technical perfection by only one thing: it meant something." It had been easy to drop Cass Mastern when there arose a danger that the research job would be marred by meaning. Though Cass Mastern had lived in time, it was not Jack Burden's time and it was easy to think of Cass as part of history, "the *done.*" But Judge Irwin is still alive and Jack loves him, and in digging up his past Jack has brushed the spider web. He tries not to know that, but cannot escape when his mother says, "You killed him, you killed him. . . . Your father, your father and oh! you killed him."

He has had his bad moments before, as when he caught himself defending what Willie Stark had done against the sincerely selfish business men at Judge Irwin's dinner party ("the bluff, burly type, with lots of money and a manly candor"). He hastened to absolve himself of responsibility ("I didn't say I felt any way," he insisted, "I just offered a proposition for the sake of argument"), but he had come very close to understanding the possibility that—as Cass Mastern puts it—"only a man like my brother Gilbert [or Willie Stark] can in the midst of evil retain enough innocence and enough strength to . . . do a little justice in terms of the great injustice." Jack Burden does not want to understand that; he wants to go on thinking that "politics is action and all action is but a flaw in the perfection of inaction, which is peace," wants to go on not knowing that his refusal to possess Anne Stanton "had almost as dire consequences as Cass Mastern's sin" with Annabelle Trice, his friend's wife, and far more dire consequences than the sin of his father, Judge Irwin, with the wife of Judge Irwin's friend Ellis Burden.

The real reason Jack Burden works for Willie Stark, just as it is the real reason Adam Stanton does, is the fascination for him of *doing* good, not just imagining it. But he does not want to recognize that to do good he must involve himself in the world where power is acquired, not without dust and heat, and what you do has all sorts of unexpected consequences for which you must take responsibility. So Jack Burden has to persuade himself that he is just Willie Stark's research man. It is not until Willie is dead and Jack discovers the part Tiny Duffy played in killing him that Jack considers acting on his own. Then he comes very close to telling Sugar Boy about Tiny. He knows that will make Sugar Boy shoot Tiny, exactly as Tiny had known that telling Adam Stanton about Anne and Willie had made Adam shoot Willie.

But Jack does not tell Sugar Boy. Before he gets a chance to, he has gone to see Tiny and given himself the unearned pleasure of setting Tiny straight. Then Sadie Burke writes him that it would be foolish to expose Duffy "just because you got some high-falutin idea you are an Eagle Scout and [Anne Stanton] is Joan of Arc." That is the truth, and it makes him think of his own responsibility for Willie's death, and suddenly he feels himself caught in a "monstrous conspiracy whose meaning I could not fathom. . . . It was as though in the midst of the scene [with Tiny Duffy he] had slowly and like a brother winked at me with his oyster eye and I had known he knew the nightmare truth, which was that we were twins bound together more intimately and disastrously than the poor freaks of the midway who are bound by the common stitch of flesh and gristle and the seepage of the blood. We were bound together forever and I could never hate him without hating myself or love myself without loving him."

That is the moment at which Jack Burden faces the truth. But until it arrives, he is a brass-bound Idealist filled with something like despair by the insignificance of the existence he has been so careful to persuade himself is the only reasonable one, so that when Anne Stanton says to him, "You are such a smart aleck. . . . Aren't you ever going to grow up?" he says, "I reckon I am a smart aleck, but it is just a way to pass the time." But it does not even do that, for he wakes each morning to look out the window and see "that it [is] going to be another day" in the endless series of insignificant tomorrows. Or he watches from a train window a woman empty a pan of water and go back into her house—"To what was in the house. The floor of the house is thin against the bare ground and the walls and roof are thin against all of everything which is outside, but you cannot see through the walls to the secret to which the woman has gone in. . . . And all at once you feel like crying." For "the soul's life is experience, a given thing . . . to be known only in living. . . ." That is what makes Willie Stark so fascinating.

Willie Stark has a gift for acting in the world. As a country boy he had studied law and history with the passionate intensity of one who instinctively feels that knowledge is, not so much a means of understanding as an instrument of power. "Gee," he says later with amiable contempt, "back in those days I figured those fellows knew all there was to know and I figured I was going to get me a chunk of it." What he knows by then is that you can use certain kinds of knowledge to make men do what you wish, but that is quite another thing. "No," he says to Hugh Miller, "I'm not a lawyer. I know some law. In fact, I know a lot of law. And I made me some money out of law. But I'm not a lawyer."

He began his political career with a farm boy's naïveté by trying to get the Mason City school honestly built. When the courthouse crowd kicked him out, he ran against them on his own. But nobody listened to his story about the school and he was badly beaten. His wife Lucy, who lives to remind him of the values power exists to serve—as Anne Stanton lives to remind Jack Burden of the power values exist to direct—reminds Willie that he did not want to be elected to a government of crooks anyway. But all Willie can remember is that the courthouse crowd had "run it over me. Like I was dirt," because they had the power. Then, with the collapse of the school's fire escape, Willie becomes a hero and it almost seems as if not mixing with crooks is the way to achieve power as well as virtue, for in no time there is the city politican, Tiny Duffy, on his doorstep asking him to run for governor. He never suspects Tiny is merely looking for a way to split the opponent's vote. "For the voice of Tiny Duffy summoning him was nothing but the echo of a certainty and a blind compulsion in him."

Willie sets out to campaign for governor with his earnest, boring, true speech, and Jack Burden and Sadie Burke watch him, full of the easy cynicism of the irresponsible wise. Yet they are reluctantly impressed by Willie. "You know," Sadie says one evening, ". . . even if he found out he was a sucker, I believe he might keep right on." "Yeah," Jack says, "making those speeches." "God," she said, "aren't they awful?" "Yeah." "But, I believe he might keep right on," she said. "Yeah." "The sap," she said. When Sadie turns out to be right, they both yield to the fascination of Willie's gift for action. Sadie gives herself wholly to Willie, enduring his trivial infidelities but reacting fiercely to the real betrayal of his affair with Anne Stanton, only to discover in the end that she has helped to kill the man who, whatever he had done, she could not live without.

Willie does keep on; but not making those awful speeches. The discovery that he is once more being run over like dirt strengthens his feeling that power is all that matters, and slowly, even unconsciously, he drifts away from Lucy's understanding of the values power exists for. We watch him—as he talks to Hugh Miller, to Judge Irwin, to Adam Stanton—developing his theory that the law and the good are things men of power make up as they go along until he is—in fact if not wholly in intention—merely a virtuoso of power, half believing that, by its mere exercise, men can give power a purpose, as Jack Burden, his counterpart, is merely a virtuoso of speculation, half believing that by contemplating an ideal men can change the world. When Willie reaches this point, Lucy refuses to live with him any more. But when their son, Tom, is paralyzed for life and Willie, like some pitiful Faustus, cries out that he will name his magnificent new hospital after Tom, she is there as always to remind him that "these things don't matter. Having somebody's name cut on a piece of stone. Getting it in the papers. All those things. Oh, Willie, he was my baby boy, he was our baby boy, and those things don't matter, they don't ever matter, don't you see?"

There is something in Willie that always recognizes that, too, even when he is exercising his political skill with the least regard for it. When his cunning but unscrupulous maneuver to save Byram White leads Hugh Miller to resign, he says to Miller in semi-comic woe, "You're leaving me all alone with the sons-of-bitches. Mine and the other fellow's"; and when he blackmails the legislature into voting down his impeachment, he says to Jack Burden that Lincoln seems to have been wrong when he said a house divided against itself cannot stand, since the government he presides over "is sure half slave and half son-of-a-bitch, and it is standing." When he begins to plan his great free hospital, he refuses to allow it to be built in the usual crooked way. He is not just remembering the collapse of the Mason City school's fire escape; he can prevent Gummy Larsen from building shoddily even if Gummy does take a cut of the school contract.

What he is remembering is what made him want that school built honestly. This insistence that the hospital be built without graft is, as Jack
Burden says, "scarcely consistent" with Willie's constant assertions that
you always have to make good out of bad, but it maddens him that Jack
Burden—who has not yet learned to look beyond reason—cannot understand why, just after Willie has saved Byram White from his deserved
punishment, he wants to build that hospital with clean hands.

Thus, in the confrontation of its two central characters, *All the
King's Men* poses what is for Mr. Warren the central problem of existence,
the irrepressible conflict between the conception of life that gives action
meaning and value and the act of living in the world in which meaning
and value have to be realized. This conflict appears unendurable. Yet both
Jack Burden, who tries to exist in the conception without accepting the
responsibility of action, and Willie Stark, who drifts into acting effectively
for its own sake, find it impossible not to know that it must be endured.

"This," as Jack says near the end of the novel, "has been the story
of Willie Stark, but it is my story, too." As Willie, living the practical life
of power, is haunted by a desire to use his power in a virtuous way he
denies is possible, so Jack Burden, prevented from acting by his concern
for the virtue he can imagine, is haunted by a desire to realize himself in
the world he denies is real. This is the story the novel tells about Jack
Burden. But the novel is Jack Burden's story in another sense: he tells it.
It was a risk to use as narrator a central character whose changing
conception of the nature of experience is the main issue in the novel. It is
like making Emma Woodhouse, Lambert Strether, and Lord Jim the
narrators of their novels. If it could be brought off, the meaning of the
action could be revealed dramatically, from within and behind the view of
a character who is limited by his own nature and does not understand that
meaning for a long time; and when this meaning finally emerges on the
surface of the novel, it will be the product of an experience that has been
fully represented in the novel and will not be arbitrarily given, as is, for
example, Marlow's view of life in Conrad's *Lord Jim.* But it is very difficult
to keep separate the limited view of the events a character has as he is
living through them and the view he finally takes, when the events are all
over and he sits down to write the story. Mr. Warren brings off this
difficult maneuver, and it is well worth what it costs. But that cost is
nonetheless the considerable one of making the novel very easy to
misunderstand.

The voice of Jack Burden conveys three distinct feelings about the
events he describes. It is, most obviously, the voice of Jack Burden the
Idealist who sardonically points out the plentiful evidence that life is

grotesquely absurd. He does that very effectively and what he shows us is hard to deny. At the same time the tone of his voice is almost hysterically extravagant. That extravagance gives a hectic rhetorical brilliance to his descriptions of the world's absurdities, but why should he care that much if the world is beneath contempt? His extravagance is really the expression of the second of Jack Burden's feelings, his longing to reach beyond reason to the secret of experience that he is debarred from by the refusal of Jack Burden the Idealist to believe experience is real.

The Idealist's rhetoric always belittles the world by contrasting the indignity of its shoddy physical nature with some dignified image of the soul.

> I'd be lying there in the hole in the middle of my bed where the springs had given down with the weight of wayfaring humanity, lying there on my back with my clothes on and looking up at the ceiling and watching the cigarette smoke flow up slowly and splash against the ceiling . . . like the pale uncertain spirit rising up out of your mouth on the last exhalation, the way the Egyptians figured it, to leave the horizontal tenement of clay in its ill-fitting pants and vest.

How silly to describe men in grand terms when they are all what Jack says Lois's friends are: "There was nothing particularly wrong with them. They were just the ordinary garden variety of human garbage"—whose "wayfaring" produces nothing but broken springs in cheap-hotel bedrooms, whose "pale, uncertain spirit" is only cigarette smoke, whose "tenement of clay" is dressed in ill-fitting pants and vest.

The Idealist Jack Burden is, then, always saying, "Go to, I'll no more on't." But just the same "it hath made [him] mad," or nearly so, and like Hamlet, once he is launched on a description of it, he cannot stop torturing himself ("Nay but to live/In the rank sweat of an enseamed bed,/ Stewed in corruption . . ."); until slowly, as we listen, we begin to feel, not that men's lives are less horrible than he says they are, but that there is some imperfectly fulfilled intention in them not unlike Jack Burden's own—some dim light—that makes them pitiful rather than disgusting. Consider, for example, Mortimer Lonzo Littlepaugh who was fired by the American Electric Power Company in order that Judge Irwin might be paid off with his job "at a salary they never paid me." Mortimer is almost as absurd as his name, and his indignation is a fantastic mixture of "confusion, weakness, piety, self-pity, small-time sharpness, vindictiveness." "I gave them my heart's blood," he writes his sister just before he commits suicide, "all these years. And they call him vice-president, too. They lied to me and they cheated me and they make him vice-president for taking a bribe. . . . I am going to join our sainted Mother and Father who were kind and good . . . and will greet me on the Other Shore, and dry every tear. . . . P.S. If they [the insurance company] know I have done what I am going to do they will not pay you." "So," as Jack Burden observes, "the poor bastard had gone to the Other Shore, where Mother and Father would dry away every tear, immediately after having instructed his sister how to defraud the insurance company"—to no purpose, he might have added, since Mortimer had borrowed practically the full value of his insurance. Mortimer Lonzo Littlepaugh was certainly grotesque, but with a passionate sincerity that is, however absurd, also pitiful.

The same double response is evoked by the tone of the narrator's voice as he describes the characteristic life of his time. "A funeral parlor at midnight is ear-splitting," he will say about a cheap joint, "compared to the effect you get in the middle of the morning in the back room of a place like Slade's. . . . You sit there and think how cozy it was last night, with the effluvium of brotherly bodies and the haw-haw of camaraderie, and you look at the floor . . . and the general impression is that you are alone with the Alone and it is His move." Or, driving past the comically tasteless and pitifully decaying Victorian houses of Mason City, he will notice "the sad valentine lace of gingerbread work around the veranda"; or he will observe the absurd and touching awe of the girl in Doc's drugstore who, seeing Willie Stark standing there at the counter, "got a look on her face as though her garter belt had busted in church." People are certainly ridiculous—vain, pretentious, foolish—as Jack Burden, who is being a smart aleck to pass the time, can see very clearly; they are also pitiful—sincere, eager, committed—as another Jack Burden cannot help feeling.

The third and most important feeling Jack Burden's voice expresses is the feeling that ultimately resolves the conflict between these two, the feeling of the Jack Burden who is telling us this story. This Jack Burden seldom speaks to us directly, and when he does it is mainly to remind us that what Jack Burden felt when he was living through these events was different from what he feels now, as he tells about them. "If I learned anything from studying history," he will say, "that was what I learned. Or, to be more exact, that was what I thought I had learned." Or he will say, "at least that is how I argued the case then"; but he does not say how he argues it now.

Only at the end of the novel do we learn that, discover that Jack Burden, without ceasing to believe in the reality of man's reason, has come to believe also in the reality of experience. Life, he now knows, is not "only a story" in the timelessness of which "the *done*" and "the *to-be-done*" are one. But if he now knows that "the *being done*" exists beyond any story man's reason invents about it, he also knows that story represents man's idea of it and determines the way he will act in it. The very existence of *All the King's Men* demonstrates that, for the controlling element in the narrator's voice is not Jack Burden the Idealist or Jack Burden the historian but the Jack Burden who has come to understand that "the soul's life is experience," and thus believes, "in my way," what Ellis Burden says as he is dying, that "the creation of evil is . . . the index of God's glory and His power. That had to be so that the creation of good might be the index of man's glory and his power. But by God's help. By His help and in His wisdom."

We sometimes hear the man who knows that in the way the narrator puzzles over an ostensibly virtuous act, as when he says of Jack Burden's conduct that night in his bedroom at Burden's Landing that Anne Stanton "trusted me, but perhaps for that moment of hesitation I did not trust myself, and looked back upon the past as something precious about to be snatched away from us and was afraid of the future. . . . Then there came the day when that image was taken from me. I learned that Anne Stanton had become the mistress of Willie Stark, that somehow by an obscure and necessary logic I had handed her over to him." Sometimes we hear it in an ostensibly accidental observation, as when he notes that "later on love vines will climb up, out of the weeds," around the sign of the skull and cross-bones put up where people have died on the highway. Jack Burden does not notice that because it is irrelevant to his sardonic description of life in the age of the internal combustion engine; it is the image of some larger meaning of experience.

This larger meaning is in fact present behind everything he tells us, as it is behind the whole description of that drive up route 58 with which the novel begins. There is Sugar Boy taking every risk he can in order to exercise his uncanny skill as a driver and satisfy his naive need to act effectively in the world by slipping between truck and hay wagon with split-second timing ("The b-b-b-b-bas-tud—he seen me c-c-c-c-c-coming"). There is Willie Stark enjoying every minute of this dangerous game. There is Jack Burden thinking it was a pleasure to watch if you could forget it was real, but not willing to know, as Willie Stark does, that only if it is real does it have what Cass Mastern calls "the kind of glory, however stained or obscured, [that is] in whatever man's hand does well."

That drive was a wholly natural event, the politician being driven at politician's speed to his home town to get himself photographed at his pappy's farm for the newspapers. But it sets Jack Burden brooding about the age of the internal combustion engine and the cars whirling along the

new slab Willie had built for them, the boys imagining themselves Barney
Oldfields and the girls wearing no panties "on account of the climate" and
their knees apart "for the cool." It is an absurd way for human beings to
behave; and yet Jack Burden knows too that "the smell of gasoline and
burning brake bands and red-eye is sweeter than myrrh" and that the girls
"have smooth little faces to break your heart." It is all very like the life
of man, which moves through time at a breakneck clip that some enjoy
too much and some are too frightened by but which is the unavoidable
condition. It is far more dangerous than the gay ones suspect, for the sheer
speed of it can easily hypnotize you and "you'll come to just at the moment
when the right front wheel hooks over into the black dirt off the slab, and
you'll try to jerk her back on. . . . But you won't make it of course."
Probably not; but, as the frightened ones refuse to admit, you have to risk
it if you are ever to smell the frankincense and myrrh.

In this way the whole story of *All the King's Men* becomes a kind of
metaphor. The events of the novel are the incidents of a journey every
man takes up that highway toward the River of Death (if not so surely to
any Celestial City beyond it). For each wayfarer the other characters
represent different ideas of how to get there as incomplete and partial as
his own is for them. Each of Willie Stark's women, for example, represents
a mode of travel he adopts for a time. Lucy, the school teacher, has the
country people's simple notion of virtue and lives by it with unfailing
integrity, leaving Willie when he discovers he cannot hold onto it and
gain power; but Lucy has to go right on believing that Willie, whom she
had loved and married and borne a son to, is, with all his faults, a great
man. When Willie discovers how to gain power, he takes up with Sadie
Burke who, having fought her way up from the bitter poverty of her
childhood, plays the game of power with fierce determination; and when
Willie takes Anne Stanton as his mistress and Jack Burden, seeing Sadie's
suffering, says characteristically, "If it's all that grief, let him go," she says,
"Let him go! let him go! I'll kill him first, I swear"—and does. Willie
makes Anne Stanton his mistress when he discovers in himself a need not
just for power but to do good with clean hands. Anne Stanton has shared
something of her brother Adam's dream of an ideal past in which those
who governed were heroic figures; she has always known it is not enough,
but it makes her able to give those who, like Willie, govern now a sense of
greatness. Anne comes to love Willie when she learns that he, whom she
had supposed a wholly wicked man because he was not perfectly good, has
done much good—"Does he mean that, Jack? Really?"—and that her
father, whom she had supposed perfectly good, had done evil. Each of
these women is for Willie Stark the embodiment of the idea he lives by

while he loves her, as Willie is for each of them. So each character is for all the others he knows.

Through most of the novel, Jack Burden is suspended between Adam Stanton, the friend of his youth, and Willie Stark, the friend of his maturity, and between Ellis Burden, the father who had loved to make the child Jack Burden happy and lived only to care for the helpless children of the world after he learned that his wife had become the mistress of his best friend, and Judge Irwin, the father who did not scare but loved Jack's mother and took her, was an upright judge all his life except once, when he was desperate, and taught Jack to shoot ("You got to lead a duck, son").

For Jack, Adam Stanton is the romantic who "has a picture of the world in his head, and when the world doesn't conform in any respect to that picture, he wants to throw the world away. Even if it means throwing out the baby with the bath. Which . . . it always does mean." Jack ought to know; it is what he did when he refused to touch Anne Stanton. Adam Stanton refuses to believe people need anything but justice. But Willie Stark who, like Judge Irwin, has the courage to act what he feels, is one of the people and knows that "Your need is my justice." Jack Burden is, to start with, too like Adam Stanton to believe that the grotesque world he lives in can be put together again, even by all the king's men, and for a long time he refuses to touch it. But in the end he is too much like Willie Stark not to understand Willie's dying words—"It might have been all different, Jack. You got to believe that"—and to know he must try. As the novel ends, he has married Anne Stanton and is living with her in Judge Irwin's house, that relatively permanent—and lifeless—expression of the values handed down to him from the past, writing the history of Willie Stark's life. But he and Anne are about to leave that house and the writing of history and to enter the process of history, the life of their times. "And soon now," as Jack says in the novel's last sentence, "we shall go out of the house and go into the convulsion of the world, out of history into history and the awful responsibility of Time."

WALTER SULLIVAN

The Historical Novelist and the Existential Peril: Robert Penn Warren's "Band of Angels"

I want to begin my consideration of Warren as historical novelist not with *Band of Angels,* which is the subject of this paper, but with the story of Cass Mastern, which is told in the fourth chapter of *All the King's Men.* It will be remembered that Mastern, the intended subject of Jack Burden's master's thesis, was a rich young man from ante-bellum Mississippi. He went to Lexington to attend college, there met Duncan Trice, seduced Trice's wife Annabelle, and survived long enough to observe the vast burgeoning of his sin and to expiate his guilt through suffering. He learned that "the world is all of one piece," that actions have consequences, having observed how a series of calamitous evils followed his "single act of . . . perfidy, as the boughs from the bole and the leaves from the bough." He sought painful death and at last found it, and at his end he thought himself more fortunate than those who remained alive.

The story occupies a secondary position in the novel, but taken alone, it seems to me to be an almost perfect piece of writing. Set seventy years before the main action of *All the King's Men,* told primarily through the device of Mastern's diary and therefore couched in the language of another era, it demonstrates a good many of the advantages that the historical perspective affords a work of fiction. The separation in time, the

From *The Southern Literary Journal* 2, vol. 2 (Spring 1970). Copyright © 1970 by the Department of English, University of North Carolina, Chapel Hill.

diction, the existence of the journal all help to create distance between the action and the reader. Because of the method, certain passages can be effectively summarized and the sweep of the story can be conveyed in great succinctness. It exists for us whole in stark terms of good and evil, sin and redemption, and these values are made more readily available by the gap in time. Not only are we willing to believe of the past what we cannot believe of the present—the grand action, the heroic character— but by employing attitudes and convictions of another age, Warren was able clearly to draw moral and religious distinctions that are blurred or even obliterated by our present stance.

But, of course, historical fiction, like all other kinds, has to be written. Whatever grand theme it seeks ultimately to exploit, it must begin—the writer must begin—with the concrete, with a few specific characters set in motion by a concatenation of individual acts. Then, as Conrad and others have taught us, if the people are truly realized, if they come to life and behave as we know human beings do and must behave, and if the truth of their situations is told, accurately and fully and with sharp sensuous detail, the philosophy of the writer, his world view, whatever larger truth is contained in his concept of the human condition will emerge. And if he is lucky and works exceedingly well, he will perhaps say more than he knew he could say when he set out on his task of creation.

I rehearse this familiar set of principles only because they seem to apply so aptly to the Cass Mastern story. Warren found in Cass an image that was almost perfectly designed to convey in microcosm the novel's theme of the unity of the moral fabric and the consequences of action. But we begin with Cass, who reads the Latin poets, and Annabelle, whose deep blue eyes sparkle above the candles. We see their gestures, we hear their voices speaking the words that we know they would have spoken. ("Yes, I am seven years older than you, Mr. Mastern. Does that surprise you, Mr. Mastern?") Her tears and the touch of the flesh are real, and the story is allowed to make its own way to the suicide of Duncan Trice and the accompanying broadening of image, the evolution of the private and individual guilt into the universal and public sin. Annabelle's sale of Phebe, Mastern's fight with ruffians in the house of the slave trader, the war, and Cass' death agony in an Atlanta hospital all support the final philosophical summation. "He learned that the world is like an enormous spider web and if you touch it . . . the vibration ripples to the remotest perimeter and the drowsy spider feels the tingle and . . . springs out to fling the gossamer coils about you who have touched the web. . . ." This is well put, but the humanity of Cass and Annabelle had to precede it: the simple truth of their lives sharply delineated had to come first. Such is the nature of all fiction, historical or not.

But Warren knows this better than most other people, and one suspects that when he came to write *Band of Angels* he must have seen in his cast of characters images fully as promising as those of Cass and Annabelle. By this time—nine years intervened between the two books—he had progressed from his original dialectic of fact and idea, the man of dreams against the man of action, to an existential and activist orientation. He had given up completely whatever notion he had previously entertained of a created universe subject to a transcendent order. Though he remained deeply interested in the dramatic possibilities of the past, and in certain theoretical aspects of the Civil War that seemed to him to bear on modern problems of race, he had grown somewhat contemptuous of history in the larger sense, for to the extent that life is absurd, it must always have been that way. He had left the South and eschewed what remained of the traditional society. All of which is to say that he was properly alienated; his concern was with the questions of individual identity and freedom, and he had come to have the ordinary intellectual's ordinary interest in social justice.

So Amantha Starr must have seemed a splendid vehicle for what he meant to do. She is deprived of identity by her mixed blood, bound spiritually by her humanity and physically by the circumstances that make her a slave, and her material condition symbolizes the anguish of her soul. Who am I? she asks in the opening passage of the novel. How, she wonders, can she be set free? Such is the overture, the introduction of theme, and then Warren sets to work with his customary skill. Initially, he allows Amantha her freedom; she looks at bondage from the outside, regarding its victims with ineffectual and pompous sympathy. The first climax of the novel comes when Amantha stands beside her father's grave and discovers that she is legally a slave, and that unless someone comes to her aid, she must be delivered by the reluctant sheriff to her new owner. That no one helps, that freedom will not come from outside, foreshadows the book's conclusion. But there is a good deal of action to be got through before this epiphany is achieved.

The fact is that someone else does assist her. Hamish Bond wanders into the New Orleans auction room, defends her honor, bids her in and takes her to his home. Bond himself is one of the lost people of the world: he is rich and self sufficient, but he knows no better than Amantha who or what he is, and his fate, like hers, is bound up with race, although more tenuously. His name is not Bond, but Alec Hinks, and the days of his youth were filled with his mother's harangues, her lamentations for the slaves who used to serve her wants and the gentility of the life she used to lead before she married and came to Baltimore from South Carolina. It was partly to spite his mother that Bond became a slave trader: with a sense of irony, he immersed himself in Negroes and arrived at his love-hate relationship with Rau-Ru, his dearest friend and his bitterest enemy, his alter ego, his *K'la*.

Since in spite of the ease of his worldly circumstances, Bond is not free, he cannot offer freedom to Amantha. Or at least, the freedom that he can give her, physical emancipation, is not the freedom that she seeks. Early in their relationship, after he has yielded to the temptation to make love to her, he offers to send her north, but she remains with him until he discloses to her the story of his shameful past. Knowing at last what he has done and seen, regarding him in the light of the vast evils he has perpetrated, she, like Rau-Ru, discovers hate where she once felt affection. Now, with cotton burning on the wharfs and Farragut waiting to capture the city, Bond turns to Amanatha in bed, but these flames, this smoke remind her of the conflagrations of African villages. She feels that to be united with Bond sexually makes her a party to his guilt, one with him in responsibility for the trade he followed with all its accompanying bloodshed and agony and degradation. He forces himself on her and thus she is released—from Bond, but not yet into freedom.

This scene which occurs halfway through the book marks the second distinct turn of the novel. At her father's funeral, Amantha was enslaved; now she is forever physically free. Bond has released her, but more than that, the North is winning the Civil War, the Emancipation Proclamation will soon be issued. Tobias Sears arrives apparently ready to lead her into the white world and even into the most powerful segment thereof, if only he can solve his own problems of loyalty. Sears, a New Englander and captain in the Union Army, is caught between his sense of reality, what he sees with his own eyes about the war and reconstruction, and the narrow capitalistic puritanism which is his heritage and which is exemplified by his father. Sears is the quintessential white man: Amantha insists on the paleness of his body at the moment of their marriage's consummation. But in his despair over the world and his argument with the self that he used to be, he parodies Bond in a noble way and volunteers to lead Negro troops and later works for the Freedmen's Bureau. He seeks a new identity in the cause of the black man.

We are to believe, I think, that Sears' obsession with the Negro's plight is the immediate reason, not the underlying cause of Amantha's deserting him. She has searched for a definition of herself in his whiteness, and basic to Warren's philosophy is his conviction that self recognition comes from within, not from without. Amantha's discovery of this principle is still far off, and she turns away from white to pursue black in the company of Rau-Ru. This effort too fails, of course, but identities do begin to be found within the framework of confrontation. Rau-Ru claims black; Bond claims white; each proclaims the reality of self and chooses death in a final and absolute exercise of freedom. But Amantha is still left, and she drifts away into the middle west with Sears, growing older in boredom and disappointment and occasional sharp grief until she and Tobias make their liberating discoveries.

Now it seems to me that the conclusion of this novel is unsatisfactory. Two Negro derelicts—one of whom remains nameless and both of whom appear only in the final pages—trigger the action. Uncle Slop is a comic figure, I suppose, though not a very original one, and he remains shadowy since we never see him directly. There is a certain effective irony in the reversal of roles: a somewhat seedy Tobias Sears is employed by the rich and black Mr. Lounberry. And what Tobias discovers is the predictable existential enlightenment. He must be himself. He must declare his own manhood. And he does so by insulting Mr. Biggers and proving thereby that he does not have to submit to the kind of persecution Mr. Lounberry has just endured.

Amantha's epiphany is a result of her believing, erroneously and against her better judgment, that an old beggar with scars on his back is Rau-Ru, escaped somehow from death in Louisiana. She gives him money she cannot afford to part with: she goes to visit his grave when he dies. There, surrounded by the sinking mounds and the parsimonious tombstones, she hears the Kansas wind whisper the truth. No one can help you. No one can set you free except yourself. Thus the questions that are raised on the first page are answered. But the conclusion does not seem to jibe with the main thrust of the book's action: the solutions do not seem to be the inevitable product of character and plot.

The failure of the ending is, in my judgment, indicative of the general failure of the novel, which is largely unredeemed by the presence of many well conceived and fully realized scenes and some truly moving passages. Warren is a splendid prose stylist, a competent craftsman, or more than that: a thorough student of his genre, a master of technique. I need not expand on his virtues, except to say that in at least one way he is as well qualified as any living American novelist to write about the past. He is a diligent researcher and his eye for costume and equipment, his feel for manners, his ear for archaic patterns of speech are unsurpassed. Open *Band of Angels* anywhere, and you will find evidence of Warren's full grasp of the surface details of life as it used to be lived. Such a talent is not to be minimized: it is exactly with such minutiae that fiction begins its journey toward the truth.

But accuracies of dress and gesture are not final, and where critical argument with Warren often commences is with the ideas that burden the dialogue and inform the scenes. Are his people really believeable in terms of the stern philosophical bases that start their yearnings and inform their impulses and govern their fates? Such a question, let me hasten to say, may be unfair and is certainly unchivalrous. It takes us immediately into a twilight area where the meanest sort of cavils remain largely unanswered and where judgments that are basically subjective are likely to be made. Whenever we debate the realism of characters, the verisimilitude of action, we must keep reminding ourselves that all fiction is distortion: otherwise it would not be fiction but merely life unrefined and formless, a mundane record not yet vivified and made revealing by the processes of art.

Still, fiction must convince us. Credibility is a *sine qua non,* and I must confess that I find it very difficult to believe that a teenaged girl on a plantation in ante-bellum Kentucky ever really wondered who she was and what it would take to make her free. Indeed, I doubt that very many people in the eighteen fifties of whatever age or sex or place of abode troubled themselves much about the problem of identity. Existentialism as a popular philosophical stance is a manifestation of the modern age, and to hold otherwise in a piece of fiction is to commit the most damaging sort of anachronism. Whatever reappraisals and revisions the historians might make, the novelist is obligated by the demands of his craft to keep to the truth in its simplest form. That is, he must be faithful to the spirit of the time. His characters must share with their now dead, but once actual counterparts a common view of life and its sources, the way it should be lived, the ends it should serve.

We know this to be true, because in the first place, if the study of literature discloses anything, it teaches us that social and cultural fragmentation are bad for art. Endowing characters in an historical novel with attitudes that are not indigenous to the age is one way of creating fragmentation or exacerbating that which already exists. But this is a lateral argument, and I shall not pursue it. More germane is the combination of uniqueness and universality that every author strives to achieve in the characters that he creates. Certain writers such as Cervantes or Dickens may lean toward the idiosyncratic, but the final ambition of every serious novelist is to create chracters so firmly rooted in our shared humanity that each becomes a kind of everyman, an example of human attributes that are and were and shall be recognizable to readers of whatever period. To succeed in this ambition is the crowning achievement of the great novelist.

But again we must remind ourselves that we proceed from the particular; or to speak more nearly in the context of the present discussion, we must first apprehend the individual in his specific time and place. Consider *War and Peace*. In the opening scene of the novel, Pierre is almost completely individualized. We are conscious of his hulking figure, his spectacles, his uncertain manners; he is uncomfortable and at odds with his fellow guests at Anna Scherer's party. His differences stand out on this most intensely Russian occasion. Frequently in the future he will be in disagreement with both friends and enemies over social and political matters. But he exists always within the limits of historical actuality: in the particulars of his life and thought, he never violates his own age. Because he has first his roots in the realities of the period, he can, under Tolstoy's genius, expand as image, until, as Andrew Lytle has pointed out, he becomes during the occupation of Moscow, the incarnation of his fatherland: he *is* the Russian bear. Nor is this all. At the very end of the novel, he along with some of the other major figures shows us the very sweep of life, the repeated patterns of human generations, so that the full implications of the book's title are made clear.

It may be argued here that my objections to Warren's characters are too procrustean. For certainty it is possible to take the position that all literature of all periods is to a greater or less degree existential, and as for the age under discussion, there is the example of Henry Fleming, who, if we can get around all the talk of Christian symbolism in *The Red Badge of Courage*, is in some ways as fine a figure of existential hero as we could demand. Men have always had to make commitments, endure crises, achieve accommodations with impending death. But self consciousness and the quality thereof count for a great deal. If the existential posture is to have any limits, then we must recognize the difference between those who postulate the absurdity of the world, the lack of identity, the loss of freedom, and others who take other views of the common human agony. Which is to say, existentialism is a way of looking at men and life, not a mere foreknowledge of mortality.

But it is a grim way of looking and it exacts its price. As Helmut Kuhn put it, in what seems to me a brilliant figure, the existentialist takes the road to Calvary, but when he gets there he finds only the crosses of the two thieves. A true belief in such a nothingness lacks both the dignity and the high sense of despair that accrued to our former postures of negation. It leads to a mock show—Faustus with no Satan to deal with, no God to betray. Small wonder it is then that only the very strong—

Camus, for example, and the early Hemingway—can regard emptiness without flinching and write about it with such stringent fidelity that every small victory is effected totally from within. Others require a more promising context, a glimmer of hope that life may be made easier by means of social action or political reform. But this, I dare to say in spite of Sartre's vast reputation as writer and thinker, is a marriage of ideas that contradict and strive against each other. If the world is truly meaningless, then its nothingness is absolute and unalterable: if, on the other hand, the human condition and the frame which defines it are subject to melioration then the universal emptiness is not complete. Consequently, images that argue against each other tend to cancel each other and in *Band of Angels*, this damaging contention manifests itself in a weakening of motivation which grows more serious as the narrative proceeds.

After the second major climax, when Amantha turns in disgust from Hamish Bond who has just told her the story of his past, the emphasis shifts from the private suffering of Amantha to the public ordeal of the Civil War. This is a common practice of the historical novelist. If his public and private actions are properly amalgamated, if his character is truly drawn in terms of the historical context, then it is essential to the scope and success of the work that the smaller, private images participate in and at best become one with the larger configurations which have been constructed out of the alarms and exigencies of the past. But once Amantha has left Bond, escaped from slavery and married Sears, the credible reasons for her anxiety are removed. She has as much identity and as much freedom as are commonly thought to be necessary. Yet out of some brooding sense of her unhappy past, some lingering agony, she abandons Sears to follow Rau-Ru, now become Lieutenant Oliver Cromwell Jones. We are to interpret this as an effort which Amantha makes to discover her ultimate self in terms of her vestigial black blood. The Freudian overtones, her fascination with Jones' shape and color, her obsessive desire to see the scars on his back do not make her flight to him more believable. She simply goes while the reader wonders why, and all the while the story is held together, allowed to happen by the historical situation which produces the chaos that will partially mask the lack of motive and the violence which keeps the novel moving along. Once Amantha has married Sears, his conduct alone makes sense. At this juncture, he comes close to knowing who he is, and his desire is to do good, to improve the conditions of human existence through political commitment and sacrificial devotion to programs of social change. His actions fit the dimensions of history in the last part of the novel even better, perhaps, than Amantha's predicament was symbolized by the larger milieu of the first. But Amantha remains the principal character of the novel and she no longer functions in terms of the book's main historical thrust.

All this brings me to a fatally simple question: can existentialism as we commonly define and practice it ever furnish the historical novelist with a proper thematic basis for his work? I am aware as I ask this that our concept of the existential may be deeply flawed. For example, Jacques Maritain warns us that anguish has no philosophical standing. It is not a function of Cartesian analysis, nor is it the stuff of a premise to be cast into an Hegelian figure. Rather, it is an emotion which is essentially religious: it represents a subjective cry unto the transcendent. When it is properly understood, according to Maritain, the existentialism of Kierkegaard, Kafka, Chestov and others issues from the "nothingness which is the nonbeing *in* the existent," which is to say in the individual, rather than from any universal meaninglessness which imposes the terms of the human condition from without. I find Maritain's interpretation appealing, but I am conscious that his is a minority report. In any event, whatever the proper meaning of existentialism may be, Warren and virtually all his contemporaries are certain that the nothingness resides *outside* the existent and that there is no God to call out to, and that the transcendent, in whatever form or dimension, does not exist.

And because life is change and nothing remains stable, our posited nothingness, be it real or imagined, closes in. Our possibilities, the choices that are available to us both in life and in fiction, are diminished; because regardless of the claims that have been made to the contrary, the death of God has grievously reduced mankind. If there is nothing beyond ourselves, and if, as we are told time and time again these days, our first duty is the simple physical perpetuation of our species, then soon there will not be anything to write about or even to concern ourselves with except whether to live or die. But I shall not dwell on this. I merely want to say that existential philosophy imposes restrictions of theme and vision on the novelist. And while it may be true that those who write about their own time cannot avoid either the philosophy or the accompanying restrictions, the historical novelist can and should.

I alluded earlier to the aesthetic or psychic distance the historical image affords the novelist, but there is a moral or philosophical distance to be achieved as well. The novelist who writes of the past is freed of the prejudices and disagreements and idiocies of the moment: he goes back into time and thereby relieves himself and his readers of their predispositions. Only the characters have a stake in the action or the outcome. The artistic vision is purified, so that, ideally at least, man and his condition are more clearly seen. Warren has given us an example of this, not only in the Cass Mastern section of *All the King's Men*, but in his first novel, *Night Rider*, which many critics consider one of his finest works. It will be recalled that *Night Rider* is based on the often violent struggle between the tobacco growers' association and the organized tobacco buyers which took place in Tennessee and Kentucky just prior to and around the time Warren was born. By 1939, when the novel was published, this was a part of the dead past: a solution had been found to the tobacco problem and the old wounds had healed.

Curiously, Warren says in a note at the front of *Night Rider* that although the story is based on actual events, the book is not an historical novel, but I think it is easy to guess what he means. I take it that he is disclaiming any interest in the surface attractions of history and emphasizing his concern with human nature itself which is the novelist's proper province. The main character in *Night Rider*, Percy Munn, is a lawyer who allows himself, almost against his will, to become involved in the tobacco growers' protest. In the course of the novel we watch Munn's deterioration. As Munn becomes more deeply involved with the association, he increasingly subordinates his individual responsibility to the will of the group. He gives up both his right and his duty to make his own moral choices, which is to say that he abdicates his birthright as a man. For Munn, one act of evil leads to another; as his sins increase in severity and number, all aspects of his life disintegrate into disorder; thus the book moves with inexorable power toward Munn's death at the end. *Night Rider* is more than a sum of its parts: it transcends its images in a way that *Band of Angels* never does. And yet, like *Band of Angels*, it takes the question of human freedom for its theme. The difference is that Munn begins free and as a result of his own weakness and poor judgment, he loses his freedom and therefore loses humanity and we in turn believe in and are moved by his death. Amantha begins postulating a lack of freedom, but except for her interlude of enslavement, this is only something we are told about, and it is hard to see how she is much freer on the last page than she was on the first.

I suppose what I am saying here is that truth for the historical novelist does not reside in the present, except as the present is a part of the eternal. The truth of history is in the past and always, but not in the restricted contemporary view. Therefore, the historical novelist must trust the historical images and the historical context. He must be willing to work with life as it was lived, knowing that history is indeed life and that human nature does not change. Above all, he must avoid the temptation to impose the errors of the present upon the past. For the present is fraught with errors: the one thing above all else that our secular, scientific culture should have taught us is that we are always wrong. Today's certainty is the instigation of tomorrow's superior smile.

Which brings me again to a point I have been insisting upon: the historical novel, like all other novels, must start with the concrete: it must be built from the bottom, not from the top. For whatever literature has to tell us about our continuing agony and glory, it must show us as individuals first, single people in the here and now or the there and then of another era. Historical or otherwise, the novelist must start with the scene, because the art of literature is not one of definition or one of gathering proof for principles that are already established in the mind of the author. It is rather a search, an exploration begun and conducted in faith, a voyage toward a shore that is at best dimly seen. Whether we look toward the past or to the present, we must take our chances: we must submit to the risks of the craft, or we fail.

ALLEN SHEPHERD

The Poles of Fiction:
Warren's "At Heaven's Gate"

All the main characters of the novel are violators of nature.
—ROBERT PENN WARREN

Fiction may be said to have two poles, history and idea, and the emphasis may be shifted very far in either direction.
—ROBERT PENN WARREN

The two quotations from Robert Penn Warren, the first from his introduction to the Modern Library edition of *All the King's Men,* the second from an essay on the short stories of Eudora Welty, provide both a statement of his intention in *At Heaven's Gate* (1943) and a scale on which to measure his achievement. In his summary of Miss Welty's accomplishment, Warren concludes that "when the vividness of the actual world is best maintained, when we get the sense of one picture superimposed on another, different and yet somehow the same, the stories are most successful." Warren is not here describing or advocating anything as pedestrian as a careful mean between extremes. He is certainly talking about depth, dimension, which the reader discovers in and through his engagement with the narrative.

How well, to undertake application, is this feat of superimposition managed in *At Heaven's Gate*? For the sake of ready comparison one may say, with considerably greater felicity than in Warren's first novel, *Night Rider* (1939). In the four years intervening he had advanced a long way in

From *Texas Studies in Literature and Language* 4, vol. 12 (Winter 1971). Copyright © 1971 by University of Texas Press.

his ability to manipulate and interweave large, contrasting masses of experience and in his willingness to permit the reader to arrive at his own conclusions. There is, for example, a partially structural matter—the narratives of Willie Proudfit (*Night Rider*) and Ashby Wyndham (*At Heaven's Gate*). The Proudfit *exemplum*, offered in the penultimate chapter of the novel, strikes one as an overly precise, detached, and rather intrusive statement of a desirable alternative to Mr. Munn's empty life and meaningless death. The *exemplum* seems to be an attempt at adaptation of a dramatic device, the play within the play, which fails largely because it is in such evident contrast to the tone of all that precedes. The intercalary chapters of Wyndham's statement, however, are from the beginning integrated with the main plot, and the relation of the subsidiary to the main plot begins to be evident by Chapter 4, while the converging of the two (completed in Chapter 23) is unforced. As "history" there is perhaps not much choice between the two stories; as a projection of "idea" in or through "history" Wyndham's is clearly the more effective narrative. There is yet one further step in the relation of *exemplum* or subplot to the main plot, and this Warren takes in *All the King's Men* (1946). Proudfit's story evokes no discernible response from Mr. Munn. Wyndham's statement awakens Private Porsum's moral sense and Porsum goes on to discredit Bogan Murdock. Here the relation of the subplot to the main plot is effected by a minor character. In Warren's third novel, Cass Mastern's record, though its author has been dead seventy years, works directly and effectually upon Jack Burden, the novel's narrator.

If in establishing the relation between the principal and subsidiary plots of *At Heaven's Gate* Warren achieved the desired stereoscopic effect, one has still to consider that gloss on the fable which he offered in his introduction to *All the King's Men*. Here Warren refers to the relation between the politician hero of *Proud Flesh*, the dramatic antecedent of *All the King's Men*, and Bogan Murdock, of *At Heaven's Gate*: ". . . Bogan Murdock was supposed to embody, in one of his dimensions, the dessicating abstraction of power, to be a violator of nature, a usurer of Dante's Seventh Circle, and to try to fulfill vicariously his natural emptiness by exercising power over those around him. . . ." At the point of reference to the Seventh Circle, Warren inserted a footnote, which states that "it was this Circle that provided, with some liberties of interpretation and extension, the basic scheme and metaphor for the whole novel."

From this account one can see quite clearly, I think, that Canto xi of the *Inferno* is indeed reflected in the "basic scheme" of the novel, that the main characters are violators of nature, practicing violence against God, themselves, and their neighbors. One may readily enough associate characters in the novel with those specific kinds of violators named in the cantos devoted to the Seventh Circle: the usurer, the suicide, the spend-thrift, and the sexual aberrant. Yet the essential question does not lie with such reflection or association, but with the effects on the novel of Warren's interpretation or construction of Dante. The principal charac-ters, Ashby Wyndham excepted, are violators of nature, that is, unnatural, and—as a consequence, in Warren's scheme of values—unreal. They are, as Warren says of Bogan Murdock, empty; they have lost their hold on the magnetic chain of humanity. They seek power, satisfaction, or fulfillment in the attempted exploitation of others, and their sense of moral responsiblity is either limited or nonexistent. All of which is to say that the characters do exemplify Warren's Dantesque thesis nicely but that they do as a result lack precisely that depth and dimension which Warren admired in the fiction of Eudora Welty. They exemplify their sins, but are largely devital-ized in the process. Such a problem is not by any means peculiar to *At Heaven's Gate*, for Warren in the application or dramatization of his theses, from whatever source derived, is inclined to this sort of constric-tion or abstraction, although he has never written a novel of ideas in the Huxleyan sense.

There are those who would interpret the "history" of *At Heaven's Gate* quite literally, and who read it almost as a *roman à clef*. Thus Malcolm Cowley in his *New Republic* review identified Bogan Murdock as Senator (Colonel) Luke Lea, who served a term in jail for his part in the $17,000,000 failure of the Asheville Central Bank and Trust Company, the unnamed city as Nashville-Memphis, and the university as Vanderbilt. The trouble with such a reading, of course, is that while it does produce a certain accretion around the characters, it quite effectively does away with the "idea" of the novel, reducing it to a fictional reconstruction, to one-dimensional "history."

That transformation of the South which Warren figures in *At Heaven's Gate* is in good part a process of deracination, a loss of the sense of the meaningfulness of the past and of its relation to the present. By some the past is used as a means to a highly practical end. Bogan Murdock casts his decrepit father, Major Lemuel Murdock, as the scarcely living embodiment of personal honor, who—because Murdock seems to honor his father—shed his reflected glory upon the son despite the fact that Major Murdock had apparently collaborated with the carpetbaggers to his own enrichment and had murdered a political opponent who had charged as much. Bogan's theory of history and of traditional values, transparent as it is, serves his purpose, since—among other things—it facilitates his plan to defraud the state by selling to it a parcel of land which will as a state park commemorate his father. To the end of assuring his social acceptability in the world of Bogan Murdock, Jerry Calhoun lets it be known, with only a little prompting from Murdock, that his great-grandfather (in fact his great-uncle) was *the* Governor Calhoun, an unknown but now thoroughly honorable ancestor. Private Porsum, another of Murdock's retainers, is in a very real sense the prisoner of his own heroic history, subconsciously courting the death he finds at the courthouse riot.

Although the past may be used or converted, most often it is rejected. Thus Jerry Calhoun, the farm-boy-turned-banker, "shut his mind resolutely to any thought of the past." And Sue Murdock, as Jerry observes, lived "like the minute was all there was, like there wasn't any yesterday and there wasn't any tomorrow" (*At Heaven's Gate*, New York, 1943, pp. 22 and 117. Subsequent quotations from this edition will be identified in the text). Slim Sarrett finds his parentage and early history inappropriate to the artist and creates an elaborate and entirely fictional past. Jason Sweetwater, the Marxist labor organizer, lives comfortably in the present because of his hopes for (or certainty of, given his theory of history) the future. Some for whom the past is real and meaningful, like Jerry's Uncle Lew, live on hate, on the recollection of injustice done them. Others, like Major Murdock, relive the horrors of the past every day, re-enacting the crime which has stopped history.

The novel is the record of a number of fathers and children, and of the rejection of father by child. Bogan Murdock uses his father, Sue Murdock violently rejects Bogan, Slim Sarrett creates both mother and father, a New Orleans whore and a barge captain, Jerry Calhoun rejects his father, attempting to find another in Bogan Murdock, and Duckfoot Blake treats his parents kindly as witless pets. The past, then, as personal history, as family history, as the repository of traditional values, has virtually no relevance to the present.

Democracy is corrupted, the novel suggests, by the evolution of the business-state, by the influence of Bogan Murdock upon the state government, specifically upon Governor Milam. Bogan, clearly a malefactor of great wealth, is the dominant character in the novel (in terms of influence, not of reader identification), and it is ironic that although he is, in one sense, what Duckfoot Blake calls him, "just a dream" (p. 373), emptied of humanity by his abstract lust for power, Murdock remains an attractive figure, not in the sense of being admirable (he is the villain of the piece), but in the sense of compelling the reader's attention. Although he is, literally and figuratively, a self-made man, he is not—the pun is justified by Warren's common practice—entirely bogus. In his Shakespeare seminar paper, Slim Sarrett observes that "the successful man [Bogan

Murdock is certainly that] . . . offers only the smooth surface, like an egg. Insofar as he is truly successful [by which Sarrett means self-fulfilled], he has no story. He is pure" (p. 196). In creating Murdock, Warren seems to have acted upon the thesis that the story of the successful man is best told from the outside, despite the fact that Murdock does not possess self-knowledge—psychological in nature but moral in focus—which is the essence of the "truly successful" man.

Early in the novel Murdock initiates a refrain later picked up by most of the characters, "If things had been different for me . . ." (p. 22), which forecasts, without a suggestion of either hope or credibility, Willie Stark's dying words, "It might have been all different." What one wants to know, and what one never finds out, is how "things" had been for him, what made him the way he is. Bogan is viewed from several different perspectives by several characters, but we are never allowed entrance into his mind, never know the inner reality of the man as he conceives it to be. "Inner reality" is perhaps an inappropriate term to apply to Murdock, for he is presented as being in a significant sense unreal. And this very unreality, however appropriate or indeed inevitable it may be in Warren's scheme of values, makes of Murdock a decidedly thin and unsatisfying character. In short, while his characterization of Murdock is faithfully representative of Warren's thesis and judgment, that characterization is itself defective, since it makes both Murdock and the power he wields less than credible.

The people gathered about Murdock, like those in Willie Stark's retinue, characterize him by reflection. Jerry Calhoun, as Sue Murdock charges, aspires to the status of carbon copy, although here, as in the evolution of Murdock himself, we see too little of the process. His is the American dream: learn the business and marry the boss's daughter. And Calhoun, for all his genuine insensitivity, is clearly representative of Murdock's boys, who are themselves set apart, by talent and prospects, from their competitors. The names and faces change, but the characters and the desires are pretty much the same—with the notable exception of Duckfoot Blake, who is a prototype of Jack Burden, in his intelligence, his Ph.D. (this time from the University of Chicago), his knowledge of economics, his breezy cynicism, his incisive commentary, his detachment as statistician. Blake is not truly one of Murdock's boys, but he is a valuable employee. He understands Murdock as well as anyone, and when he discovers Murdock's financial plight he moves on to safer employment. His abrupt conversion from detachment to a belief that "everything matters" (p. 372) is among the most important in the novel. Private Porsum, who like Calhoun is a courageous man but a moral half-wit, is used by Bogan Murdock to calm the mountain men who are in danger of being organized and to preside as president over one of his banks. And like Calhoun, Porsum is vaguely and uncomfortably aware that Murdock's ethics might not stand close and impartial scrutiny, but tries not to know his responsibility. Murdock's wife is what he has made her, "a drunken, sodden, self-abusing, middle-aged bitch" (p. 347). His daughter, Sue, openly revolts against him, but she never has (or Warren never seems to give her) much of a chance, and Murdock uses, with apparent success, the public sympathy evoked by her death.

Within the lives of most of the principal characters in *At Heaven's Gate* there are two spheres of influence, that of Bogan Murdock and that of Slim Sarrett. It is Sue Murdock who makes the ultimately futile attempt to escape from one sphere, that of her father, and to find fulfillment in the other, that of Slim Sarrett. What she discovers before her death, however, is that the two men are almost mirror images: in its own way Sarrett's art is as dessicated, abstract, and sterile as Murdock's finance. Sarrett's analysis of Murdock, which resembles that which Blake offers, is incisive but could as well be applied to Sarrett himself. The essence of Sarrett's statement of the artist's creed is that "he finds in facts ample occupation, and he can afford to face them. He doesn't have to 'make up' himself or his own life" (p. 150). But as Jason Sweetwater observes, Sarrett's life is a lie, he is himself a lie. The need for the lie derives from his internal division, that of the sexually ambivalent boxer-poet whose lust for power complements Murdock's own, but who has turned inward to a private dream world for fulfillment.

Although at the end of the novel Sarrett and Murdock appear still to be in control, it is evident that Sarrett's expertise as boxer, as poet, as critic, as murderer, as New York literary person, is, like Murdock's association of himself with the Jacksonian tradition, a final ironic comment upon or travesty of success, as the term is properly conceived. Bogan Murdock beneath the portrait of Jackson and Slim Sarrett in his New York hotel room are two tableaux, inscriptions for which might read: "They all want success. What is success?"

Success as the affirmation of traditional, essentially agrarian values in twentieth-century American society is the problem of Ashby Wyndham's narrative. Does his hard-won fundamentalist faith constitute a tenable alternative to the violence, arrogance, and abstraction of Murdock's and Sarrett's worlds? In his treatment of Wyndham, Warren decreases the considerable distance indicative of his apparently minimal involvement with his other characters, and the profundity of Wyndham's struggle emphasizes the moral tragedy besetting the others; but what, one wonders, is the nature of his success, the outcome of his pilgrimage? Warren's own formulation of the dual function of Wyndham's statement is as follows:

> First, the story provides one of the various views which are contrasted in the novel, the naive religious view at one end of the scale. Second, the story serves a purpose in the over-all organization of the plot. Ashby is driven out on his pilgrimage by two forces: by the effect, even in his remote corner of the world, of the financial speculation and corruption in the city, and by his own repentance and vision. When he finally reaches the city, he, in his innocence, brings down the house of cards which is Bogan Murdock's empire.
>
> (*Spearhead*, New York, 1947, p. 415.)

This is enlightening, in its association of history and idea and in its representation of Wyndham as a latter-day Joshua, but it does not define Wyndham's end. One of his companions has murdered a policeman, has lost her faith, and will probably be executed, and he has himself, without intending it, been the indirect cause of the death of his kinsman, Private Porsum. Worst is the fact that in prison he finds himself unable to pray. Without prayer, with God's face turned away, he is nothing.

The significance of Wyndham's progress is best considered apart from its specifically religious context as one manifestation of that search for identity which concerns most of the novel's characters. Each of the other principal characters puts on a mask to conceal or distort his identity. Sue is Jerry's respectable fiancée, Sarrett's bohemian creature, Jason Sweetwater's tough lover. Calhoun is farm-boy, All-American college man, Sue's respectable lover, banker and broker. Sarrett is the boxer-poet, the perceptive critic of Shakespeare, possessed of romantic and entirely fictional antecedents. Bogan Murdock wears the mask of omniscient power. Concerning all of these characters one may speak of development or revelation, but they are all, in varying degrees and essentially for thematic reasons, moral drifters, spiritually eviscerated. Ashby Wyndham differs from them not in degree but in kind, and it is perhaps for this reason that he is almost capable of carrying the novel himself. Wyndham is the maskless man, totally committed to the achievement of self-knowledge. To Wyndham the meaning of his life is all in all; his every thought, his every action, is referable to the end of his pilgrimage. That he does not achieve it (the source of self-knowledge, in his life, being God) says little about the glory of his effort. And since, in Warren's formulation, self-knowledge is dynamic and not static, it can be said that he will never achieve it. Thus the apparent bleakness or indecisiveness of his final situation does not so much lack affirmation as bear witness to the nature of his search.

At *Heaven's Gate*, as Warren has remarked, is about "social justice." The character in the novel one most readily associates with the idea
is probably Jason Sweetwater, Warren's Marxist labor organizer. After Sue
Murdock has given up her successive attachments—to her father, to Jerry
Calhoun, to Slim Sarrett—Sweetwater is her last hope. The reason for his
failing her is central to Warren's conception of the inadequacy of his
philosophy. Sweetwater is neither a despot (Bogan Murdock) nor a dupe
(Calhoun) nor a poseur (Sarrett). He is neither empty nor self-worshipping,
for he has found a goal outside himself in union organization. Life has
become for him "an objective problem, complicated in its detail, but
susceptible to solution in terms of a single principle" (p. 293). Sweetwater
has developed a kind of working association with the past, for he has
come to believe that his father, an Episcopal bishop, was in part right,
that a man cannot believe in himself unless he believes in something else.
Sweetwater has sympathy for those whose lot he is trying to improve, and
to them he has a sense of obligation. But when Sue announces that she is
pregnant with his child, he knows that he cannot marry her and continue
to be Sweetie Sweetwater. For "he honestly believed that if he and Sue
got married he would be making a concession to something to which he
could no longer afford to make any concession" (p. 312). Sweetwater's
system is what Warren—speaking of the Marxists of the 'thirties—has
elsewhere called "the one-answer system," the possession of those who
have "got hold of one key to the universe." For Sue, Sweetwater's sense of
self-definition is more satisfying and more therapeutic than that of her
father or Calhoun or Sarrett; he fails her because his sense of himself is
static, because his philosophy is too limited and inflexible, because he
cannot adjust a general thesis to a particular instance. While Sweetwater is
of all the characters the one overtly and professionally concerned with the
implementation of "social justice," it is apparent that in a society ruled by
such figures as Bogan Murdock and Governor Milam, and supported by
such retainers as Jerry Calhoun, there cannot come into existence a just
social order. And what Sweetwater, ironically, shares with his antagonists, is a deficient sense of moral responsibility. For the mass of laboring
men in their quiet desperation Sweetwater acknowledges and acts upon a
strong though somewhat abstract sense of responsibility (life is for him an
"objective problem"), but for Sue Murdock, in her clear and present
distress and danger, he can—finally—make no allowance.

In his review of *At Heaven's Gate*, Malcolm Cowley concludes that
"the trouble with the novel as a whole is that it tells too many stories in
too many different styles," in proof of which he quotes five dissimilar
passages. There is a sense in which one can agree with Cowley, for Warren

readily turns aside from his narrative to fill us in—at unnecessary length—on the backgrounds of some of his characters, and these diversions often become stories in their own right. What Warren accomplishes with the novel's multiplicity of characters, however, is at least equally important, for by the use of a relatively large cast he achieves a more solid and extensive relation between "history" and "idea" than he could manage in *Night Rider*. Precisely because each of the characters is separate and distinct, because each is involved in and responds to the central situation, Warren is better able to resist that inclination toward the editorial commentary which weakens *Night Rider*.

Yet concerning the characters through whose actions ideas are made to live, there are two other observations to be made. The main characters, with the exception of Ashby Wyndham, are distinctly unsympathetic (although one might also exclude Sue Murdock), and a number of them are almost repulsive. It is of course not necessary that we like or admire the characters, but we must be able to believe in their integrity, that is, we must believe in the words Warren puts in their mouths. It is thus decidedly disconcerting to note, repeatedly, that Warren cannot convincingly attribute his insights to Jerry Calhoun, one of the principal characters. This is important not only because Calhoun is frequently on stage but because his regeneration (Ashby Wyndham is to a considerable extent *sui generis*, and Duckfoot Blake's enlightenment is very cryptically described) is central to the novel's conclusion and thesis. Calhoun is in the end left back at home in bed, aware at last of the extent, if not the meaning of, his rejection and betrayal of his father. Yet one is not prepared even for this limited perception. While the ambiguity of the novel's conclusion is inherent in Warren's thesis, one does have to believe—to accept the novel's conclusion—that Calhoun has made a start in his ascent from egocentricity. The problem is, it would seem, that our dissatisfaction with Calhoun, and hence with the conclusion of the novel, derives from our perception of its achieved rather than its intended meaning. And this split is directly attributable to Calhoun's insensitivity, to his inadequacy as a central intelligence.

Yet Warren is in *At Heaven's Gate* both the philosophical and the observant novelist, possessed of a rich store of recollection, of voices, of faces, of clothes, of tools, of the lay of the land, perhaps of an almost excessive appreciation of life. Thus the vividness and overall effectiveness of the novel's minor characters: Marie, who is Wyndham's wife; Calhoun's Uncle Lew and Aunt Ursula; Anse, who is Bogan Murdock's chauffeur; Private Porsum, Major Murdock, Duckfoot Blake. The problem with these characters—and it is an unusual though, I think, explicable one—is that they tend to overshadow the principal characters. Why this is so, is hard to say, but it may be that shortly after the introduction of each of the major characters one attaches to or associates with him an idea or thesis (one quickly sees through Bogan Murdock, for example: he is the man of power, the capitalist). Thus, although one does not know what is going to happen to him, one senses what he stands for and anticipates Warren's judgment of him.

Throughout *At Heaven's Gate* Warren pursues a rather uneasy and uneven course between the poles of history and idea. Warren's Dantesque construction of the principal characters is consistent, though ultimately, it would seem, self-defeating. The character best situated to make an investigation of Bogan Murdock's world, Jerry Calhoun, is patently inadequate to the task. Ashby Wyndham's narrative, on the other hand, achieves that success which Warren attributes to "the sense of one picture superimposed on another, different and yet somehow the same." Here history effortlessly implies idea. The noteworthy effectiveness of minor characters in the novel derives from their possessing in full measure "the vividness of the actual world," while not being thesis-bound.

In his Modern Library introduction to *All the King's Men*, Warren establishes a plausible relation between Bogan Murdock and Willie Stark (the two, despite their emptiness, vicariously fulfilling the needs of others) and recalls that "the effort of *At Heaven's Gate* had whetted my desire to compose a highly documented picture of the modern world." Despite its own considerable intrinsic merit, *At Heaven's Gate* will likely continue to be read as the immediate precursor of *All the King's Men,* in which Warren achieved that near perfect focus which unites documentation and depth, history and idea.

DANIEL AARON

The Meditations of
Robert Penn Warren

Robert Penn Warren began his "medi-
tations" on the War about the same time as Tate. From the start, however, he was less determinedly sectional than Agrarian friends like Donald
Davidson, that self-appointed guardian of the Southern shrine. The Nashville brethren agreed on no single program ("geography and poetry" and
"mutual respect and common interests" held them together, Warren reminds us), and even his contribution to the Agrarian manifesto, *I'll Take
My Stand* (a title he abominated), betrayed a concern for moral issues
transcending regional bias. Reflecting in later years on his article, written
during an interlude at Oxford University, Warren remembered "the jangle
and wrangle of writing the essay and some kind of discomfort in it, some
sense of evasion." The explanation for this "discomfort" closely bears on
Warren's attitude, then and subsequently, toward the War.

He once explained it this way. After 1918 Southern intellectuals
experienced a "cultural shock" comparable in intensity to the shock felt
by their New England counterparts in the 1830s. Most of the writers
associated with the Southern literary "renascence" lived or traveled outside of the South. Upon their return, they had to cope with tensions
within themselves and their society, particularly the one growing out of
race, and to resolve an internal debate. Two loyalties were in contention:
the old "pieties" bound up with kinship, manners, regional pride, history, and what Warren called "a religious or moral sense," a phrase he did

not define but which suggests values above and beyond loyalty to race and place. The conflict between them demanded a redefinition and re-examination of that fount of piety—the past.

With *John Brown, the Making of a Martyr* (1929), Warren took his first plunge into history. Substantively a swift and competent retelling of the story of that "ungodly godlike man," it is plain from the first pages that this is no ordinary biography. Warren is systematically demythologiz-ing a myth, replacing the divinely inspired hero of the hagiographers with what Warren regards as the "historical" John Brown: the deceiving and self-deceived fanatic, shifty appropriator of other people's money, moral bully, cunning intriguer, and cold-blooded killer. Yet *John Brown* is far from being a debunking exercise. Warren is not untouched by Brown's courage or by his "different but haughty and self-reliant nature." Con-ceived simply as phenomenon, a kind of human earthquake or tornado, Brown is an object of his wonder if not veneration. Warren's animus is not directed so much at Old Ossawattomie as at the society that hatched him and exploited his martyrdom.

Then and later Warren reserved a special scorn for a type he once described as "a certain breed of professional defender-of-the-good who makes a career of holding right thoughts and admiring his own moral navel." New England abolitionists, he implied, were largely composed of that breed, and in *John Brown* Warren engaged in a considerable amount of Yankee nose-pulling. In fact, his effort to scrape off the crust of legend from the "real" John Brown might be likened to Henry Adams's impious assault against the legend of Pocahontas in 1863. Like Adams, Warren aimed his arrows against the gods of his enemies. Brown's mental instabil-ity and his claim to be the Lord's lieutenant (sailing "with letter of marque from God," as Wendell Phillips put it) exposed the "Higher Law" men for what they were: believers in the doctrine that the ends justify the means. Brown's chicanery, financial and otherwise, made all Yankee philanthropy suspect. His timorous allies may have stalemated the senatorial committee looking behind the agents of the Harper's Ferry episode for the alleged Yankee conspirators—but not his biographer. Warren more than fulfilled the Neo-Confederate task of exposing Yankeeism as a corrupt blend of materialism and abstract idealism.

In some respects *John Brown* was hardly less tendentious than the biographical narratives of Tate and Lytle. Warren simplified abolitionists and abolitionism to the point of distortion, played down the grimier and unpatriarchal side of slavery that aroused the Garrisons and Mrs. Stowes of the North, and took for granted the "Southern" view on Negro talent and character. The slave in *John Brown* never bothered his "kinky" head about the right or wrong of slavery. Of course "the system was subject to grave abuses," but generally speaking the blacks enjoyed tolerable conditions, if only for their cash value. Good-natured and irresolute, they harbored no hatred for their owners, as their unrancorous behavior during the War clearly proved. Warren neither condemned the North nor romanticized his own section, yet his biography invidiously contrasted two societies, one agitated by bloody-minded idealists, the other controlled by a pardonably impulsive but relatively stable gentry.

It also hinted of complexities and ironies unsuggested in the more frankly partisan "histories" of his friends. If Warren's New England humanitarians failed to "visualize the barbarous and pitiful consequences" of "divinely inspired" ends, neither did the great theoreticians, Calhoun and Webster, perceive how issues so clear to themselves would be translated into violent and savage action by wielders of bowie knives. Although Northern fanaticism kindled the great War, Southerners who mistook the passions of a handful for the will of an entire nation heaped on the coals. The South, Warren argued, rested its case on the rule of law; the North transposed the terms of disagreement into theology. "There is only one way to conclude a theological argument: bayonets and bullets."

Warren weighed, qualified, revised, and expanded his thoughts on the War during the next twenty-five years, holding on to some of his youthful convictions while emancipating himself from parochial myths. The longer he studied it, the more dense, paradoxical and ambiguous it seemed to him. Gradually he shifted a larger share for the responsibility of the War onto the shoulders of history without absolving the participants. "Contingency" now became a more revelatory word than "Blame."

Increasingly fascinated with the etiology of the War, Warren probed the American past and discovered the virus of the disease in the nation's origins. The United States, unlike other nations which were "accidents of geography or race," began as pure idea, a grand abstraction operating without benefit of deep-rooted traditions and institutional controls. Hence its susceptibility to epidemics of romanticism, of which transcendentalism and the cult of the Higher Law were characteristic samples. The Nashville Agrarians had saddled the North alone with the sin of Abstraction, the separation of life from thought. Warren in his mature view no longer exempted the South from its contagion. The Southern *mystique* of Legality was no less abstract. "It denied life also, and in a sense more viciously, in its refusal to allow, through the inductive scrutiny of fact, for change, for the working of the life process through history."

So the War emerged in his eyes as a tragedy of unconscious complicity, as a fusion of nobility and beastliness, and the virtue and

defects of its principal actors were inseparably intertwined. Without con-
doning the "personal absolutism" of the abolitionist mind, he now acknowledged abolitionism's just cause and conceded the darkness of the
"anachronistic and inhuman" institution it sought to overthrow. A comparable sincerity and rigidity marked the defenders of slavery. "If in the
North the critic had repudiated society, in the South society repudiated
the critic; and the stage was set for trouble." At such moments in history
the way is clear for terrible simplifiers like John Brown, who explode like
dynamite and break up the moral log jam. Warren appreciated how the
madness of martyrs can enthrall, but "who can fail to be disturbed and
chastened," he asked, "by the picture of the joyful mustering of the darker
forces of our nature in that just cause?"

Only one figure loomed over the War's *personae*—Abraham Lincoln, whom Warren alone among the Neo-Confederates had honored in
1929: "humane, wise, and fallible," he called him, "but learning from his
own failings." Meditating on the War centennial, Warren found in Lincoln's principled practicality and serene common sense both a rebuke and
an answer to the mad logic of extremism. Yet even that shrewd empiricist
had no inkling of the "slick-faced fixers" who would take over in the
post-War years or "the uncoiling powers of technology and finance capital-
ism, the new world of Big Organization."

Writing as a Southerner and a moralist, Warren reflected on the peril
of righteousness and totaled up the physical and psychological costs of
"the great single event of our history": the immense drain of life and
property, the rise of a new class of millionaire as brutal as any South
Carolina Lord of the Lash, the eruption of industrial strife exceeding the
terrors of slave insurrections, the spread of venality through public and
private sectors of American life. Even one of the primary ends of the
War—the abolishment of black servitude—was only partially realized, for
the defeat of the Confederacy failed to liberate the liberated, and the
Negro won at best "a shadowy freedom." North and South fell prey to
their self-engendered illusions. To the North, the War signified sectional
redemption, and thereafter it supplied the national "Treasury of Virtue"
with an endless supply of fraudulent spiritual capital. It furnished the
defeated with the "Great Alibi" by which the South could deny its culpability for social and racial iniquities and blame malign outside influences
for every Southern ill.

These were some of the unsavory consequences a smug America
chose to ignore. But Warren was equally sensitive to the "nobility gleaming
ironically, and redeemingly, through the murk." Men ungodlike in their
weaknesses displayed in their best moments extraordinary independence,

bravery, and self-control. The American *Iliad* had no shortage of heroes or marvels. It was almost too "massively symbolic" and "sibylline," however, for literary condensation as all truly incestuous civil wars are likely to be. Warren tried to unravel its mystery in his one novel with a War setting. He succeeded better in his centennial meditation. There he persuasively showed why the dimensions and ambivalences of our Homeric war have yet to be imaginatively encompassed.

RICHARD HOWARD

Dreadful Alternatives:
A Note on Robert Penn Warren

In all our societies, the hold the dead have over the living is the subject of literature; in the American South, or in the mind of that South, which made the discovery for America that when you live without the past you do not live in the present but in some imaginary (and unpromising) future—in the South, the hold the dead have over the living is the subjection of literature. Death is perceived, of course, as a standstill, life as a falling away from such perfection. The tension generated between that immobility and that erratic descent is the famous tension of poetry, its irony, even its disease: one tends to turn to stone, or to water. One petrifies, or one liquefies. Though he has his lithic moments, they occur early on in Robert Penn Warren's abundant oeuvre—back in the poems of "Kentucky Mountain Farm":

> Instruct the heart, lean men, of a rocky place
> That even the little flesh and fevered bone
> May keep the sweet sterility of stone.

And from almost as long a way back, the impulse is against the stone, and toward the water, against what stands and toward what runs. This poet is of course a novelist, a teller, and the poems which constitute such a continuing part of his production are just that: they continue, they persist against their own concretion, their own calculus. "This book is conceived as a single long poem composed of a number of shorter poems as sections

From *Georgia Review* 1, vol. 29 (Spring 1975). Copyright © 1975 by University of Georgia.

or chapters," Warren carefully tells us at the beginning of *Or Else,* and the very alternative of such a title ominously suggests what bothers him into poetry: on the one hand, we exist only by getting on with it, only by continuity; yet on the other hand, "only in discontinuity do we know that we exist." And surely poetry is the knowledge of our existence! Yet just as surely poetry is more than death, more than discontinuity, more than one damned thing next to another: poetry is one damned thing *after* another, it is what happens next as well as what has happened once and for all. The tug of these polarities, the tactic of concessions now to this extremity, now to that one, are the matter of all Robert Penn Warren's various manners—are why he has so many. With *Promises* (1954–56) came a great renewal, and for the past twenty years the poems have been "brought in" in a steady stream, eagerly receiving signals from the deciduous world: the golden sycamore, the white dogwood, emblems of an acknowledged mortality, a complicity with death accepted by life, the narrated detail and the abstract knowledge made one.

The stream can be traced to its source fifty years back, when in 1924, Allen Tate wrote to Donald Davidson: "That boy's a wonder—has more sheer genius than any of us; watch him: his work from now on will have what none of us can achieve—power." Well of course "any of us" meant not only Davidson and Tate, but John Crowe Ransom as well, and in such a case we are as reluctant as Warren would be to measure out the "sheer genius." But if by "power" Tate intended that honorable skirmish between life and death, between the hold the dead have over the living and the hopes the living have over the (mere) dead, then he was prophetic and not only in the sense of seeing what was coming, but in the sense of saying what was there. Robert Penn Warren has indeed the power to keep himself going, to write with an ease and outrage which cancels out rather than conceals the strictures which operate between poetry and prose (I mean that *verse* means very little to him now; what means very much is the movement of the voice as it glows over images, a prose voice most of the time, obstructed only at transcendent moments into the stoppages of significant line-breaks). It is a poetry, often, of statement below the tension of the lyre, though it acknowledges that tension as, indeed, above itself; toward the end of *Or Else* comes this statement:

> This moment is non-sequential and absolute, and admits of no definition, for it subsumes all other, and sequential, moments, by which definition might be possible.

Warren is talking about ecstatic recognition, which takes place out of time, against time, which takes the form of a kind of death ("this moment is . . . absolute"), and he cannot endure to versify such recognition, though the lines I have just quoted as prose here are set up on the page in a kind of fancy articulation which has nothing to do with that ceremony of recuperations we have agreed to call verse. He cannot bear, I think, to bring together the statement of death with the form of death (Tate's poems, Ransom's), for at such a confluence the flow will cease, he will stop writing poems, the ecstatic identification will choke him off. He says this very deliberately, very gently, at the end of one of the poems about his dead and their possession of him:

> All items above belong in the world
> In which all things are continuous,
> And are parts of the original dream which
> I am now trying to discover the logic of. This
> Is the process whereby the pain of the past in its pastness
> May be converted into the future tense
>
> Of Joy.

Such conversion is the effort and is the success, by and large (largeness is what most interests Warren now, his impatience with the finicky characterizes a man who knows his own mind, who knows what to expect of his own senses), of this newest installment of Warren's *poème-fleuve,* though installment is scarcely the word—let me say this new view from the next bend in the river, always the same water in which we can step any number of times: "he is telling himself his own old story."

The invoked masters for the present pursuit of joy are Dreiser and Flaubert. Dreiser because "his only gift is to enact/ all that his deepest self abhors"; and Flaubert because he offers "a solemn thanksgiving to God for the fact he could perceive the worth of the world with such joy." Abhorrence *becomes* joy by the perception, the enactment, and of course by a kind of reverence in receiving what I have called the signals from mortal things: "Reality/ is hard enough to come by, but even/ in its absence we need not blaspheme/ it." The two great realists, the Frenchman transfiguring even Egypt and syphilis ("Man lives by images. They lean at us from the world's wall . . ."), the American failing, and in his abasement coming to a kind of glory ("let us note how glory, like gasoline spilled/ on the cement in a garage, may flare, of a sudden, up/ in a blinding blaze, from the filth of the world's floor"), are superb emblems of invocation here, psycho-pomps, and the rest of the poem/poems hence fall or flow under the sign of the one redemption or the other loss. The paradox is that it is the redeemed experience, the transfigured image which literally stands for death, and that it is the lost experience, the abased and abhorred continuity which melts away into a life merely lived and thereby eluded. "Virtue is rewarded, that/ is the nightmare," the book begins, and characteristically goes on: "and I must tell you . . ." Such telling, then, is the way out of the nightmare, the clue to the labyrinth:

> All day, I had wandered in the glittering metaphor
> For which I could find no referent.
> All night, that night, asleep, I would wander, lost in a dream . . .

whereas "the glittering metaphor" is no more than the scandalous image of death, the patience, the suffering, just so, of the ecstasy.

The drama of a life's work *resumes*, then, in both senses of that verb—continues and is summed up—in these new poems which are so much anti-verse because they seek to be universe, poems of autobiography and devotion, despairing illuminations of a man who turns from the rock, from the crystal, from the death, and at the end of the very poem addressed to John Crowe Ransom adjures himself and his old friend and all of us with that half-century of his "power":

> I advise you to detach your gaze from
> that fragment of rock. Not all witnesses
> of the phenomenon survive unchanged
> the moment when, at last, the object screams
>
> in an ecstasy of
>
> being.

So may the revelations of a man be cast, the energies of metonymy, continuity, prose opposing the energies of metaphor, ecstasy, verse (or at least separation), the water running out of the rock, the narrative escaping mere (mere!) being. *Survive unchanged*—who would want to?—the terms are contradictions, survival requires just that change which can withstand the scream of the object in its ecstasy. I said earlier that the impulse is against the stone, and toward the water; it is reassuring to notice that at the front of his poem/poems Robert Penn Warren has taken, from Psalms 78, this line as an epigraph: "He clave the rocks in the wilderness, and gave them drink out of the great depths." Not only reassuring to my assessed phenomenology of the poet, but reassuring that there is more poetry to come.

RICHARD LAW

Warren's "Night Rider" and the Issue of Naturalism: The 'Nightmare' of Our Age

A year prior to the publication of
Night Rider (1939), Warren was working on the materials which eventually
became *All the King's Men*. Among the many elements which shaped the
early versions of those materials were a series of related issues which he
later characterized as ". . . the theme of the relation of science (or
pseudo-science) and political power, the theme of the relation of the
science-society and the power state, the problem of naturalistic determinism and responsibility. . . ." The links suggested here between a "pseudo-
scientific" world view and the huge dilemmas of the modern world not
only inform Warren's famous Pulitzer Prize-winning work, but provide the
major themes for his ambitious first novel as well.

The core of these issues which Warren was pondering was the crude
determinism popularly derived from scientific assumptions; empiricism,
narrowly understood, had, he felt, become the ruling premise of the
modern world, the mythology of the "science society." In his views of the
consequences of that mythology, Warren is clearly the student of John
Crowe Ransom. Both mistrusted this mythology they called "scientism,"
and both traced a good many of the ills of the modern world to its
destructive underlying assumptions. In 1930, Ransom had devoted an
entire book, *God Without Thunder*, to the problems posed by the acceptance of this deterministic or "naturalistic" world view. "Naturalism" he

From *The Southern Literary Journal* 2, vol. 8 (Spring 1976). Copyright © 1976 by the
Department of English, University of North Carolina, Chapel Hill.

asserted, is based on the "belief that the universe is largely known, and theoretically knowable. . . ." It means accepting what William James called a "block universe" in which everything is finished and predictable and where effects flow inalterably from definable causes. The determinism inherent in such a world view must lead, Ransom felt, to an alarmingly truncated view of experience and of the nature of man. No system of values or ethics can be founded upon such a narrow empiricism; no reason for being or motive for action is implicit in it. It not only leaves out the chief part of man's subjective experience, it reduces the whole cosmos to meaninglessness. The consequence for the individual life, he implied, must ultimately be nihilism.

While Warren agreed substantially with Ransom's assessment of the problem, his use of these assumptions in his fiction has been surprisingly tentative and skeptical. *Night Rider* is characteristic of Warren's best work in that such ideas—his own or opposing ones—are treated as hypotheses to be tested rather than as conclusions to be demonstrated. In his first novel, Warren explores a world view he hates but cannot entirely repudiate, and which he disbelieves but cannot satisfactorily disprove. *Night Rider* is thus a philosophical novel in the best sense of the term: it does not argue a position; the action dramatizes, intelligently and comprehensively, the major facets of a philosophical problem—one which Warren was later to call the "nightmare" of our age.

I

The novel opens with a description of the crowded train that brings the protagonist to Bardsville for a rally of tobacco growers who are protesting against the monopolistic buyers. The scene is emblematic of the uncertain relationship between human will and the impersonal forces of history. In a sense, it presages the action of the entire novel. The protagonist, Perse Munn, packed in a coach with a crowd of passengers bound for the same rally, is hurled against the man in front of him by an unexpected change in the velocity of the train. He is caught up by a "pressure that was human because it was made by human beings, but was inhuman too, because you could not isolate and blame any one of those human beings who made it" (*Night Rider*, 1939; reprint New York: Random House, 1958, p. 1. Referred to hereafter by page number in the body of the text). Munn strikes the man in front of him because he "was not braced right," and the other man blames the anonymous and invisible engineer—a figure who stands perhaps for all explanations of how things come about. The whole passage is a complex emblem which parodies both the problem of knowledge and the venerable issue of free will.

As we have seen, Warren associated the acceptance of scientific determinism as a philosophy with the rise of totalitarianism—partly, one supposes, because that philosophy appears to be merely an expansion of the idea of cause and effect into a universal principle as applicable to human affairs as to the motion of billiard balls. Such a view *seems* scientific and therefore carries with it the implicit authority of science—an awesome authority, since the laboratory has become in our time the only "sanctioned" mode of intercourse with the world and our only criterion of truth. If, in an historical context, determinism tended to bolster non-ethical forms of authoritarianism, on the level of the individual life, Warren felt, with Ransom and Allen Tate, that such a view of the world took man dangerously near the abyss. Warren's strategy in exploring that issue in *Night Rider* is to take a single catastrophic action (such as is imagined in the first scene in the novel) and to examine it in as many of its facets and implications as possible. The underlying question throughout is whether naturalism, as a frame of reference, is adequate to the "data" thus discovered: Does it encompass and account for all that we see? To borrow a phrase from William James, what is its "cash value" as an explanation of the action either to the reader or to Perse Munn, who himself comes to adopt a naturalistic view?

The issue of determinism is raised at several levels in the novel, most obviously in the political elements of the plot. Warren sets the action in a time of acute crisis analogous to the period in which he wrote, and the urgent and practical questions raised there translate very readily into more modern terms: is it possible to resist "outside" forces which threaten to plunge one's community into catastrophe? And if the community fights for certain idealistic values it holds dear, is it possible to preserve those values successfully on the battlefield? Significantly, once the tobacco growers' association in this rural, turn-of-the-century Kentucky community turns to terrorism, to "night riding" in the phrase of the countryside, the large moral issues of the conflict are immediately submerged in the confusion and fury of civil war. The conflict proves to have a logic of its own and rules of development and extension independent of the aims which brought it about. Under the pressure of the war's logic, the antagonists commit acts inimical to their own aims and ideals of justice expressly in order to obtain justice. Furthermore, the violence initiated by the night riders intensifies and spreads in unpredictable ways, returning with fitting irony to plague its inventors. Munn's own house is burned to the ground by a group of poor whites who, infected by the fever of violent reprisal, demonstrate their resentment of Munn's Negro farm hands in the manner they had learned from their "betters." In short, once the terror is unleashed, all the issues in the conflict are submerged in a single overwhelming imperative, the necessity to win.

The bearing of these political events on the issue of naturalism seems clear: the antagonists seem unable to match the consequences of their actions with their intentions; they cannot control or predict the results of what they do, and they cannot act in the cause of "good" without committing "evil." There appear to be two worlds of experience which intersect only imperfectly in the action. The one, the external world, is deterministic, or largely so, and the other is subjective and internal. Human "will" in the latter does not translate simply or easily into action in the other. There is, in fact, as Warren has noted elsewhere, an "irony of success," something "inherent in the necessities of successful action which . . . [carries] with it the moral degradation of the idea."

At the political level, in fact, the evidence of the plot seems to point toward naturalism. Taken at face value, Munn's private fortunes also seem to confirm and illustrate the operation of deterministic forces. Initially, Munn's aims are partly idealistic. He shares with most of the other farmers in the association in ideal of economic justice. But as he is drawn deeper into the conflict, those ideals are among the first casualties of the war. Indeed, under the impact of what he feels forced to do, his very sense of identity becomes a casualty of the war. Munn's disintegration in turn calls into question the traditional, simplistic notion of will, for that conception presupposes a holistic entity or agent capable of volition. Warren's depiction of Munn's decline is a careful testing of our popular and largely unexamined mythology of self, especially as it relates to the larger issues of will and determinism. The calculated ironies between what Munn intends to do and what he achieves are illustrative of the problem. Munn becomes preoccupied with discovering or defining his own "real" nature, "a more than intermittent self." But in his search for self-identification, he kills a former client whom he had saved from hanging, rapes his own wife, helps lead a raid on tobacco warehouses, and betrays his best friend by committing adultery with his daughter. At the end, in an ironic inversion of "poetic justice," Munn is sought for a murder he did not commit, is betrayed because of an imagined offense he had not given, and—immediately after his first redeeming act—is ambushed and shot by soldiers sent to restore order to the community.

Like all the other events in his career, Munn's death is ambiguous, its actual nature an impenetrable mystery. It is impossible to determine whether it is a suicide "willed" by Munn himself or is rather the inevitable

conclusion of a chain of events outside himself. His raised pistol and
unaimed shot the moment he is killed describe, as it were, a large question
mark in the evening sky. There is a strong suggestion that his death may
be an unconscious fulfillment of a longing for oblivion which much of his
previous behavior had implied. But it may, on the contrary, represent a
sudden revulsion on Munn's part against the shedding of more blood and
may be, therefore, a conscious gesture of compassion and a reaffirmation
of his ties with mankind. Or like Melville's whale, the gesture *may* be
devoid of any significance.

The ambiguity of Munn's death-scene merely focuses the larger
ambiguities which pervade the novel. If the outer world is a meaningless
flux of forces as impersonal and amoral as the law of gravity, what of the
human antagonists? There is the fact of their consciousness (the importance of which is continually emphasized through Warren's control of
narrative perspective). But are the human actors in the drama nevertheless helpless atoms hurled this way and that in spite of their awareness?
Warren raises several possibilities, ironically posing them for us in the
consciousness of his baffled protagonist. In one of his periods of introspection, Munn explores the possibility that his entire existence may well be
the product of random forces:

> . . . looking across the big, pleasant room with its soft carpet and fine
> furnishings and at the leaping firelight and the known faces, he was
> aware how strong accident was—how here he was, warmed and fed and
> surrounded by these people who, if he spoke a single word, would turn
> pleasantly to him, and how cold it was snowing outside, all the country-
> side filling up with snow that would blind all familiar contours, and how
> but for the accidents which were his history he might be out there, or
> elsewhere, miserable, lost, unbefriended. How anyone might be. That
> made the room, and all in it seem insubstantial, like a dream. The
> bottom might drop out; it was dropping out even while you looked, maybe.
>
> (103)

The significance of this reverie emerges gradually as Munn's subsequent
fortunes prove its accuracy. What he sees in the friendly, well-lighted
room *is* insubstantial; the bottom is dropping out even as he stares.

Character and fate, however, are as symmetrically aligned in the
novel as in Greek tragedy, and Warren seems to imply by that alignment
yet another, and contrary, line of causation adequate to explain the
action. What happens to most of the characters in the novel represents
what they are at the deepest level. Their actions are a progressive and
involuntary revelation of their inner natures, and death comes as a final
epiphany of character. "Did you ever notice," Dr. MacDonald asks Munn,

"how what happens to people seems sort of made to order for them?"
"One way or another, that's what a man does. What's in him. A man goes
along, and the time comes, even if he's looking the other way not noticing,
and the thing in him comes out. It wasn't something happening to him made
him do something, the thing was in him all the time. He just didn't know"
(355–56). Professor Ball's often repeated platitude, "You never know what's
in you," becomes an almost choral reiteration of this theme.

Moreover, as if this opposing line of causation were not irony and
complication enough, "what's in a man" turns out to be another mysterious quantity not easily susceptible to analysis or definition. Munn frequently feels himself driven by impulses which are in him, but not, in a
sense, *of* him. Even though they help to destroy him, Munn does not
seem reducible to the mean of his unconscious drives. He is partly aware
of his own darker impulses, and he often feels strangely entangled in a
pattern of behavior not of his will; or, if of his will, it lies at a level
inaccessible to his comprehension. His decision to join the night riders,
though it surprises him, seems "inevitable, like a thing done long before
and remembered, like a part of the old accustomed furniture of memory
and being" (148). Later, while riding out to warn Trevelyan of his danger,
Munn experiences a feeling of *déjà vu* and senses again that he is fulfilling
a pattern which is outside his comprehension and which, if it does not
contradict his will, encompasses and drowns it (191).

The starkest image of character unconsciously "fulfilling" itself in
the novel is Munn's aunt, Ianthe Sprague. In her method of coping with
the world by isolating herself from it, she bears a significant resemblance
to her nephew. Her mode of living is an implicit denial of all coherence
and purposefulness. It is as if she deliberately chooses what is forced upon
Munn. Her nephew recognizes in her an image of fate as the fulfillment of
one's deepest wishes (213), for when he tries to picture her as a young and
lively woman—that is, as a different woman—he cannot: "She had really
always been as she was now. . . . Her present being was a sort of goal
toward which, confidently, she had always been moving. This present
being had always been, he was sure, her real being, and now she was
merely achieving it in its perfection of negativity and rejection" (210).
But whether one may speak of such "fulfillment" as actually willed or
simply as a consequence of the given qualities of one's nature (like the
behavior of a toy soldier constructed to march only in straight lines) is
never made clear. For the problem is complicated by yet another factor:
Munn's deepest desires are often at war with one another and hence, with
what he "is." His most fundamental concept of what he is also changes
radically in the course of the novel, so as a result, there seems to be

neither a center nor continuity to Munn's being. "The things you remembered," he concludes at one point, "they were what you were. But every time you remembered them you were different" (352).

The inner, unconscious drives which help to destroy Munn propel him as impersonally as any of the forces outside himself; they are as alien to him as the anonymous powers behind Senator Tolliver. Munn, who is aware of his self-division, seeks constantly to impose or discover some coherence in himself. But the difficulty of discovering that elusive "center" of his being is inextricably bound up with the difficulty of getting the outside world into focus. Munn poses this problem to himself with some insight:

> If I couldn't know myself, how could I know any of the rest of them? Or anything? Certainly he had not known himself . . . ; if indeed the self of that time could claim any continuator in the self that was to look backward and speculate, and torture the question. Then, thinking that the self he remembered, and perhaps remembered but imperfectly, and the later self were nothing more than superimposed exposures on the same film of a camera, he felt that all of his actions had been as unaimed and meaningless as the blows of a blind man who strikes out at the undefined sounds which penetrate his private darkness.
>
> (113–14)

But if the self does not exist continuously over time, it can scarcely "fulfill" itself in action. Munn, as the image of the camera film indicates, comes to accept a naturalistic version of his own experience which virtually denies his own selfhood. But the reader, who watches Munn consciously arrive at this self-negation, cannot so easily dismiss that selfhood. The thread of the argument thus seems to ravel out into irreconcilable strands. Warren's technique here is to construct a tangled dialectic of possible positions, the terms of which are continually called into question. Alongside the hard logic of the case for determinism and beside the vexing haziness of our conceptions of self and self-realization, he constructs a tentative case for freedom of the will. Ironically, that case rests largely upon the fact—absurd and anomalous as it may seem—of Munn's painful awareness of his predicament. Munn *knows* he is "selfless," knows he is a divided, alienated creature helplessly in the grip of forces beyond his understanding or control. There remains to be accounted for, however, the paradoxical "knower" of these things, the existential consciousness which, as it is hurried to annihilation, has power at least to recoil in disgust and nausea from what it cannot control. And that knower is, of course, left unaccounted for in the naturalistic hypothesis. Admittedly, none of Munn's attempts to direct his destiny is sufficient to break or reverse the pattern of his decline. But on the other hand—if we may paraphrase Dr. MacDonald—while a man may do merely "what he must," what is in him, the simple fact of his consciousness may, as a contributing factor in the situation, alter the nature of what one "must" do.

During the scene of the Bardsville rally, the possibility of such a radical alteration of reality through a simple alteration of consciousness, the grasping of an idea, occurs to Munn as he swelters on the platform:

> Behind all the names he was hearing without attention were other men, scattered over the section, in other countries [sic], perfectly real men, all different from each other in their own ways, but drawn together by the fact that their names were on the pieces of paper which Mr. Sills held. From that paper invisible threads, as it were, stretched off to Hunter County and Caldwell County and into Tennessee to those men. They were all webbed together by those strands, parts of their beings, which were their own, different each from each, coming together here and becoming one thing. An idea . . . seized parts of their individual beings and held them together and made them coalesce. And something was made that had not existed before.
>
> (16)

An idea in the collective consciousness and will of these various men constitutes a new "thing" in the world; reality has been altered.

Warren suggests yet another way in which consciousness may be consequential in a remark Professor Ball makes to Munn while attempting to persuade him to join the night riders: "You won't be making the trouble. . . . You won't be making it, but you'll be making it mean something. You can't stop the mountain torrent, but you can make it feed the fruitful plain and not waste itself" (142). In this simple dichotomy between what must be and the definition of creation of its significance lies a traditional resolution of the problem of free will. It is roughly the same distinction which Milton implies in *Samson Agonistes*: events may be predetermined (either by God or by History), but the meaning of those events depends upon the will with which the acts are performed. Even, presumably, if that will is mysterious and complex and divided against itself. The will may then, in turn, operate as a cause out of which other consequences grow.

We are dealing here with the most elusive of arguments, but one which Warren poses repeatedly throughout his career, paralleling rather than imitating the stubborn and contorted positions of the European existentialists. Warren's intention in his first novel, however, is to pose these issues rather than resolve them. The most that one may properly claim is that, in spite of the artist's careful objectivity, there is some pressure exerted upon this "dialectical configuration" of "truths" to cohere in

Truth. And the Truth which is being asserted is a definition of freedom of the will which transcends rather than denies the logic of naturalism.

Such a notion of truth, however, is so relative that it becomes nearly synonymous with "myth," as Warren has consistently used the word, and presages his later large affinities with the philosophy of William James. A myth is simply a version of reality, a construct by which the confusing welter of experience is reduced to order and significance. Warren, like James, seems to posit a "pluralistic" universe where no construct, however complex, is ever adequate to contain *all* of experience. Therefore, knowledge, in the sense of a self-orienting and meaning-giving myth, is difficult to obtain and precarious once found. Munn, for instance, "finds himself," in the popular meaning of the phrase, as a bold leader of guerrilla raiders. But his certainty about what their struggle against the tobacco companies has meant disintegrates in collision with other people's certainties concerning the same events:

> The truths of the others, they were not his own, which was, if any one thing seizable and namable, that reeling moment of certainty and fulfillment when the air had swollen ripely with the blast. But that had gone. Like the blink of an eye; and would not come back. Even that self he had been had slipped from him, and could only be glimpsed now, paling and reproachful, in fits as when the breeze worries a rising mist.
> The truths of these people [who testified at Doctor MacDonald's trial] were not the truth that had been his that night; but that truth was his no longer. The truth: it devoured and blotted out each particular truth, each individual man's truth, it crushed truths as under a blundering tread, it was blind.
>
> (365)

One of the largest obstacles, then, to a straight naturalistic interpretation of the novel is the implied relativism and tentativeness of truth which is apparent throughout. No simple or single version of events seems adequate to account for them. Scientific determinism, the very notion of cause and effect, is (as Ransom had argued in *God Without Thunder*) no more founded upon demonstrable premises than Christianity is. Hence (in the words of William James), ". . . why in the name of common sense need we assume that only one such system of ideas can be true? The obvious outcome of our total experience is that the world can be handled according to many systems of ideas. . . ." The nature of things appears to be *inherently* mysterious and elusive, and man's fate is therefore to act in the darkness of uncertainty.

II

In *Night Rider,* the issue of naturalism obviously flows into the problem of defining the self, of discovering some entity capable of willing or of being acted upon by mechanistic forces. Controversy over the novel has centered from the first on Warren's characterization of Munn, but usually on other grounds. Most critics have judged Munn inadequate as a center of consciousness for the novel. It seems clear, however, that the obvious and severe limitations of Munn's awareness, rather than being the result of a defect in Warren's skill, are the point of the novel. One may as well condemn Melville for the moral obtuseness of Amasa Delano as charge Warren with Munn's insufficiencies. The characterization of Perse Munn is a brilliant device which involves the reader in a direct perception of that incongruity between intention and act, intellect and feeling, self and world, which so bewilders Munn. The reader's close-up view of Munn's disintegration is further calculated to dispell any predisposition toward a simplistic determinism or facile assignment of causes or motives in his decline, and should dissuade most readers from the view that the world is unitary and knowable.

Munn is indisputably an enigma, but he is an enigma to himself as well as to the reader, so the sources of his puzzlement are thematically significant. The narrative voice is limited, except in three or four instances, to a perspective approximately identical with Munn's, and those limitations seem expressly intended to convey the boundaries of Munn's vision. Munn, for instance, does not see very far into his own motives, and in nearly every case where he engages in baffled introspection, the narrative forces the reader to confront the same invisible barriers which encompass the protagonist. Through such means, the gradual crumbling of Munn's sense of identity is perceived directly by the reader, who is allowed, as it were, to participate in the very process of his disintegration.

In the first few scenes of *Night Rider,* Munn is established as a seemingly trustworthy center of consciousness and a ready object for the reader's sympathy. Warren then proceeds to undermine that too readily granted confidence until, by the end of the novel, the reader is largely alienated from what Munn has become. Precisely as alienated, in fact, as Munn is from himself. It is interesting to note that from the perspectives of most of the other characters in the novel—from the crowds at Bardsville to intimate acquaintances such as Benton Todd, Willie Proudfit, and Lucille Christian—Munn seems an admirable, self-assured man. During the crisis in his community, he is selected as a leader almost as a matter of course. And it must be said in his behalf that he acts his part credibly.

The point is, however, that Munn's public behavior is a part which he acts, an unconscious role which both his community and he take for granted. Munn is the very figure of the Southern gentleman, and Warren manages to convey Munn's sense of his role very adroitly. He displays a dignified reserve in speech and carriage, pays chivalrous court to the ladies, and is deferential to all. He takes with commendable serious ness the obligations which his talent and social position confer upon him; he saves a poor man from the gallows out of his own conviction of the man's innocence, and he refuses payment for his services. Outwardly, Munn represents his culture's version of the decent, enlightened gentleman.

Perse Munn is not the kind of man to engage frequently in deep soul-searching or introspection, but that, too, is part of his self-image as Southern gentleman. Munn's unexamined assumptions about his social identity unconsciously modify his every gesture and attitude. The furniture of his life, and even his wife May, seem selected according to the exacting specifications of that identity. In his public appearances, such as the raid on Bardsville, one can almost sense the way Munn sits a horse and hear his easy tone of command. The narrative voice also reminds us of his ideal of himself through its insistent reasonableness and gentility. Both the imperturbable reserve of that narrative voice and the consistent use of the appellation "Mr." before masculine proper names are echoes of Munn's own habits of address, and they suggest further how far he is imprisoned in a superficial public identity. Because he has no language—and no con cepts, apparently—adequate to his inner life, Munn seems intolerably passive and emotionless. It is not that Munn lacks passions, but that he lacks a way to acknowledge and deal with them.

Where he differs dramatically from Mr. Hardin of Warren's earlier "Prime Leaf," whose self-image somewhat resembles Munn's, is in his lack of that solid "moral certainty of self" that Henry Adams attributed to the Southerner of his own day. Why Munn's image of himself and his tradi tional role fail to provide him with a comprehensive mode of feeling and with values for dealing effectively with the world is left for the reader to infer. While he seems to embody important agrarian virtues and is the product of an agrarian culture, Munn is not immune to nihilistic doubt; he succumbs as easily as the Buchan family in Tate's The Fathers to the forces of cultural change and upheaval. His social role and myth of himself become, under stress, a suffocating mask which distorts his vision and disguises him from himself.

The depth of Munn's uncertainty is usually concealed by his habitual reticence and manifests itself only indirectly. He is not one to agonize or indulge in displays of emotion. But his actions speak eloquently of his problems. He is continually drawn, for instance, to figures like Captain Todd and Senator Tolliver and Lucille Christian, to whom he attributes a strength and self-assurance he lacks. Ironically, the inner certainty of each of these characters proves to be as fragile as his own. Late in his life—too late for the knowledge to be of benefit—Munn learns that Lucille Christian had sought in him that same elusive assurance which he had supposed existed in her. All the characters in the novel, with the possible exception of Willie Proudfit, seem to suffer the same insecurities.

Munn's desperate desire for certainty is also manifested in his compulsion to explain himself. The frequent need which Munn feels to discover the exact equivalent in language for some event in his experience is analogous to Warren's notion of the artist's task of rendering the world. To discover a language adequate to convey one's experience is to discover the meaning of that experience and to reduce it to coherence. But Munn finds in the constant disparity between word and event that same mysterious gap between conception and act which confronts him elsewhere. The "definition" of things on a page, he finds, is inevitably different from the things themselves (173). And that difference produces in him a despairing lack of conviction in any construct or definition of reality. The significance of what he does escapes him because the world eludes the categories he imposes upon it. There is no "word," he discovers, for any of it (312). "It did not matter what name a man gave it" (149), his constructs do not stick. As a result, his power to order or mythicize his experience fails, until he can "connect nothing with nothing."

The seriousness of Munn's disorientation is at first disguised by the apparent normality of the doubts that plague him. His commitment to his work in the association seems phony to him; he discovers he does not really know his wife. But his reactions are always in excess of their proximate causes, and the ordinary actions he performs begin to grow detached from his sense of the actual. He inflicts small cruelties upon his wife in order, it would seem, to exort from her some glimpse of what she really is and therefore what *he* really is. Unconsciously, he is thrashing about for some solid and tangible contact with a world which is becoming ever more chimerical to him: "He tried to imagine her lying there, her posture, the expression on her face, remote and rapt, but could not. The image would not stick in his mind. It would flicker and be gone. But the almost inaudible breathing, that was steady, was real, was everything. Anonymous, nameless in the dark, it was the focus of the dark. There was nothing else" (109). In spite of his efforts, she seems progressively to withdraw from him, "fading, almost imperceptibly but surely, into an impersonal and ambiguous distance" (124). Later, the newspaper accounts which he reads of the acts of terrorism he himself has committed seem to possess the "same unreality, the same lack of conviction," as if they described "something in which he had had no part, . . . something that had happened a very long time before" (173). In trying to reduce his affair with Lucille Christian to some comprehensible category by asking her to marry him, Munn is described as being "like the man who tries to find in the flux and confusion of data some point of reference, no matter how arbitrary, some hypothesis, on which he can base his calculatons" (251).

As Munn becomes detached from his own emotions, the language of the narrative becomes progressively detached and impersonal. There are provoking silences at crucial occasions in which both the reader and Munn are puzzled at Munn's inability to feel anything. The continuing uncertainties which nag Munn, his odd tendency to perform acts he has just decided not to perform, and his moments of inexplicable elation or depression, all signal a deepening malaise.

The increasing separation of Munn's knowledge of facts from his emotional response to those facts culminates appropriately in his midnight execution of Bunk Trevelyan, the man whom Munn had previously saved from hanging. Munn's complete emotional dissociation from the act is rendered by the insidious calm of the narrative: "he felt removed, even now, from the present experience, as though it was a memory" (191). But on his way home, he suddenly and unexpectedly vomits, as if some submerged part of him had recoiled violently from the deed. When he arrives home, Munn completes his repudiation and desecration of everything he had previously felt himself to be and to stand for. In a scene which is described with a strange, dispassionate objectivity, Munn brutally rapes his uncomprehending wife. It is but a short and inevitable step from this psychological state to the nihilistic lethargy to which he succumbs while hiding at Proudfit's farm. By then, whatever threads of continuity had existed among the confused and disparate elements of his being are irreparably snapped; the "seed of the future" has died in him, and he is numb to both the past and the future, able to exist imaginatively only in the present moment (385). Toward the end Munn is startled by the unrecognizable face that stares at him from the mirror.

Munn's difficulty in sustaining his conviction of his own identity seems to imply the ultimate inadequacy of all such "myths," whether of self or of the world. The novel is thus not merely a depiction of the quest for "self-knowledge" that it is usually taken to be, but a depiction of the illusory and partial nature of all knowledge. The novel examines systematically the consequences of a loss of conviction in one's unconscious sense of self and all the unspoken, unexamined assumptions about the world which proceed from it. Toward the end, Munn cannot maintain the simplest connection among things in his mind: "the past . . . , which once seemed to have its meanings and its patterns, began to fall apart, act by act, incident by incident, thought by thought, each item into brutish separateness" (390). By the time he has his last interview with Lucille Christian, Munn can scarcely attend to the sense of what is being said; the incoherent sound of insects buzzing nearby rises instead to dominate his consciousness: "That dry rasping sound from the insects in the dark trees yonder, that unpatterned, unrelenting sound, drew him, and enveloped him. It was as though it was in him, finally, in his head, the essence of his consciousness, reducing whatever word came to him to that undifferentiated and unmeaning insistence" (431).

Perhaps the best image of Munn's experience lies in his remembered glimpses in childhood of the world seen through the lenses of a stereopticon (161). Removed from the viewing apparatus, the stereopticon card's dull, depthless confusion of images closely resembles the world of Munn's perceptions. He confronts everywhere the same blurred, unintelligible patterns that refuse to focus. The stasis and clarity of the small world within the stereopticon, however, provide (like the figures on Keats's Grecian Urn) a perfect image of the elusive certainty which is denied Munn, and an emblem of his obsession for permanence and meaning. It adumbrates also the half-understood motives behind his every violent collision with the world, all of which are attempts to clarify his experience. Nearly the last act of his life, his abortive attempt to murder Senator Tolliver, is a final effort to make the meaningless pieces of his life fall together, to *force* them into coherence with a single blow.

Munn's chief motive throughout the novel is the relatively modest hope of understanding what his life is about; it is the mainspring even of his atrocities. In this, and in his "restless appetite for definition," Munn is most typically human, most like ourselves, and like our conventional heroes. But everything Munn tries to grasp eludes him; for all his pain and effort, knowledge is not ultimately his. The naturalistic view of events at which he arrives late in the book clearly contributes to his problems rather than provides a solution. At best, naturalism can offer only an oversimplified model of Munn's actual experience; in fact, such a view leaves Munn himself and all his efforts to find moral vindication unaccounted for. Although he justifiably repudiates his early, unexamined sense of self, his subsequent behavior, his disintegration and death, all imply the impossibility of living "naturalistically" without some such self-concept. To take the straight look at Nothing, at the abyss undisguised by our myths of order, is fatal. There is thus, finally, a pragmatic inadequacy in naturalism; it offers Munn nothing he can use, nothing he can live by.

HAROLD BLOOM

"Brother to Dragons"

Warren's *Brother to Dragons: A Tale in Verse and Voices* was published in 1953. A quarter century later, he gives us a new version that is, as he says, "a new work." His poetic style changed radically with *Incarnations: Poems 1966–1968*, a change that continues in his increasingly distinguished canon of poems. He stands now, at almost 75, as our most impressive living poet because of his work since 1966. Reading *Brother to Dragons* in this new version, side by side with the 1953 text, is an instructive experience, particularly in regard to the vexed problem of poetic revisionism. The famous dictum of Valéry, that a poem is never finished but is abandoned, is severely tested by Warren's rigorous reworking of his longest poem.

I myself was one of the readers, previously cold to Warren's verse, who converted to him on the basis of *Incarnations* and the subsequent long poem *Audubon: A Vision*. Reading *Brother to Dragons* in 1953, I was made uneasy, acknowledged the poem's vigor, disliked its ideological tendentiousness, and gloomily admired the Jacobean intensity of its more violent passages. The poem seemed then a good enough extension of the tradition of T.S. Eliot, sounding at times the way Eliot sounded when he was deliberately closest to Webster and Tourneur. Warren's quite explicit argument seemed to be another churchwardenly admonition that original sin was indeed the proper mental burden for *our* poetry. Thus, poor Jefferson received a massive drubbing, for being an Enlightened rationalist, and the drubber, a tough interlocutor named R.P.W., prodded the author of the Declaration of Independence into saying: ". . . I once tried to contrive / a form I thought fit to hold the purity of man's hope. / But I did not

From *The New Republic* (Sept. 1 & 8, 1979). Copyright © 1979 by *The New Republic*.

understand the nature of things." The nature of things was that Jefferson's nephew, wielding a meat-axe, had butchered a 16-year-old black slave, in December 1811, for having broken a pitcher belonging to his deceased mother, Jefferson's sister. In his "Foreword" Warren dismissed with polemical gusto the evident fact that Jefferson never referred to this family debacle:

> If the moral shock to Jefferson caused by the discovery of what his own blood was capable of should turn out to be somewhat short of what is here represented, subsequent events in the history of America, of which Jefferson is the spiritual father, might still do the job.

A reader more Jeffersonian and Emersonian than Warren was could be forgiven for muttering, back in 1953, that if there was something nasty in the meat-house, there was something pretty nasty in the "Foreword" also. But I too am a quarter-century older now, the age indeed that Warren was when he first published the poem. I am not any happier with the implicit theology and overt morality of *Brother to Dragons* than I was, but subsequent events have done the job all right, to the degree that I am not tempted to mutter my protest anymore. Warren does seem to me the best poet we have now, and the enormous improvement in the poem's rhetorical force is evident upon almost every page. I am never going to love this poem, but I certainly respect it now, and a poem that can overcome one's spiritual distaste probably has its particular value for other readers in my generation besides myself.

The difference in the tale comes in both verse and voices, especially in the voice of R.P.W., which has an authority and resonance that little in the 1953 text prophesied. I could argue back at what seemed only another Eliotician, but I just want to listen to this sublime sunset hawk of 1979:

> . . . and lift our eyes up
> To whatever liberating perspective,
> Icy and pure, the wild heart may command,
> And so the glimmering night scene under
> The incalculable starlight serves
> As an image of lethal purity—
> Infatuate glitter of a land of Platonic ice.

In the 1953 version those six and a half lines appeared as eight and a half and between the "lethal purity" and "Infatuate glitter" came, most tendentiously, "the incessant / And whirling dream of desperate innocence." Warren now trusts his reader to interpret the trope of the passage's final line on his own, and a poem of 216 pages has been reduced to 133.

In the central poem of *Incarnations*, "The Leaf," Warren has celebrated being blessed by a new voice "for the only / Gift I have given: *teeth set on edge.*" This grim Biblical trope epitomizes the ethos and the style of Warren in his major phase, and is realized in the new *Brother to Dragons*. Our teeth are set on edge by the harsh power of this verse.

Warren, in his revised "Foreword," asserts that the dramatic effects of his poem have been sharpened, which is true, particularly in the exchanges between Jefferson and R.P.W., where the poet no longer maintains a rhetorical advantage over the president. That Warren is still dreadfully unjust to Jefferson could go unsaid, except that I fear no one else is going to say it. If presidents were morally responsible for their nephews, then our twice-born incumbent would have to confront a parody of Warren's dramatic situation, since I believe a son of one of President Carter's sisters is currently serving an extended term for armed robbery.

Warren might argue that his sense of Jefferson's greatness is dialectically demonstrated throughout the poem, in much the same way as there is a projection of Emerson's adversary power in the ironic sequence "Homage to Emerson, on Night Flight to New York," which preceded the *Incarnations* volume. Still uneasy with his ideological ferocity, I content myself here with expressing admiration for the revisionary skill and intellectual persistence he has shown in this new *Brother to Dragons*. There is a greater Warren, the poet of "Evening Hawk," "Sunset Walk in Thaw-Time in Vermont," "Red-Tail Hawk and Pyre of Youth," and scores of other visions of an authentic American sublime, including *Audubon* and the work in progress, a volume intended for his 75th birthday. That greater Warren compels homage, and has transcended his polemics against Jefferson and Emerson.

DAVID WYATT

The Critic as Artist

Warren's novels read like essays about themselves. His fictions continually resolve into apologues. It is scarcely possible while reading them to have the experience but miss the meaning. Where commentary does not preempt drama, it quickly intrudes to explicate it. While in "Pure and Impure Poetry" he acknowledges that ideas may "participate more fully, intensely, and immediately" in poetry by being implicit, his own work typically incorporates ideas "in an explicit and argued form." Such a habit of mind stations Warren on the border between two modes of imagination, between the artist who works from experience and the critic who works toward meaning.

Warren's double career in the creative and critical establishments seems to be the central fact here. There is nothing remarkable about a divided allegiance in a man who set out to devote himself to both worlds. But had Warren never written his major articles on Frost, Faulkner, Conrad, and Coleridge, or his textbooks on *understanding* poetry and fiction, we would still need some term for a writer so concerned to usurp, within the body of his own fictions, the critic's task. Warren has revived interest in Wilde's claim that "it is very much more difficult to talk about a thing than to do it." His works constantly "talk about" themselves. His characters achieve integration in a moment with its own self-reflexive grammar: *"I am me."* How can one both feel and say this? In such climactic formulations, wholeness asserts itself against a syntax which splits the self into the nominative and the accusative case. The self remains the object of its own *critical* awareness. Oneness proclaims itself in a language doomed to doubleness.

From *Prodigal Sons: A Study in Authorship and Authority.* Copyright © 1980 by Johns Hopkins University Press.

Warren's characters are placed out of themselves, the bemused or obsessive spectators of their own wayward acts. So his newest narrator tells us: "Something is going on and will not stop. You are outside the going on, and you are, at the same time, inside the going on. In fact, the going on is what you are. Until you can understand that these things are different but the same, you know nothing about the nature of life. I proclaim this." We abstract; we embody. Warren has dedicated his career to proving the indivisibility of the critical and the creative imaginations. Even where the self stands next to itself, he tries to convert self-consciousness into ecstasy. He thus joins that central American tradition of speakers— Emerson, Thoreau, Henry Adams, Norman Mailer—who are not only the builders but the interpreters of their own designs.

The stance of a critic is the stance of a son. Both are fundamentally indebted as both take up their positions in response to prior achievement which surrounds and defines them. The price of understanding is belatedness, a sense of remove in time. If the creative spirit repudiates as much of the past as it possibly can, the critical sensibility conserves as much as it possibly may. Warren's central character is a son (or daughter) whose only hope lies in not rebelling against father, tradition, home. In 1960 Leonard Casper nominated "exploration of unbroken years of home-sickness" as Warren's central theme. Warren has not been coy about proving him right. *A Place to Come To* depends upon a place one has come *from.* Warren's most recent novel explores once again the psychology of exile and return.

Adam's first word to Eve in *Paradise Lost* is "Return," and it is upon her reluctant but ultimately obedient response to this command that Warren models his plots. The voice of one's origin keeps calling one homeward. Satan wanders; Eve returns. While Warren's strongest characters wander also in aimless selfhood (in *A Place*, through what Jed's mentor calls the *"imperium intellectūs"*), none of his readers is left to doubt the pointlessness of such quest. Warren the critic always shepherds us toward the destination the artist knowingly withholds. The best way out is always back.

In the character of Jed Tewksbury, Warren has found his perfect hero. As if in passing a last judgment upon himself, Warren writes a novel about a critic writing a novel. Just after Jed introduces himself by retelling the primal memory of his father's death—drunk, he fainted while pissing in the road at midnight before the very wagon which then rolled over his neck and broke it—he steps out of his autobiography to tell us how it reads to him:

I wrote that part very fast. It came rushing out, my ball-point pen rushing ahead—a new experience for me who am accustomed only to scholarly and critical composition and who, not being of a quick mind or ready to trust my early notions, am inclined to be painfully slow and careful in my formulations.

"Rushing ahead" on into experience is, unfortunately, just what this Dante scholar repeatedly fails to do. Too much the spectator and too little the actor, he prefers telling to doing. Potential ecstasy becomes mere alienation as we read on into this book full of "the passion for the big ideas." Considerable scorn is heaped, as usual, upon abstractions untethered to fact. But Warren goes far beyond his earlier judgment in *World Enough and Time* that the world must redeem the idea. It is no longer a question of working from the concrete toward the abstract; there seems little hope here that the two can be brought into any relationship whatsoever. The author of this novel seems to have rejected Wilde's boast and embraced Faulkner's apparent dismissal: "those who can, do, those who cannot and suffer enough because they can't, write about it." All writing comes under indictment here as an evasive sublimation, a criticism of, rather than a participation in, life. When Warren shares this mood, he tries to make it convincing by reducing writing to a merely critical impulse. This book displays a contempt for learning that is downright redneck. Scholarship feeds on the death of life: as Jed's first wife dies, his essay on "Dante and the Metaphysics of Death" grows. Never are we made to feel Jed's work as interesting, let alone valuable. Jed suffers an alienation of word from world that he is never fully allowed to resolve.

This alienation arises from Jed's attempt to use words as a defense against origins. He begins as sick *of* home. Jed's parents confront him in embarrassing postures. His father dies not only drunk but clutching his penis of legendary size. His mother, having worked for a decade to free her son of Dugton, Alabama, is rewarded by having him return from college to find her in bed with a man of somewhat lesser proportions. Such things must be put behind one. When the distancing power of words fails him, Jed tries to escape the continuities of the self through the discontinuous joys of sex.

The best writing in the book is reserved for the return of Rozelle, Jed's rejected high school prom date who becomes his middle-aged mistress. A past rejection becomes a future one must inevitably face; through this fateful and wish-fulfilling logic Warren guarantees that one must return not only to the abandoned parent but to the spurned girl friend. No explanation is offered for this highly coincidental reunion other than the implicit appeal to the return of the repressed. Sex proves, however, less a way to redeem time than to stay it. The critic who would return gives way to the artist who will escape. Sex becomes an antimetaphysic. Making love leads to "the death in life-beyond-Time without which life-in-Time might not be endurable, or even possible." Jed's impossible project here stands revealed. Sex, which promises a transcendence of duration, stands defined by the original repression it undoes and the eventual interpretation it generates. The worlds of before and after catch such a moment up to interrogate and place it. Jed comes to realize that a love founded solely on the instant of conjunction is "nothing":

> What had I had of her? Only what I had had, and that seemed, in that instant, nothing at all. It was as though there could be no possession, not even blind and timeless pleasure, unless confirmed by the sight of a sleeping face.

A Place to Come To is Warren's most ambitious attempt to study "the relation of the concept of Love to that of Time." Love finally proves subordinate to time; the only abiding love is a repetition, not a revolution. Thus Jed must return to the mother before he can begin to live. The conclusion which has been lying in wait consequently presents itself, and this wandering son of Alabama, standing for the first time since a boy in his dead mother's front room, not only returns but understands: "after all the years I was returning to my final self, long lost."

A reviewer of this novel might well feel cheated in having nothing climactic to give away. Surprise endings are impossible in a book which knows from the beginning that there is finally only one place to come to. Home hovers over Warren's novels like the threat of death—it will get you in the end. What one may come to resent about Warren's fiction is not its end but its means. The necessity for return few will question, but where it emerges as inevitability rather than option, we are deprived of the very chance to wander and even lose our way, which makes arrival seem an achievement rather than a gift.

PERPETUAL RETURN

Warren's career as a novelist departs from the Miltonic assumption that "true autority" begins and ends in "filial freedom," in the freedom to be and remain a son. In the lines that first introduce Adam and Eve, Milton feels it necessary to make (for the onlooking Satan's benefit?) just this point:

in thir looks Divine
The image of thir glorious Maker shone,
Truth, Wisdom, Sanctitude severe and pure,
Severe, but in true filial freedom plac't;
Whence true autority in men

The works of both authors are filled with Satans, but in every case narrative logic, symbolic structure, and overt commentary intrude to undercut even the most charming. "I was the thing that always came back": Jack Burden's self-judgment can be taken as Warren's definition of the human. Any unconscious desire to rebel (Blake's caveat still stands) is played out within a larger myth of accommodation that eventually exposes prodigality to ridicule. Paradise is regained in the apparently modest but heroically strenuous closing of a circle: "he unobserved/Home to his mother's house returned."

The critical question for Warren studies could become the one which has vexed Miltonists: is Warren of the prodigal son's party without knowing it? Does a career so dedicated to revealing the poverty of filial ingratitude not protest too much? The answer probably awaits a full biography, as well as further study of the ways in which the dogmatic aims of the novels are compromised by formal lapses and excesses. It is finally his own originality that Warren's ethical position sets out to curtail, and in a writer of such energy and gifts, this occasions some suspicion, even where it does not actively hobble his prose.

Warren and his various proxies characteristically see the entire circle of falling, wandering, and returning in a flash, as, regardless of their station along the way, a story already complete. So "R.P.W." domesticates Robert Warren's history in *Brother to Dragons*:

in a cafe once, when an old friend said,
"Tell me about your father," my heart suddenly
Choked on my words, and in the remarkable quiet
Of my own inwardness and coil, light fell
Like one great ray that gilds the deepest glade,
And thus I saw his life a story told,
Its glory and reproach domesticated,
And for one moment felt that I had come
To that most happy and difficult conclusion:
To be reconciled to the father's own reconciliation.

After such understanding, what forgiveness? To *begin* at the end is to assume a limiting responsibility, since an author so knowing can never digress into the least indulgence of revolt without seeming merely to mark time. If Agee suffers a nearly perpetual case of arrested development,

Warren's as a novelist is strangely preempted. Warren's novels echo his father's self-judgment, as expressed in "Reading Late at Night, Thermometer Falling": "I reckon I was lucky enough to learn early that a man/can be happy in his obligations." The prototype is "Anchises' son," and in his fiction Warren has never failed to shoulder the *cura pater*. Perhaps an immense pride underlies Warren's position, since to begin with such a powerful identification with the father implies that one has but fleetingly accepted one's status as a son. Warren's repeated humiliations of the erring child are so consistent, so predictably cathartic (or tragic when they fail), as to take on the quality of a regimen he has assigned himself for fear of more vagrant impulses.

The climax of *All the King's Men* reveals a fascination with the way fathers exercise authority rather than with how a son gains it. These are the moments of true suspense in Warren. There is little question that the son will enjoy his opportunity for accommodation. There is some as to how the father will arrange it. In ignorance of their true relation, Jack has returned to Burden's Landing to complete his blackmail of Judge Irwin. Standing over his surprisingly calm adversary, Jack thinks the Judge has started to reach for a gun.

> He must have guessed the thought, for he shook his head, smiled, and said, "No, don't worry. You needn't be afraid."
>
> "Look here—" I began angrily.
>
> "I wouldn't hurt you," he said. Then reflectively, added, "But I could stop you."
>
> "By stopping MacMurfee," I said.
>
> "A lot easier than that."
>
> "I could just—" he began, "I could just say to you—I could just tell you something—" He stopped, then suddenly rose to his feet, spilling the papers off his knees. "But I won't," he said cheerfully and smiled directly at me.
>
> "Won't tell me what?"
>
> "Forget it," he said, still smiling, and waved his hand in a gay dismissal of the subject.
>
> I stood there irresolutely for a moment. Things were not making sense. He was not supposed to be standing there, brisk and confident and cheerful, with the incriminating papers at his feet. But he was.

Jack walks out of the house, and that night the Judge shoots himself.

The Judge certainly steals the show. Here a father acquires nobility by *not* conferring upon a son a knowledge of origins. We admire the judge for not telling Jack what Jack needs to know. It is a scene almost unique in American fiction, where fathers usually prove so strong (Sutpen) that they overpower their sons or so weak (Compson) that they unman them.

Judge Irwin suspends his fatherly prerogatives and creates a situation in which the unwitting son can triumph, can even, in the words of Jack's mother, "kill" his father. This may seem a mere reversal of roles, a violently *unresolved* Oedipal conflict. But, in part because of Jack's ignorance that he is caught in a hidden triangle, the father's sacrifice of himself does not lead to further conflict. It does not lead, that is, to the destruction of the son through guilt but to the son's acceptance of his role as a son.

What looks like kindness may disguise, however, a crushing magnanimity. Jack only gets a stronger father in addition to his weak one (the Scholarly Attorney), even if the intensity of this collision begins to crack the ice in which he has long frozen. Almost as if to acknowledge that he has rescued Jack from alienation only by further indenturing him to authority, Warren rewrites and inverts this scene at the end of *A Place to Come To.* There a stepfather, Perk Simms, asks that the "son" he has never seen accept him as the parent he has never had. If we understand Jed's coming home to his mother's house as significant for the husband who survives her, the inevitability of his return may matter less than the quality of the father's welcome.

> "I'm Perk Simms, I'm Perk what had the luck to find your ma in this dark world and I declare I will love her till the day I die."
> By this time, forgetting his abortive handshake, he was grappling for my neck like a spookily inept Strangler Lewis returned from the shades, the formidable old hands on their pipestem wrists getting a grip, and with both arms around my neck, he pressed one of his great, bony, leathery, imperfectly shaven cheeks, as raw as a clutch of cockleburs, against my own, all the while saying it was God's blessing to see me, there was so much to tell piling up inside him, and he claimed me like a blood-kin son, with my kind permission, for he had loved her so. And meanwhile I felt the dampness on his cheek.

Rembrandt could have painted this.

In its gentle recovery of the long lost, this penultimate scene becomes one of the most moving in Warren's fiction, and takes much of its own power from a sense that Jed and Perk accept each other because of their willingness to share their absent third. The adopting proceeds without a hitch, and old Buck Tewksbury seems long forgotten. But Jed's Ma had made one last request, as Perk reveals that night over his empty glass of whiskey:

> "All she done for me—" he burst out, croakingly.
> I waited, for I caught the peculiar inflection.
> "And then what she did," he said, "and on her dying bed."

I waited, for I now could tell that whatever it was, it had to come.

"Holding her hand," he said, "setting close to the bed, that's where I was, and she said it. Ast me did I know she loved me. I nodded my head, being a-sudden choked up. Then you know what she said?"

I shook my head.

"She said for me to forgive her," he managed to get out, "she loved me and declared she never knowed a better man and more fitter for her, and she said she prayed God I'd come to know it was not to kick dirt up in my—in my—" He did a few contortions in his chair, then took it head on: "To kick dirt in my—in my sweet ole face—no, don't make no mistake. Perfesser, them was the words she spoke, not me."

After a little: "Do you know what it was on her mind?"

"No."

"She wanted to be buried out in Heaven's Hope graveyard," he said. "Next to—to you know who." Then "What kin a man do! You do the best the Lord lets you, and it is like all yore love, it is in vain."

So Perk exacts his last request—that Jed scatter whatever remains of him after his cremation in some place "not too unhandy to Ma." On the day when Jed returns to carry out is promise, he will constitute a perpetually oscillating triangle's living fourth. By ending his novel with an image that blurs distinctions between the first and the second, the natural and the adopted, Warren lays questions of priority and authority quietly but firmly to rest.

Warren's sustained identification with paternal authority, however qualified in his most recent novel, contributes to his anticipatory stance toward the development of his plots. One of his favorite narrative devices is to foretell an outcome that must then be awaited through pages of exposition. In *Flood*, Brad Tolliver actually writes a movie script that heralds the climax of the novel containing it. Casper calls this abbreviated foreshadowing an *"exemplum."* The most famous is the Cass Mastern episode in *All the King's Men*. Faulkner thought this the only part of the novel worth saving: "The Cass Mastern story is a beautiful and moving piece. That was his novel. The rest of it I would throw away." Faulkner's objections to the body of the novel had a good deal to do with the contrast between the heroic past and the banal present. But one wonders whether this master of the twice-told tale was not also urging Warren to tell his story only once. Had Faulkner been challenged on this point, he might have answered that while in his novels multiple narrative strands are kept unraveled until and even beyond the last page, in Warren's the story within the story, or the telegraphing of the novel's destination, occurs at some one point along the way. His foreshadowings are not, like

Hemingway's, implicit in hauntingly unsure beginnings, but explicit, calculated, *understood.*

The problem comes down to the manipulation of narrative time, and here again Warren displays almost paralyzing insight into the technique of his immediate forefathers:

> . . . The frozen moment. Freeze time. Somewhere, almost in a kind of pun, Faulkner himself uses the image of a frieze for such a moment of frozen action. It's an important quality in his work. Some of these moments harden up an event, give it its meaning by holding it fixed. Time fluid vs. time fixed— In Faulkner's work that's the drama behind the drama. Take a look at Hemingway; there's no time in Hemingway, there are only moments in themselves, moments of action. There are no parents and no children. If there's a parent he is a grandparent off in America somewhere who signs the check, like the grandfather in *A Farewell to Arms.* You never see a small child in Hemingway. You get death in childbirth but you never see a child. Everything is outside of the time process. But in Faulkner there are always the very old and the very young. Time spreads and is the important thing, the terrible thing.

This brilliant comment designates both authors as impatient with the medium that defines origins and limits originality. By turning this impatience into an overt theme, Warren almost stands aside from an experience of it. The rejection of origins is the given of Warren's fiction, but the fact that nearly every strong character rejects them, and the reason why, remains to be explained. In Faulkner, the past explains the present; in Warren, the present is explained by the *reaction against* the past. But whence the reaction? The violent departures of his sons seem more perverse than motivated. Here too Warren is Miltonic; Satan's rebellion against the very concept of origin ("That we were formed then say'st thou?") springs out of nowhere. It is the first, the "original" sin. Warren seems to agree that further explanation of such revolts is not possible: "Explanations can only explain explanations, and the self is gratuitous in the end." As a philosophical rather than a psychological novelist, Warren is interested less in motivation (an instigating act) than in definition (a concluding act). This interest (along with all the other attitudes and devices that mitigate a dynamic unfolding) renders his novels curiously static, since definitions are not so much earned through time as they are formulations which, however frequently reconceived, remove us from it.

"There will be an end but you cannot see it": if this line from "The Ballad of Billie Potts" fails to capture the experience of Warren's novels, it does ample justice to his career as a poet. In his best poems, he does not stand at a critical distance from the very themes he wishes to affirm.

Warren does not develop in his novels, as I have been suggesting, because in them he converts any authentic rage against authority into its opposite, a thoroughly rationalized myth of filial dependence. Warren's poems are the medium through which his true development takes place. "Poems are," he wrote in the preface to *Selected Poems* (1966), "in one perspective at least, always a life record." In his statements about writing poetry versus writing fiction, Warren usually casts the difference as a matter of degree:

> Both fiction and poetry became—poetry very early—for me a way of life. I had to live into them, had to have them. But there is a difference. Poetry is a more direct way of trying to know the self, to make sense of experience.

In the same year he told another interviewer that

> I started as a poet and I will probably end as a poet. If I had to choose between my novels and my *Selected Poems,* I would keep the *Selected Poems* as representing me more fully, my vision and myself. I think poems are more *you.*

Because Warren practices poetry as a running life record, he had to write poems as assignments made to him by experience, not as tasks he set himself. As the ongoing history of a life, his poems asked him to submit to whatever happened next. In his poetry Warren lives through as life what he may already, as evidenced by his fiction, have comprehended as thought. The drama of his career is in watching his life draw his art into time.

THE FATHER'S SUBLIME

The end of Warren's *Selected Poems: 1923–1974* defies prediction. One usually reads such a volume with a gathering sense of a poet's hard-earned maturity. But this selection begins with the poems of 1975 and ends with those of 1923–43. As one reads into the book, the past looms up as if were the future.

> This
> Is the process whereby pain of the past in its pastness
> May be converted into the future tense
>
> Of joy.

This inverted presentation of his poetic development is Warren's most profound act of criticism. It is also his biggest lie against time.

The most obvious motive for such reversal is to present the best work first. Warren has had the luck to live a long life. It took sixty years for his poetic voice to ripen into his great volume, *Or Else*. Naturally he might wish to begin with his triumph. More compelling, however, must have been the impulse to revolt against a career dedicated to the awful responsibility of Time. (Warren had inverted and jumbled chronology in his two previous *Selected Poems*, but never to such dramatic effect. The last line of all three books has remained the same, and reverberates backward to sum up our passage through these wayward measures: "Borne in the lost procession of these feet.") This is a book in which poem after poem defines man as a creature caught up in irreversible history. Yet all these propositions inhabit a structure which belies chronology. The arrangement of the *Selected Poems* constitutes a rebellion against the priority of an earlier self, and, by extension, earlier selves. Through an illusion of presentation, early Warren becomes indebted to late Warren. In throwing off the yoke of time, the critic/son finally becomes the artist/father.

Watching Warren assume fatherhood creates the drama of his book. If we restore chronology for a moment, the following pattern emerges:

I	Poems 1923–43 (The Fugitive and After)
II	Ten year gap (The Novelist)
III	*Brother to Dragons* (The Poet as "R.P.W.")
IV	*Promises:* 1954–56 (The Birth of the Son)
V	Poems 1957–60 (*Mortmain:* The Death of the Father)
VI	Poems 1960–68 (The Falling Off)
VII	*Audubon* (The Recovery)
VIII	*Or Else:* 1968–74 (The Father's Sublime)

Brother to Dragons, with a density of metaphor never again equaled in Warren's poetry, marks his turn into direct self-presentation. Not until *Promises*, however, does Warren achieve a fully personal voice over the length of an entire book. The birth of his son and daughter suddenly converts the abstractions of Time and History into a continuity of blood in which he has directly chosen to participate. The son is named Gabriel. Warren's paternal grandmother Martha, wife to Gabriel Warren, had died giving birth to Robert Warren, the poet's father. By naming his son Gabriel, Warren celebrates the survival and triumph of the line in the wake of family disaster. He also revives the suppressed "Genealogy," the poem that had once pondered this inheritance:

> Gabriel, Gabriel, if now together
> With Martha you keep any sort of weather
> In fragrant hair and dissolute bone adrowse,
> Your grandson keeps a broken house.
> There's a sticth in his side no plasters heal,

> A crack in the firmament, maggots in the meal;
> There's a mole in the garden, fennel by the gate,
> In the heart a curse of hell-black hate
> For that other young guy who croaked too late.

This poem is almost unique in Warren's canon in voicing an active grievance against a personal past. I take it that the "other young guy" is Warren's father, and it is in documents like this that we should look for the authentic filial ingratitude that Warren chastens so thoroughly in the novels. Victor H. Strandberg argues that this poem expresses "such a *personal* trauma concerning entry into the ruined world" as to explain its deletion from the *Selected Poems* (1944). If so, by 1956 the personal has become the promise. The joy of two successful births seems directly proportional to the curse of that earlier one. In the moment of watching his infant son asleep, we can hear all the voices of Warren's past absorbed into the poet's own:

> Moonlight falls on your face now,
> And now in memory's stasis
> I see moonlight mend an old man's Time-crossed brow.
> My son, sleep deep,
> For moonlight will not stay.
> Now moves to seek that empty pillow, a hemisphere away.
> Here, then, you'll be waking to the day.
> Those who died, died long ago,
> Faces you will never know,
> Voices you will never hear—
> Though your father heard them in the night,
> And yet, sometimes, I can hear
> Their utterance like the rustling tongue of a pale tide in moonlight:
> *Sleep, son, Good night.*

Metrical restraint here still chastens Warren's reach toward a more untrammeled rhythm. This father conserves as much as he invents: this is a lullaby. The poise of these poems is shattered in *Mortmain*, where Warren returns to the bedside of his dying father. The death of his origin releases even more in the poet then the birth of his future. So intensely felt is this sequence that we scarcely notice its beginnings in *ottava rima*. As the dying father reaches out to the awaiting son, perhaps in blessing, the motion stops:

> But no. Like an eyelid the hand sank, strove
> Downward, and in that darkening roar,
> All things—all joy and the hope that strove,
> The failed exam, the admired endeavor,

Prizes and prinkings, and the truth that strove,
And back of the Capitol, boyhood's first whore—
Were snatched from me, and I could not move,
Naked in that black blast of his love.

This failed embrace had to wait nearly twenty years for requital. The falling off after *Mortmain* is due to the blunting of any possible sublimity through bathos. "There was a time," Warren tells us, "in the middle of the forties and for the next 10 years almost when I couldn't finish a poem." The poems of 1960–68 are finished, but they rebel against any sustaining conclusions. Simply put, "Delight is not to be trusted." Then, in *Audubon*, ugliness becomes the parenthesis of "delight," the poem's last word. The sublime has been established as inclusive rather than exceptional. Now it only remains to make it a Father's Sublime. Warren accomplishes his embrace of the father not through a return but through a repetition with a difference, by doing for his own son what had not been done for him:

When my son is an old man, and I have not,
For some fifty years, seen his face, and, if seeing it,
Would not even be able to guess what name it wore, what
Blessing should I ask for him?

That some time, in thaw-season, at dusk, standing
At woodside and staring
Red-westward, with the sound of moving water
In his ears, he
Should thus, in that future moment, bless,
Forward into that future's future,
An old man who, as he is mine, had once
Been his small son.

For what blessing may a man hope for but
An immortality in
The loving vigilance of death?

In this act of forgiveness, Warren heals the past by blessing the future. He realizes the great possibility of reversal, and in so doing recovers a sense of rhythm more sure than anything he has previously known. To use Warren's words from "Knowledge and the Image of Man": "The form is the flowing of that deep engagement of spirit, the discovery of its rhythm." Sometime in the late sixties Warren acceded to the fact that his concern with rhythm could best test itself in a genre written in lines rather than paragraphs. In poetry, rhythm is return, and all the pleasure in *Or Else* depends upon Warren's resisting the pull toward premature closure.

Suspense builds as he tolls the self forward into an amassing harmony rather than backward into perpetual refrain.

The Poem which immediately follows the reconciliation of the generations in "Sunset Walk" testifies to renewed possibilities for a happy timing of response within the generations. In "Birth of Love" Warren develops into what is perhaps most difficult, because least determined: a faithful lover. This is so arresting a poem that I want to read it at length:

> Season late, day late, sun just down, and the sky
> Cold gunmetal but with a wash of live rose, and she,
> From water the color of sky except where
> Her motion has fractured it to shivering splinters of silver,
> Rises. Stands on the raw grass. Against
> The new-curdling night of spruces, nakedness
> Glimmers and, at bosom and flank, drips
> With fluent silver.

This is a poetry of the verb rather than the noun. Warren rediscovers the power of words that enact over those that abstract. Our fate in the poem depends upon its verbs. Stationed at the beginnings and ends of lines, granted a full and measured breath of their own, these carefully positioned action words reach forward to create an anticipation which carries us through the poem. They draw us, like enduring love, into time.

Love is also born here in an onlooker:

> The man,

> Some ten strokes out, but now hanging
> Motionless in the gunmetal water, feet
> Cold with the coldness of depth, all
> History dissolving from him, is
> Nothing but an eye. Is an eye only. Sees

> The body that is marked by his use, and Time's,
> Rise, and in the abrupt and unsustaining element of air,
> Sway, lean, grapple the pond-bank.

Suspended in an undifferentiated medium, cut off from shore, the man here contracts into a mere seer. For a moment he seems in the world but not of it, but Warren allows him only a momentary stay. Simple eyesight quickly becomes historical consciousness as seeing leads to remembering. To see "the body that is marked by his use, and Time's" is to dissolve back into awareness of history. However much the eye may enjoy visions unmarked by time, the objects of its sight insist upon their subjection to time's usages. Warren rejects Blake's visionary claim that "the Eye sees more than the Heart knows." However much the heart longs for immutability, it can only feel the loss of memory as the loss of love.

This is a poem of suddenly perceived grace. Love comes back unannounced, as surprise:

> Sees
>
> How, with the posture of female awkwardness that is,
> And is the stab of, suddenly perceived grace, breasts bulge down in
> The pure curve of their weight and buttocks
> Moon up and, in that swelling unity,
> Are silver, and glimmer.

With each "and" conclusion is here delayed while loving attention is extended. These conjunctions testify to her sheer bodily abundance. Within the ingathering the beat comes momentarily to rest upon "grace," and we are given time not only to see "how" she moves him but to feel how she moves us. What may have only penetrated to the eye now stabs to the heart.

The poem now precipitates us toward a fall:

> Then
>
> The body is erect, she is herself, whatever
> Self she may be, and with an end of the towel grasped in each hand
> Slowly draws it back and forth across back and buttocks, but
> With face lifted toward the high sky, where
> The over-wash of rose color now fails. Fails, though no star
> Yet throbs there.

As she withdraws into her private history, the light fails. "Fails," Warren repeated, to emphasize that no fiction of arrest comes between this failure and the acknowledgment of it. Her ongoing withdrawal turns upon the "The's" which begin the next four sentences. Throughout the poem, the formality of definite articles replaces the intimacy of personal pronouns to create a sure sense of otherness. Here the articles build toward a vision of her as an "it," drawing "to itself . . . what light/In the sky yet lingers." What then shall we further be able to see? An abstraction:

> This moment is non-sequential and absolute, and admits
> Of no definition, for it
> Subsumes all other, and sequential, moments, by which
> Definition might be possible.

"This" closes the growing gap between the man and his vision, the reader and the poem. "This" testifies to the presence of a thing and our familiarity with it. We have had our moment; now we savor it through commentary. An immediacy becomes an example. Yet the poet speaks of this moment as still happening. It "is." We again question whether one can speak of a moment and still experience it. The poet's way of saying contradicts the force of his statement. He advances a definition about the inadmissibility of definition. He denies sequence in a poem dependent on it. The moment, we are told, subsumes and dissolves history. And yet the poem, as we have seen, involves us in a necessary sequence of seeings. Our movement through it is as much like walking as stationary looking. In its own words, it is "stair-steep." It is torn between asserting its moment as "nonsequential and absolute," and the necessity of entrusting any such experience to the mediation of language and emotion working in time.

The genius of Warren's poem is to locate this lapse from unconscious grace not after but *within* the swelling present moment. The abstraction interrupts rather than completes the poem's movement. So it is with relief that the reader returns to the unfolding of the actual scene. The woman must still wrap, glimmer, and go. For five syllables the poet prolongs departure and restores her to our sight through repetition: "Glimmers and is gone." This is the freedom of poetry, the power of its repetitions to reassure us that all is not quite yet lost. What the man now hopes for is not so much to stay her going as to stay her forever:

> and the man
>
> Suspended in his darkling medium, stares
> Upward where, though not visible, he knows
> She moves, and in his heart he cries out that, if only
> He had such strength, he would put his hand forth
> And maintain it over her to guard, in all
> Her out-goings and in-comings, from whatever
> Inclemency of sky or slur of the world's weather
> Might ever be. In his heart
> He cries out.

Here repetition works not to recover but to remind, to remind that what he cries out for he cannot really achieve. Yet what we are moved by is not the impossibility of the hope but its stubborn persistence. (Readers of Warren will note that "Birth of Love" rewrites "A Vision, Circa 1880," perhaps Warren's most beautiful poem to his father, and one in which he first tries to "cry out" to a "hieratic" figure who glimmers in a clearing and then "is gone.") That he cries out again—that is what matters. So he ends as the poet has proceeded, by raising his hand against the very medium—time—through which he expresses his love.

"Birth of Love" confirms the love between men and women which makes generation possible. Any enduring love is profoundly historical, growing through change, confirmed through repetition. Yet poetry represents love less in its confirmation through repetition than in its freshness through transformation. Warren's poem is a repetition *experienced* as a beginning. It fuses, as fully as one might ever wish, the imagination which conserves and the imagination which creates. This birth is really a rebirth. The man has again fallen in love with this woman, as he will, with grace, again. He falls in love again, however, *as if* for the first time, *as if* he were free to choose, apart from all the historical obligations determining such a choice. The whole poem is structured to be experienced as "the non-sequential" moment of which it speaks. It is given greater force than a poem of actual beginning by virtue of the very history it excludes, and yet which surrounds this moment to define and give value to it. We know that the body has been marked by time's use; we know that the day is late. Yet we are left with another image of beginning:

> Above
>
> Height of the spruce-night and heave of the far mountain, he sees
> The first star pulse into being. It gleams there.

Of course the star is Venus; of course the poem is a repetition in modern time of the myth of her birth. But Warren's mode of indirect allusion frees us from a mere rehearsal of the archetypical—the poem was originally called "The Birth of Love"—and preserves the illusion of an original event. What is lost for mythic inevitability is gained for imaginative free play.

The poet ends by refusing to answer an unasked yet implicit question posed by the evening star:

> I do not know what promise it makes to him.

Is this a question on our lips? Not if we have attentively read the poem. For by the end we should realize that the fact of the star's pulsing forth every night, not what it might symbolically promise, *is* the promise. It too marks a pattern of repetition, yet it too, in its nightly pulsing forth, is always ready to be seen and felt as if for the first time. In this quiet refusal to interpret his own imagery, Warren acknowledges the critic's desire to know while protecting the poet's will to present, a resolution worthy of his most mature and beautiful poem.

T. R. HUMMER

"Audubon" and the Moral Center

. . . and what is your passion?
—AUDUBON

In his essay on Katherine Anne Porter, "Irony with a Center," Robert Penn Warren makes a sweeping judgmental statement on a perennial question: what separates "great" writers from those who are merely competent? Warren says of Porter that "she belongs to the relatively small group of writers . . . who have done serious, consistent, original, and vital work in the field of short fiction." Against this group of the elect, Warren opposes another "very large group of writers who have a great facility, a great mechanical competence, and sometimes moments of real perception, *but who work from no fundamental and central conviction*" (emphasis added).

While it is important to realize that Warren is writing in a particular context here, his statement is so categorical that it can only be intended to have broad application. If Warren uses this criterion as a basis for judging other writers' work, he is surely willing, insofar as he considers himself striving toward "serious, consistent, original, and vital work," to have it used as a yardstick against his own. Any writer who makes such a statement surely first considers *himself* to be working from a "central conviction"; and if we can discover what conviction is central to Warren, we will have gone a long way toward understanding his art.

Later in the same essay, Warren considers a conclusion that he says many readers of Porter have come to: that Porter's "underlying attitude is one of skepticism, negation." To this, Warren replies that, while the "skeptical and ironical bias is . . . important in Miss Porter's work . . . her irony is irony with a center, never irony for irony's sake." In attempting a definition of the center Porter's irony revolves around, he says that her skepticism "simply implies, I think, a refusal to accept the formula, the ready-made solution, the hand-me-down morality, the word for the spirit. It affirms, rather, the constant need for exercising discrimination, the arduous obligation of the intellect in the face of conflicting dogmas, the need for a dialectical approach to matters of definition, the need for exercising as much of the human faculty as possible." It is this refusal and this affirmation, Warren says, that give Porter's work "philosophic urgency" and "thematic integration": "the mark of the masters."

Several important facets of the "central conviction" that Warren is talking about emerge here. On the negative side, it involves refusal to accept authority, dogma, any kind of easy morality, at face value. On the positive side, there is an emphasis on "discrimination": the writer must make decisions, and not simply aesthetic ones but decisions about such things as "conflicting dogmas" and "definition." To put the matter, for the moment, in a rather simplistic nutshell, Warren seems to be saying that the writer, if he is to be of the first rank, must not be afraid of getting his hands dirty grappling with the big questions. He must plunge arduously into the "dialectic" of things—must attempt to encompass all the contrarieties of the world—before he can begin the essential task of forging definitions. And he must be engaged in this process with his whole being, "exercising as much of the human faculty as possible."

That is all tidy enough, and has the comfortable thump of good rhetoric in the bargain. It is just the kind of thing we want to hear writers say, particularly our older writers, about whom we like to feel certain. But if we leave it at that—if we fail to examine Warren's statement scrupulously and try to decide precisely what it means, what it defines, in theory as well as in practice—then we will commit precisely the error that Warren is warning us against. We must not take Warren at his word here. We must try to discover the spirit of what he is saying, and so doing, decide whether Warren himself practices what he preaches.

Though there might be other ways of getting inside Warren's notion of a "central conviction," there are two points in his statement that cry out immediately for exploration and definition. The first is morality—for if a writer should eschew "hand-me-down morality," there is an implication that another kind of morality exists which a writer should embrace. The second is the "human faculty" Warren says a writer should exercise "as much of . . . as possible." What, exactly, does Warren mean by this "human faculty," and how are we to know when it is being exercised?

Clearly, these are knotty questions—questions to which there will be no easy answers. But that in itself is a hopeful sign. They are big questions of the kind Warren has admonished us to grapple with. And, more importantly in the present context, they are questions we must assume Warren himself has grappled with and brought to at least provisional definition. Otherwise, he would not be so willing to apply them in the judgmental way he does.

"Moral" is a word that writers have not been comfortable with for a long time. Yet when we look at Warren's considerable body of essays, we discover that the word crops up with significant frequency; and it is never, unless qualified by "easy," "hand-me-down," or the like, used in any pejorative sense. For example, in his essay "A Poem of Pure Imagination" on Coleridge's *Rime of the Ancient Mariner*, Warren quotes Mrs. Barbauld, a poet contemporary with Coleridge, as attacking *The Ancient Mariner* on the grounds that it has "no moral." Warren's reply is that while he disagrees with Mrs. Barbauld's contention, he can "sympathize with the lady's desire that poetry have some significant relation to the world, some meaning." Here, then, is a bold definition of the moral content of a poem: it is bound up, for Warren, with a poem's "significant relation to the world," which is furthermore synonymous with a poem's meaning. Hence we can infer that, as far as Warren is concerned, a poem without some kind of moral content—whatever he may mean by that particularly—is without significant relation to the world and is therefore meaningless.

It should be immediately clear that the definition of "moral" Warren is pointing toward here is not that of the Mrs. Barbaulds of the world, whose "Presbyterian sensibility leaves something to be desired in the way of subtlety." That is hand-me-down morality, morality that has not been tested in the crucible of experience but merely swallowed whole. It is only a word, and as such has no "significant relation to the world" in the life of the person who uses it so. It is therefore, finally, meaningless. But "moral" is not meaningless for Warren, as we can see. He has redefined the word for himself, given it a new spirit. While the equation he presents in the Coleridge essay—morality equals significant relation to the world equals meaning—is not a final definition, it points us in the direction we must follow to find out what that new spirit is. If we can discover how Warren believes a poem "means," how it establishes a significant relation with the world, then we should begin to be able to decide whether the central conviction Warren is working from is, in his terms, a moral one. We can only begin to suspect that it is, since it appears that Warren's definition of moral purpose in a poem is identical with his definition of the poem itself.

In *Democracy and Poetry*, Warren advances "the notion of the self as the central fact of poetry"—poetry here representing "art in general." Warren writes,

> poetry—the work of the "makers"—is a dynamic affirmation of, as well as the image of, the concept of the self. . . . the "made thing"—the poem, the work of art—stands as a "model" of the organized self. . . . The "made thing" becomes, then, a vital emblem of the struggle toward the achieving of the self, and that mark of struggle, the human signature, is what gives the aesthetic organization its numinousness.

To work backward through this statement, we see here that art has, or has at best, "numinousness," a power that the reader or viewer experiences as though he were in the presence of something sacred. Furthermore, we learn that this power is the consequence of the artist's "struggle toward the achieving of the self," which "marks" the product with "the human signature." Here we are reminded of our second question about the passage from the Porter essay: what does Warren mean by the "human faculty?" Can it be that the human faculty, whatever it is, is what the artist exercises in "the struggle toward the achieving of the self"; and that the human signature Warren refers to here is the outward sign in the artifact of the inner exercise of that faculty—just as the artifact itself is the "vital emblem" of that struggle?

But let us complete our scrutiny before we attempt to answer this question. Warren has also told us that the work of art "stands as a 'model' of the organized self." Warren is quick to say that the artist is not necessarily a completely organized self; rather, the poem comes to be "the image of the 'ideal self,' the 'regenerate self,' as it were, of the disorganized man." We can now see how the work of art can be a " 'model' of the organized self" and at the same time a "vital emblem of the *struggle toward* the achieving of the self": it is so because, for Warren, selfhood and the struggle to achieve selfhood are, at bottom, the same. That is why the artwork is both "a dynamic affirmation of, *as well as* the image of, the *concept* of the self" (emphasis added). Notice Warren never says the artifact is the direct image of the self. If that were the case, the self would have to be seen as complete, and thus static. The poem is rather the model of a *possible* self; and finally it is the emblem of the struggle toward the achieving of that self, a struggle that never ends.

There are several important implications here. First, Warren would say, the artist must be self-reflective enough to have realized the need for, and to have evolved some sort of concept or model of, a self to strive toward. And if he has done that, then—no matter how much or how often that model may change, as change it undoubtedly will—he is already neck-deep in the struggle. For to attain that degree of self-reflection, to be what in *Democracy and Poetry* Warren calls "a more or less aware individual" who recognizes "the self as a development in time, with a past and a future"—surely a recognition of continuity is a prerequisite for one who is *struggling toward* a model of selfhood—is already to be struggling with the prime matter of human nature.

This, I think, is what Warren means by the human faculty: the ability—that, as far as we know, is uniquely human—to turn in on ourselves, with all the energy and all the means at our disposal, and *remake* ourselves. Perfection is, of course, impossible; therefore the struggle should go on all our lives—for, to arrive at some state of being that we conceive of as "final" would be to abdicate, to give up the struggle, to rest in some preconceived notion. The concept of the self, the "model" we are striving toward, changes constantly as we move toward it; it recedes infinitely. But it is the struggle that counts, anyway, the process, the attempt. And this struggle is essentially moral; for, as Warren tells us, part of the sense of self as "significant unity" is the self's ability to recognize "itself as capable of action worthy of praise or blame."

Here, in the idea of action, is where the work of art comes in. There are, as we know, two kinds of action: inner and outer, subjective and objective. The first is what we have been talking about, primarily, up to this point: action by the self aimed at the self. The second is action by the self aimed at the world. Both kinds of action are clearly necessary—and the execution of a work of art is a special kind of action because it is both at once. For the true artist, the artist of the "first rank," creation is a part of his struggle toward the achievement of selfhood. It is, Warren says in "A Poem of Pure Imagination," "as much a process of discovery as a process of making. A poem may, in fact, start from an idea" or a "phrase, a scene, an image, an incident," but the main thing is that the creative "process for the poet is the process of discovering what the idea" or image or whatever "'means' to him in the light of his total being and total experience." In other words, the creation of a work of art, for Warren, is in large part a process of discovering *meaning*; it is, then, a process of making significant contact with reality. And that implies that it is equally a process of discovering the self, the "felt unity" that experiences the meaning, contacts the reality. Therefore, for the artist, the process of creation is a tool par excellence in the struggle to achieve selfhood: at once a lens to see the raw stuff of existence through, and a hammer to shape it with. But the work of art, as it exists for an audience, is an outward act as well. The artist is not alone in the world, and he is not the only one who is struggling within himself. Therefore, the reflection of his struggle, as it exists in the "vital emblem" that the artifact is, has the power to strike a chord of recognition in its audience. That chord, when it strikes, is the "numinousness" of the artifact; and that numinousness, that energy, can become useful for the reader or viewer in turn. The artist has succeeded, when that happens, in passing energy to his audience to aid in the struggle for selfhood. It is this transfer of energy that we call *meaning* in a work of art. It is the artist's, and finally the audience's, contact with reality through the artifact. And it is, in Warren's terms, the moral content of the work. It is the thing that is the most worthy of praise, or the absence of which is the most worthy of blame, in a work of art. Such a work has value only insofar as it helps us through what Warren, in "Melville's Poems," calls "the necessity for action in the face of the difficulty of knowing the truth." If hand-me-down morality, dogma, is inadequate, then each of us is at sea; we cannot know what must be done unless we somehow find our own way into the living heart of things. "In this situation," Warren says in the same essay, "man becomes fully man only if he submits himself to the inwardness of life in order to be returned, chastened and enlightened, to the objective world of action." This is what the artist attempts each time he creates; and if he succeeds, he not only points the way for us, he also passes on the will and the energy to follow his example.

This explains why Warren is impatient with writers who, he feels, have "mechanical competence" but who "work from no fundamental and central conviction." That central conviction, for Warren, is a reflection of the self, which is a vortex of struggle; it constantly dismembers itself and regenerates itself in its unending battle to *create* itself. Hence, the true artist, for Warren, is artist second and human being first. For himself, he is only an artist insofar as being an artist helps him in his struggle. For us, his greatness resides in his ability, his moral ability, to help us all. This, too, is why Warren has no use, as he makes clear in *Democracy and Poetry*, for the notion that art has no effect in the world. Art, he says there, is "the voice of the passion of the soul. . . . Even a nourishment of the soul, and indeed of society, in that it keeps alive the sense of self and the correlated sense of a community."

This, then, is Warren's central conviction, the moral center of his art: the deep engagement of the artist with human growth, in himself and in other men.

II

Louis Martz hailed *Audubon*, on its appearance in 1969, as the embodiment of "the accumulated power of a lifetime's skill and wisdom." Indeed, there is much to indicate that *Audubon*, whatever else it may be, is a kind of summation of everything Warren had been struggling with through the entire course of his career. Several critics have seen similarities between the art of Audubon and Warren's own; Norman Martien goes further and says that the Audubon of Warren's poem seems "a type of the American artist."

If Warren is in fact presenting a character conceived in this way—a character who is at once an analogue of himself and of artists in general—then it is logical to assume, given the pronouncements concerning art and artists we have just been examining, that *Audubon* would be a remarkably good place to test the definition we have arrived at of the "moral center" in Warren, and to see, if we can, what grows out of it in the practice of his art.

In order to put *Audubon* to this test, we must always keep before us the dynamics of Warren's idea of a poem's relation to the self. To repeat: the poem is a bodying forth of the poet's *concept* of a self which is not static, but is in constant disequilibrium—is not something arrived at by the intellect alone but by the engagement of all the artist's faculties with experience. The "made thing" should be a reflection of the maker's continual restless struggle toward an infinitely distant but irresistibly attractive selfhood—a state of being that is unattainable, perhaps unformulable, but that must be pursued if life is to have any meaning. This struggle is the poet's only hope of making contact with reality beyond the mass of ready-made solutions and hand-me-down moralities we all live with; and so, in Warren's terms, it is the artist's (and anyone else's) moral responsibility to enter the struggle as fully as possible. What we should expect to find in *Audubon*, then—if we have been correct in what we have concluded—is the spectacle of Warren's creating, out of the already enviably rich fabric of Audubon's story, a paradigm of that striving toward selfhood.

It is thus interesting, and from our point of view hopeful, to note what Warren does with Audubon in the opening lines of the poem: he immediately sets about stripping away all the false identities associated with Audubon in the blurb that precedes the poem. These are fictive selves that surround Audubon. Some have grown up of their own accord, some he has actively encouraged; but Warren strips them all away with a clean stroke: "Was not the lost dauphin . . . was only / Base-born . . . was only / Himself, Jean Jacques, and his passion." Thus Audubon, on leaving the everyday world behind him and entering the forest—which, as we shall see, is a magical place where he is to have a decisive adventure—also leaves behind every unessential trapping of identity. He takes with him only his name, which is his connection with the past and the world he has left behind him, and his passion, which is his sense of direction, of purpose, of motion into the future.

In one way, Warren is demythifying Audubon at the beginning of the poem; he is stripping away secondary fictive selves that obscure the central self, myths in the negative sense of the word. But by doing this he is simultaneously *remythifying* Audubon. With this removal of the "secondary effects" of the world at the threshold of a magical realm, we enter the paradigm of what Joseph Campbell, in *Hero with a Thousand Faces*, calls the "monomyth": the story of the growth of the hero, which is, in symbolic language, the story of the growth of the self.

This is not to say that Warren is making *Audubon* into a myth or fairy tale. On the contrary, Warren is careful to keep the action and imagery of the poem in *this* world and to keep the characters flesh and blood. But part of the beauty of *Audubon* is Warren's (conscious or unconscious) ability to put real, earthly flesh on the bones of the monomyth: for underneath the story of Audubon as man, as underneath the story of Warren as man and all of us as human, there reverberates the structure of the myth of self as hero. What this myth signifies is the symbolic death and dismemberment of the self, its regeneration, and its resurrection in a higher form, as Campbell demonstrates. It concerns, then, the very thing we have identified as the "moral center" of Warren's work: engagement with the growth of the self. So it should come as no surprise that we encounter this mythic structure in Warren's work.

The pattern of the monomyth, as Joseph Campbell identifies it, is quite simple: the hero undergoes "a separation from the world, a penetration to some source of power, and a life-enhancing return." The separation entails, first, a journey toward the "source of power," which, as C.G. Jung tells us in *Psychology and Alchemy*, is generally some deep, dark place: "watery abyss, cavern, forest, island, castle, etc." Warren, in keeping with the truncated style of *Audubon*, collapses the first and second steps. Thus, when the poem opens, Warren separates Audubon from the world of men, as already described, and simultaneously places him in the "place of power," the primeval forest.

Warren is careful to describe the setting in exceedingly raw terms: "the dawn / Redder than meat." But at the same time we see, juxtaposed against this naturalistic imagery, the pattern of the myth: for the dawn is also "the color of God's blood spilt." This can only refer us to Christ, who is, as Jung shows, Western man's hero par excellence and who therefore participates, like all heroes, in the pattern of the monomyth.

But there is also a third thing juxtaposed to the others in this scene: the heron, moving across the sky "in slow calligraphy . . . as though pulled by a string." The bird here mediates between the raw naturalism of the forest and the pure spirituality of the Christ allusion. It is the focus of the passion, the directedness in time, of Audubon. As soon as he sees it, Audubon is plunged into "the tension of the world," a dialectic which here takes several forms but is basically the tension between the physical and the spiritual, the outer and the inner. Just as the bird is the focus between naturalism and myth, which is one kind of outer/inner tension, so it is also the focus of the tension between what Audubon *sees* ("On that sky it is black") and what he *knows* ("In my mind it is white"). As focus, the bird becomes "the great one." The bear in the following section performs a similar function. Through observation of these creatures, Audubon begins to feel his way into the world of the forest, until he realizes "how thin is the membrane between himself and the world."

There is another layer to the constructive tension between animal and human, physical and spiritual, at the beginning of *Audubon*. It is easy enough to see how a man could, realistically, be led through careful and empathic observation of nature to a realization like the one Audubon comes to. That is realistic enough, and well precedented. But there is also a suggestion of the motif of the "helpful animals" that occurs frequently in myth and fairy tale. Such animals often aid the hero in getting to the place he has to go, the "source of power," and help him through his ordeals there. In the Grimms' tales, two favorite "helpful animals" are the bear and the stork. The affinity of the hero with animals symbolizes his ability to contact more or less unconscious parts of himself—those parts of himself which are still "natural," and mysteriously powerful, because they are outside the bounds of the ego. To contact that part of the self, by whatever means, is to contact nature in its subjective form; and it is clear that, on both the inner and the outer level, the animals help Audubon "enter" the forest subjectively. Once he has come to this realization of his own participation in the world, his closeness to the natural, he is plunged instantly (as far as the structure of the poem is concerned) into the center, the place of power.

The scene in Part II is again couched in naturalistic images: "Shank-end of day, spit of snow . . . / The clearing: among stumps, ruined cornstalks yet standing, the spot / Like a wound rubbed raw in the vast pelt of the forest." The "wound rubbed raw" recalls the dawn "redder than meat" of Part I, and again, as there, there is an immediate suggestion of other levels: "There / Is the cabin, a huddle of logs with no calculation or craft." In this hyperbole, the squalor of the place is reinforced; but on the other hand, there is the real sense that this place is sunk in nature, that the cabin has grown there, unconsciously, like a plant. This duality is made explicit in the following line: the clearing represents "the human filth, the human hope." On the realistic side, this conveys the relief of the wanderer at finding a human habitation in the wilderness, no matter how unsavory. But there is another side as well. In myth, the way to the great treasure, or to the center of things where the place of power lies, often leads through filth—ashheaps, dunghills, and the like. As Jung puts it, "the cheap, unseemly substance . . . rejected by all" stands for "the distressing darkness of the human psyche," the part of the human soul that is sunk in nature, where monsters and treasures go, as it were, hand in hand. This, as we shall see, is just the situation Audubon has walked into.

In Part II–B, we see that Audubon has some premonition—or perhaps *deja vu*—of what this place represents. And it is no wonder, for he has entered a classical fairy-tale situation: the house in the forest, which is always a central ordeal for the hero. The house is generally a witch's lair or a robber's den (in this case both); if the latter, the robbers are usually out when the hero arrives, and an old woman, analogue of the witch, is minding the house. This encounter with the female is crucial. It represents the center of the mythic journey of the hero, for the "source of power" in the monomyth is almost invariably the seat of the Magna Mater, the Goddess.

Joseph Campbell writes that

> the ultimate adventure, when all the barriers and ogres have been overcome, is commonly represented as a mystical marriage of the triumphant hero-soul with the Queen Goddess of the world. This is the crisis at the nadir, the zenith, or at the uttermost edge of the world, at the central point of the cosmos, in the tabernacle of the temple, or within the darkness of the deepest chamber of the heart.

But this marriage is not always triumphant; for the Goddess has two faces, one beautiful and one terrible. Sometimes she herself (like Grendel's mother in *Beowulf*) takes the form of an ogre who must be overcome. Either way, she "encompasses the encompassing, nourishes the nourishing, and is the life of everything that lives"; at the same time she is "also the death of everything that dies. . . . She is the womb and the tomb: the

sow that eats her own farrow" (Campbell). The Goddess is the power of
life and death, the central mystery the hero must come to terms with in
the place of power. It is this knowledge that Audubon approaches,
realizing that "The dregs / Of all nightmare are the same, and we call it /
Life."

Appropriately, it is at first difficult to see the Goddess in the old
woman Audubon meets. After all, this old woman is *real* (i.e., human);
we can encounter her, in almost identical guise, in the pages of Audubon's
journal. But there, as in *Audubon*, she strongly resembles the fairy-tale
witch, who is an incarnation of the Goddess; her eyes, in Warren's poem,
"glint as from the unspecifiable / Darkness of a cave." Caves, as we have
seen, are among the typical "places of power" encountered by the hero. At
the same time, the cave association gives the old woman an animalistic
aura. She, like the cabin built "without calculation or craft," is sunk in
nature; she is human and yet not human, unspecifiable: subhuman in her
animalism, and superhuman in her mythic associations.

The scene that follows is a strange one. Why does Audubon, in
such a situation, take out his watch? This is another event that comes
straight from Audubon's journal. But a very subtle transmutation takes
place between the fact of the journal and the artifact of the poem. There,
it really seems to be a thoughtless act. Audubon writes, "I drew a fine
time-piece from my breast, and told the woman that it was late, and that I
was fatigued." In the poem, though this is by no means overt, it almost
seems that Audubon taunts the woman with the watch:

Takes his watch out.
Draws it bright, on the thong-loop, from under his hunter's-frock.
It is gold, it lives in his hand in the firelight and the woman's
Hand reaches out. She wants it.

In the journal, this happens quickly; in the poem it is stretched out,
intensified. And while in the journal the watch was simply "a fine
timepiece," in the poem it "lives" in Audubon's hand. It is talismanic;
and it recalls the heron in Part I that moved across the sky "as though
pulled on a string": the watch, in the same way, is drawn on its thong.
Like the heron, the watch is a transmuting focus. It is *time*: a kind of time
that did not exist before in that place. It represents a kind of consciousness that was not there before, that the woman lacks. Holding the watch,
she is grotesquely transformed. Something in her grows young, girlish,
sexual, and Audubon is revolted by what he sees. Here the dual nature of
the woman becomes overt. Beneath the naturalistic surface of this creature, who is in many ways pathetic but who is also a witch of sorts and so

represents the fatal side of the Goddess, we catch a glimpse of the "Queen Goddess" of the world, with whom the hero makes his "mystical marriage."

But why did Audubon take out the watch in the first place? Could he have really wanted to know the time? What difference could the time make, in a literal sense, there? Could it be that something in Audubon wanted to precipitate the situation? It is finally impossible to tell—but the whole incident smacks of the Freudian slip, the random act that turns out not to be random at all, but the crux of the situation, dictated from beyond conscious knowing, like the killing of the Albatross in *The Rime of the Ancient Mariner*. It is as though the kind of knowing, the type of consciousness, that Audubon represents could not help asserting itself.

And so the damage is done. Audubon is brought, as a direct consequence, to the nadir (or is it the zenith?) of the poem. He is brought to the moment when the old woman holds life and death—*his* life and death—in her hands. Here again we have the juxtaposition of realistic and mythic details. The woman sharpening her knife, allowing the "great glob of spit" to fall on the whetstone, is naturalistic; but the woman with the knife in her hand is the Goddess in her wrathful guise, and the knife is her traditional sacrificial blade.

Brought to the verge of death, Audubon suddenly is plunged directly in the myth, the tale. He

> . . . knows
> He has entered the tale, knows
> He has entered the dark hovel
> In the forest where trees have eyes,
> Knows it is the tale
> They told him when he was a child, knows it
> Is the dream he had in childhood, but never
> Knew the end of, only
> The scream.

And now that the outer and inner situation have come into overt focus, Audubon, who only a moment before had his gun cocked and was ready for action, is "unmanned." He cannot move to defend himself—does not *want* to defend himself. The proximity of death gives life a new intensity: "even in this moment / Of fear—or is it fear?—the saliva / In his mouth tastes sweet." He is unmanned by *guilt*—a guilt he does not understand. And he waits for his "punishment," which is death—but which is also revelation. In the moment of death he will learn, at last, the "name of the world."

If *Audubon* were truly a myth clear through, from center to surface, what would follow would be revelation indeed. The pattern of the monomyth calls for the hero to be killed (like Christ) and possibly dismembered (as Christ is symbolically and Dionysus literally); then he is regenerated and resurrected—put together in a new way, reborn. For the guilt that Audubon feels is the guilt of the unregenerate ("un-reborn") man. It is the guilt of original sin, which can only be overcome by drastic rebirth.

But *Audubon* is not a myth, or not *only* a myth. If the strands of myth and reality have united here, at the poem's dramatic center, they do not remain so long. Reality insists on maintaining its surface; and so reality intrudes on the scene. Three men, in the nick of time, burst in. But for now, Audubon can only think of the revelation he has lost: "Thinks / That now he will never know the dream's ending."

Still, if reality will assert itself, so will the pattern of the myth that lies beneath. Audubon does not die, but he is not spared death either. The knife, as it were, changes hands. Audubon and his allies now deal out death to the old woman and her sons. And if the strands of myth and reality have parted again, if Audubon has been denied his chance to enter wholly into myth—if now he has to be *only* a man—so the old woman, faced with certain death, now becomes truly united with myth. Now she "is what she is": the Goddess. Audubon sees that her face is "beautiful as stone, and / So becomes aware that he is in the manly state."

This last is an absolutely pivotal point in the poem. It is, as a three-tiered pun, a master-stroke on Warren's part. On the most obvious level, Audubon is paradoxically aroused by the woman who formerly revolted him, and so has an erection—the ironic consummation of the "mystical marriage" (with the added twist that it is usual for a man being hanged to have an erection—as though somehow Audubon is himself partaking in a physical way of the hanging he has brought about). On another level, Audubon knows that the old woman is about to learn "the end of the dream"—that she is *in* the myth which reality has drawn him, for the moment, out of. He is in the manly state as opposed to the godly—but the woman is about to enter, once and for all, one way or another, the realm of the superhuman. But on still another level, the "manly state" is Audubon's selfhood: for this is the moment of regeneration. Previously, Audubon had been "unmanned"—a word that contrasts interestingly with the phrase "manly state." It carries connotations of dismemberment, specifically castration, which is sometimes the hero's fate. But now Audubon is healed. From this point on, he will begin the third part of the mythic pattern; the return to life in the world, which is itself the "manly state." This experience is part of Audubon's "struggle toward the achieving of the self," and at this point he becomes aware, in a way he never has before, of what that struggle is about.

And so he sees the old woman hang—indeed, he has hanged her himself, having first precipitated the whole situation by displaying his watch, then in effect acting as her judge (think of the similar predicament of Jack Burden in *All the King's Men*)—sees her "ecstasy of iron" as she hangs, knows "this was the dream that, lifelong, she had dreamed toward." He stands until the snow begins to cover the corpses, the old woman hanging between her two sons like Christ between the thieves, and he "yearns to be able to frame a definition of joy." For, out of this experience of the opening and closing of the dialectic of life and death, out of his realization of the "manly state," which might also be called the "exercise of the human faculty," out of the knowledge he has gained, Audubon is learning to love the world.

Appropiately for a poem with three strands—"reality," myth, and art—*Audubon* has three endings.

The first is the realistic ending. Here, Audubon the man comes to the end that all men come to. This, on an ironic level, is the third part of the monomyth: the return of the hero to the world, to the arms of his mortal wife, and to the grave. But there is, for him, a simple satisfaction: he knows he has been "what he had to be," that he has stalked his selfhood relentlessly, has seen

> As though down a rifle barrel, lined up
> Like sights, the self that was, the self that is, and there
> Far off, but in range, completing that alignment, fate—
> . . . The quarry lifts, in the halo of gold leaves, its noble head.

This, surely, is the perfect metaphor for that infinitely receding model of the self that Warren speaks of in his essays. And in this pursuit of self, Audubon participates in the eternal, in the myth and the dream, for, as we are told, "This is not a dimension of Time."

The moral question arises: has Audubon, a ne'er-do-well in the practical eyes of the world, lived his life as he should have? He was "not even able / To make a decent living," and so as some may have said was "of weak character." But this, for Warren, is the cowardly hand-me-down morality of men who have not tested themselves in the real moral exercise of the human faculty. For a man like Audubon, "The world declared itself . . . necessity / Blooms like a rose." His is a self continually testing itself, in the unending disequilibrium of growth, and so he can tell himself, even near the end of his life, "I do not even know my own name." Though he dies quietly in bed, there is still a continuity after his dying, a continuity between the man and the life that goes on after him which has been established by his struggle. When he died, "Night leaned, and now leans /

Off the Atlantic, and is on schedule." Audubon extends beyond the night of his death into the present: for he is not only Audubon the man, he is also Audubon the artist-hero, the man who "ventures forth from the world of common day," as Joseph Campbell says of heroes generally, "into a region of supernatural wonder: fabulous forces are there encountered and a decisive victory is won: the hero comes back from this mysterious adventure with the power to bestow boons on his fellow men."

Thus we come to the second ending of the poem: the ending of Audubon as artist-hero. The title of this section, "Knowledge and Love," tells the tale in microcosm: knowledge and love are the poles of the dialectic that engages the artist, the hero, and all of us finally, insofar as we are "more or less self-aware." The analytical impulse, the desire to know, is divisive, as Coleridge wrote (and Warren knows his Coleridge). This divisiveness "strikes death through all things visible and invisible." But love, on the other hand, is unitive and regenerative. Thus the hero, in order to gain some new knowledge, is himself dismembered; the knowledge he gains is of himself: he takes himself apart to know himself. But because of his Christ-like love of the world, or perhaps because of the world's godlike love of him, he is regenerated. His self-knowledge becomes world-knowledge. He is now ready to perform great deeds in the service of mankind. Likewise the artist, in order to create, must first *know*; and so he takes things apart. But because he loves, he puts things back together again, in a new way. This is what we see Audubon doing. In order to paint birds, Audubon first kills them, then mounts them (dismemberment), and finally paints them. "He slew them at surprising distances, with his gun. / Over a body held in his hand, his head was bowed low, / But not in grief." If not grief, what? Surely curiosity, in part—the will to examine and to know. But also, there is something sacramental about the image. Audubon loves the world; and the boon he, as the hero, can grant other men is the regeneration of the nature he has destroyed. He destroys to recreate, and thus give both knowledge and love to all the world. But as hero, he is himself destroyed and recreated in the process (the above passage about the gun recalls an earlier one in which Audubon takes sight on himself and "his fate"). For, as Campbell tells us, in the mythic realm, "where we thought to find an abomination we shall find a god; where we had sought to slay another, we shall slay ourselves; where we had thought to travel outward, we shall come to the center of our own existence; where we had thought to be alone, we will be with all the world." Here, in Warren's terms, is man submitting "to the inwardness of life in order to be returned, chastened and enlightened, to the objective world of action." Symbolically for the hero, actually for the artist, ideally for us all, this is the struggle for selfhood.

The third, and *really* final, ending of the poem belongs to Warren and the reader directly. Warren enters the poem now as a first person presence. Appropriately this section is divided into two parts, one directed inward, the other outward. In the first, Warren shows us the beginning of his own journey, his own struggle—different, on the surface, from Audubon's, and yet the same underneath. In the second, he challenges the reader to undertake this struggle too: for the command "Tell me a story" is a command to know and to love the subject and the object of the story. To tell a story is first to *make* a story; and the story is the story of our lives, our selfhood. It is poem; it is myth; it is life. It has no humanly discernible beginning or end, for "the name of the story will be Time." But if the story is told well and truly, no matter how terrible it may be—like a life lived well, with full exercise of the "human faculty," no matter how tragic—it will be a "story of deep delight." In the end, the responsibility is on us all to become "Makers"—makers of our own selfhood, participating full in the "manly state." That is the responsibility—the moral responsibility— that Warren leaves us with at the end of the poem.

If we accept the notion that Warren's "moral center" is a deep engage- ment with human growth, with the growth of the self, then surely *Audubon* can be seen as a product of such a center. In the figure of Audubon, Warren found a perfect medium to embody his aims, a figure able to bear both the human and the mythic (which are finally, at bottom, the same) aspects of the struggle.

One of the epigrams to the poem reads, "I caught at his strict shadow and the shadow released itself with neither haste nor anger. But he remained silent." Warren, in calling these pieces of Audubon's story "A Vision," announces his intention to transform the subject of the poem. That subject is not really Audubon but his shadow—the shadow he casts, as an artist, across time. And thus Warren transforms himself in the process as well; for, though Audubon and Warren are different men, as fellow artists and fellow human beings engaged in the struggle for selfhood they stand in the same light and cast the same shadow.

CALVIN BEDIENT

"Truth's Glare-Glory"

Like love, glory is what a man makes himself worthy of, and what makes him worthy. But love eases the way, where glory challenges his fortitude and ingenuity and proves his genius. Save for its vigilante role, love is feminine; glory, masculine. A loved man is given admiration, a glorious man compels it—he carves it out, exacts it, coerces it into being; it is his. Love: a sometimes airy, sometimes physical "osmosis of being." Glory: a hard triumph of the will to power, proof of ontological heft, utmost distinction.

For the Greeks, glory meant standing in the light, a resplendent appearing. It was the crown of the pagan view of things: "Glory was not something additional," notes Heidegger, ". . . it was the mode of the highest being." A pagan Appearance amorously coincident with Being, light and singleness and radiant bursts of time—this is no less Warren's realm, and standing in the light no less his joy. Apostate as soon as he makes to cross to the other side, into transparent purities of Being, he looks back, as in "Evening Hawk," and speaks with tell-tale generosity of "the gold of our error."

A love of glory is in any case a natural accompaniment, if not indeed the cause, of poetry; for, as Pindar said, the essence of the art is to glorify, to place in the light. Heidegger elaborates: "The poet always speaks as though the essent were being expressed and invoked for the first time. Poetry . . . has always so much world space to spare that in it each thing—a tree, a mountain, a house, the cry of a bird—loses all indifference and commonplaceness."

To delight in the world as Audubon does is to see now this one, now that one of its creatures glimmering in the light. He himself is in the shade of obscurity, an audience; his attention is all applause. Warren plays down this painter's presumptive need for personal glory, plays down his art. The appearances that matter are those of the birds, whether in "air that glitters like fluent crystal" or "In our imagination." Where is the all-important middle term, the work of art itself, *that* glory, in "He puts them where they are, and there we see them / In our imagaination"? Nondescript, it is merely nodded to, as a "where," a "there," a convey-ance like a library shelf on which books are placed to be taken down. Yet would Warren have been drawn to Audubon, have written about him, had it not been for his fame, the heroism in and behind his glory?

It is not in Warren's nature to be secretive (at least not in the long run) about his excitement over a "name." If he took Audubon's artistic splendor for granted, it was less out of rivalry or disingenuousness about the importance of personal glory than out of fidgetiness over the precisions and patience of his painterly eye. In Warren, an appearance is above all a symbolic action (as in the great trumpeter swan's clangorous ascent to incandescence) and not a stylishly limned, minutely lined, finely shaded, "static" intricacy. Besides, if *doxa*, which emphasizes sight and aspect, was one of the Greek words for glory, the other was *kleos*, which stresses hearing and calling; and in *Audubon* when the world declares itself, it does so as—"oh, arch on arch"—a voice. His seeing ablaze, Audubon appeases our terror of darkness, but not our terror of silence. His voice is not distinctive enough to stave off the "roar" of time and untime; the hooting geese over Kentucky are more audibly arresting. Warren's own "spoken" work tries to perfect their call. "Tell me a story," raise yet another forceful cry of human destiny. Glory to the man who, like "our Milton," makes words hum and hive in his name.

In "Old Nigger on One-Mule Cart," Warren is equivocal, yet vehement, about his desire to end by "holding, / I trust, in my hand, a name." On the one hand, he feels that his vanity rates a rebuke. Surely others—for instance, the old black man carting junk on the backroad those many years ago, the one he almost drove into—surely others put down vanity. In his mind's eye, he can see the old man going home to his "askew / Shack," where he

> Unhitches the mule.
> Stakes it out. Between cart and shack,
> Pauses to make water, and while
> The soft, plopping sound in deep dust continues, his face

> Is lifted into starlight, calm as prayer. He enters
> The dark shack and I see
> A match spurt, then burn down, die.

Why does he, the poet, lack this prayerlike calm? Why does he feel he must *eat* stars? Why can't he pee in the dust and lie down in the dark, and so call a truce to his rage? Perhaps he will, at that:

> And so I say:
> Brother, Rebuker, my Philosopher past all
> Casuistry, will you be with me when
> I arrive and leave my own cart of junk
> Unfended from the storm of starlight and
> The howl, like wind, of the world's monstrous blessedness,
> To enter, by a bare field, a shack unlit?

On the other hand, his noble heart, his will to power, his love of glory, of "the grandeur of certain utterances," will not put up with such meekness. A shudder overcomes the poem at the point of "a bare field, a shack unlit," as the poet feels the pall in the old man's lack of protest. To be black as the spaces among the stars; a casualty of silence, the same that earlier in the poem, after the dance music stopped, raged in the poet's liquored ears ("it ranges the world, it will / Devour us"), to be one of Melville's "mob of unnecessary duplicates," a "nigger," even—a man without so much as a social face! (Throughout the poem, from the title on, and not least with its terrified "Man-eyes . . . white-bulging / In black face," the old man is an objectionable stereotype.) Born to revert to dust! Intolerable. So, hardly pausing to take a breath, and casuistically, the poet continues:

> Entering into that darkness to fumble
> My way to a place to lie down, but holding,
> I trust, in my hand, a name—
> Like a shell, a dry flower, a worn stone, a toy—merely
> A hard-won something that may, while Time
> Backward unblooms out of time toward peace, utter
> Its small, sober, and inestimable
> Glow, trophy of truth.

> Can I see Arcturus from where I stand?

Man has created glory to save both himself and the universe from nothingness. But for Warren this pertinacious pursuit—this starting with the world and seeing how near the stars one can go—is redeemed from vanity only if consecrated, at the same time, to the truth. The "glow" of a poem, a name, a painting, is sign of its "trophy of truth." However harsh the truth may be, it is sacrosanct, all reverence is due it, because nothing is more utter, nothing else real. Truth, together with its beauty, is all we know of God, and all we know of glory. The task of the philosopher is to shine a light on the truth, that of the poet to see the truth itself as a splendor. The poet will succeed in this insofar as he can see the truth through his longing and his ability to be the medium of its beauty.

"Learning to face Truth's glare-glory, from which our eyes are long hid," is distressing, and "It is hard sometimes to remember that beauty is one word for reality." But at other times it is not, especially to one with a feral thirst for glory. To see truth in a blaze of joy is less a choice than a glad and terrible compulsion.

"Red-Tail Hawk and Pyre of Youth" is another apologia, or reaffirmation, of this thirst. It is even, though far more clandestinely than that star-climbing monolith "Old Nigger on One-Mule Cart," another defense of the "name" a "A hard-won something that may"—because built on words—"utter" its "Glow, trophy of truth." In this poem the slain-and-stuffed red-tail hawk becomes a muse of the fallen glory of the word:

> Year after year, in my room, on the tallest of bookshelves,
> It was real, perched on its bough-crotch to guard
> Blake and *Lycidas*, Augustine, Hardy and *Hamlet*,
> Baudelaire and Rimbaud, and I knew that the yellow eyes,
> Unsleeping, stared as I slept.

Eventually, the poet burns his first published poems together with this former "king of the air," this victim of his "crime of I." He also throws on the pyre his "first book of Milton, / The *Hamlet*, the yellow, leaf-dropping Rimbaud, . . . not to mention / The collection of sexual Japanese prints—strange sex / Of mechanical sexlessness." Yet, like Yeats, he would be content to live it all again—in his case because shooting the hawk, writing poems, and sexual passion were his chief share in power and glory, all the life there was. The rest was death.

This is to contradict Dave Smith's description of the poem as a "mini-Mariner in plot, vision, and construction." Granted the murder of the hawk is a parable "of man's Fall." But it is no less a parable of his "blood-marriage" with power and glory. In consequence, Warren's poet does not want the slain bird's blood washed away. For him there is no "dear God who loveth us," who "made and loveth all." Only man loves all, and man's love is by nature transgressive. You feel it as an electric irony in

> How my heart sang!
>
> Till all was ready—skull now well scraped
> And with arsenic dried . . .

What binds "air-blood and earth-blood" together is, in this poem, "The old .30-.30," not prayer. "And I pray that . . . all will be as it was" is not penitence, but greed for the crime (and *its* punishment, for this crime was costly). To bring a marvelous otherness near enough for a mingling, we must destroy it, as we do each time we look at beauty, or read a poem. It is thus that we make it our own, a regalness perched on the bough-crotch we provide for it, stiff but "moulded as though . . . to take to the air." Always the rifle must swing up, our leaden eyes sink after staring at "unapprehensible purity" of silver air, for such is the destructive rhythm of the imaginative life.

The hawk is every fall the poet himself has endured, the fall that life somehow essentially is, that love is, that passion for truth and beauty is. And if at last he earns the right to address this "hot blood of the air," intimately, as "you," it is because, like any man, he has tumbled from the sky of his own expectations of himself, of life; has become shabby, bandy winged, "commensurate."

So it is that the plot of "The Ancient Mariner" is turned upside down—one might say, refuted. The sum total of the poet's wisdom is that, to taste or know a fate "Whose name is a name beyond joy," he would shoot the hawk again.

Indeed, he is eager, even rapaciously so, to do it:

> And I pray that in some last dream or delusion,
> While hospital wheels creak beneath
> And the nurse's soles make their *squeak-squeak* like mice,
> I'll again see the first small silvery swirl.
> Spin outward and downward from sky-height
> To bring me the truth in blood-marriage of earth and air—
> And all will be as it was
> In that paradox of unjoyful joyousness,
> Till the dazzling moment when I, a last time, must flinch
> From the regally feathered gasoline flare
> Of youth's poor, angry, slapdash, and ignorant pyre.

What he transcribes here, in a language of ecstasy, is the rhythm of his fate. So, then, he has found it; it is clear to him now; and having found it he must love it. What else is he but what his fate is? What other chance for being does he have? The remorse accreted from this fate might require the burning of a pile of criminal evidence. But this is really no sacrifice. Neither is it the promise of a new start. It is only a ritual acknowledgment of "the cost of experience." It reduces the decayed body of what was loved to ashes, but the love itself hasn't worn. The will awaits its next occasion; the .30-.30 still hangs on the hand "As on a crooked stick"; and memory—the poem shows it—grows rank at the first drop of rain.

Numbered among the costs of experience are both metaphysical and Oedipal chagrins. The first are more distinct. Just as Goethe questioned how he could be alive if others were, this poem questions how there can be life if there is God. It chooses life. The hawk is first a forced symbol of God incarnate, spinning as it does out of the unapprehensible purity of the silver afternoon sky, its "Gold eyes, unforgiving, for they, like God, see all." Then it is shot; God is dead. Later, thinking of its wicked-yellow eyes staring in vengeance, the poet will ask: "Could Nature forgive?" So the bird has been demoted to nature. The transcendent is retained only as the thrill and terror of transgression.

In this God slaying, this God denying, there is both sorrow and elation. On the one hand a man cannot endure the white albatross of idealism, so murderously pure. Better, even, endure the predatory hawk of conscience. So he flees from innocence and toward his guilt, like Jeremiah in *World Enough and Time*. He makes "the crime of self" his familiar, "the crime of life" his passion. "If we can have knowledge, if we can know the terrible logic of life, if we can only know!" True, knowledge "is not redemption, but is almost better than redemption." Jeremiah, like Camus's stranger, "will shake the hangman's hand, and will call him my brother, at last."

Appearance, not the unapprehensible, is our sphere. And here the soul hawks, or else is mouse. The mouse squeak of the nurse's shoes will (so the poet imagines) set his soul to hawking once again. Glory here below lies in triumphs, even Zen miracles of the will:

> There was no choice in the act—the act impossible but
> Possible. I screamed, not knowing
> From what emotion, as at that insane range
> I pressed the cool, snubbed
> Trigger. Saw
> The circle
> Break.

In *Brother to Dragons*, "R.P.W." relates the story of Kent, a boy who shot a wild goose, "seized it, hugged it, ran / Three miles to town and yelled for joy and every / Step cried like a baby and did not know why." He comments: "the only thing / In life is glory," and that "knocks society's values to a cocked hat." Salvation-by-glory is a "terror." It means that ours is a "reality of decreation," in Wallace Stevens' phrase—our revelations not those "of belief" but portents "of our own powers." Fear, grief, and joy mingle in its wicked, life-justifying transgressions. Kent cries, the boy in "Red-Tail Hawk" cries ("in / Eyes tears past definition") because transgression—so congenial—yet injures the dream of innocence. This injury is a shock, worse than could ever be imagined. Blood on the albatross, on the wild goose whose flock-mates still bestride the icy altitudes, or on the king of the air, master of the element that sings to the soul, is blood on the soul.

The will shows a "fearful resolve," notes Coleridge, "to find in itself the one absolute motive of action." It weeps to do so, but does it. Clasping the bleeding body of the hawk to his bare chest, the boy would instinctively nurture it back to life:

> Heart leaping in joy past definition, in
> Eyes tears past definition, by rocky hill and valley
> Already dark-devoured, the bloody
> Body already to my bare flesh embraced, cuddled
> Like babe to heart, and my heart beating life love:
> Thus homeward.

There is more than God grief, there is father-grief, mother-grief, self-grief in this fleshy embrace. Or there is a real father in the fictitious God, the fiction of God in every father. Hate alone would not have shrieked in transgressive joy to bring this hot-blooded father down; terribly, love wanted the transgression just as much, and love weeps in the tears past definition.

As the unforgiving father-god falls, as the winged phallus plummets, the boy's heart leaps in joy—but short-lived triumph, for every son is his father's father's father, his father's fall is his own but one, his own in advance. And now that the king is dead, his eyes filmed, his "lower beak drooping, / As though from thirst," is he not the very image of Oedipal deprivation? Does he not take after his son? Hug him, then, to the maternal breast of nourishment and sympathy. The boy imitates his mother in order to succor his father, who is now himself.

None of this is real, unless as the truth that "can only be enacted, and that in dream, / Or in the dream become, as though unconsciously, action." What is real is the sad body that must be wrapped in a newspaper and hidden like a crime in an ice chest in the appallingly empty-at-afternoon family home. Shut far from the admiring airy spaces. Far from the thermal paradise of both sky and breast. And now, allowing for the demigod taxidermist's joy of scraping the skull and flesh joints, anchoring the bone joints, driving steel "through to sustain wing," and so on ("Oh, yes, / I knew my business"), the killer must begin to pay.

In time, his living father becomes bankrupt, as foretold in parable. His mother dies. As for him, he seems athirst, "whiskey / Hot in [his] throat." His heart no longer leaps, but is "slow in the / Meaningless motion of life." Almost, he might be stuffed. So out come the battered bird, the books, and the sensational, pathetic "sexual Japanese prints." But the expiatory burning does not lead to a fresh start. "What left / To do but walk in the dark, and no stars?"

What would bring back "joy past definition"? Shooting the hawk would. Writing the same old passionate early poems. Feeling the same dirty excitement over the pictures. The only phoenix that could rise from the ashes of the pyre is the bird of his youth, all earthly will to glory.

Done, if a wish were a will.

There could be no greater happiness, so the conclusion suggests, than to experience again this passage from dazzling moment to dazzling moment, beginning and end all adazzle, chasing off the darkness in between. The line "youth's poor, angry, slapdash, the ignorant pyre" ritualizes and consecrates the period of youth, even as it deplores it. This is not anathema, but a grieving love; the pell-mell adjectives are youthfully rich and eager in number, a joyfully joyless homage. The paradox, once more, of an affirmative pathos. "My formula for greatness in a human being," Nietzsche said, "is *amor fati:* that one wants nothing to be other than it is, not in the future, not in the past, not in all eternity. Not merely to endure that which happens of necessity, still less to dissemble it—all idealism is untruthfulness in the face of necessity—but to *love* it."

The artist is helped to *amor fati* by *amor operandi, amor operis.* Discovering, as he does, the rhythms of destiny in the rhythms of his art, he can turn "even fear and disgust" into love. If in no other way, art would war on God through what Yeats called the joy of always making and mastering, which like all joy wants itself, redundantly. Burning the books along with the hawk—even the yellow leaf-dropping Rimbaud (the same Rimbaud who, notes Enid Starkie, "determined to leave God's love behind him and to keep his personal freedom at all costs")—only confesses this aspect of art, its formula of affirmation born out of its own fullness.

In the poem, life repeats itself at a gulp, at a gallop, in uncompromised passion. The same life is twice within it, mirrored back to itself, freeingly reflected to its own and the poet's glory. So it is that the love of the making overflows as love of the life it remembers—love of life as a general thing and love of a specific story. Yet *amor fati* was doubtless the soil and rain and sun in whose mingling the desire for the work originally germinated. This circularity is passion's plenty and redundance, illustrating again how joy "bites itself," "wants itself eternally."

The glory of a "name" remains too implicit to seem either an incitement or a comfort; the will to power must achieve an ecstasy without it. Elsewhere it is even more deeply implicit—merely an inference from the publication of the poem. In "Trying to Tell You Something" and

"Unless," profane passion and glory consist, on the surface, only in courage and sublimity. But, as Nietzsche said, "we find remedies in our courage and sublimity as well as [in] the nobler deliria of submission and resignation." To stand beneath the unseeing stars and be drenched by their acid light, yet be happy and assured of one's individual dignity, is a kind of inverted glory, a glory *despite* . . .

Where the image of the pissing black man failed to convey this—he seemed an Uncle Tom even to the stars; lacked ferocity; carted junk—the solitary oak in "Trying to Tell You Something" and the solitary poet in "Unless" (both the "image of man") are tragic protagonists. One might say they assume the *posture* of courage—for courage is never other than a self-reflective virtue. The category of the tragic is, in great part, aesthetic; the tragic is a spectacle of will, suffering, misfortune, or endurance, with the cosmos for audience, and the viewer or reader or listener the audience of it all. The tragic exists only as a creation of art; and art cannot get around itself—around its showcasing, its foregrounding, its expectation of admiration, its calling upon everything in sight, from a comma to a context, for witness.

In "Trying to Tell You Something" the immense old Jamestown oak has been stripped of the agreeable, delusory leaves of youth and summer and is naked before "the crackling absoluteness" of the icy skies. Nonetheless, it chooses this moment to sing:

> It is ten below zero, and the iron
> Of hoops and reinforcement rods is continuing to contract.
>
> There is the rhythm of a slow throb, like pain. The wind,
> Northwest, is steady, and in the wind, the cables,
>
> In a thin-honed and disinfectant purity, like
> A dentist's drill, sing. They sing
>
> Of truth, and its beauty.

In this tragic variant of the romantic trope "necessity / Blooms like a rose," what rings one round is what, in the musical sense, rings. Fate is a cadence.

Unclouded by atmospheric enrichments, past deluding thermal joy and generative fervor ("splitting / With its own weight at the great inverted / Crotch, air-spread and ice-hung"), and singing in a thin-honed voice like a very old man, reduced to being a stiff statement of its own structure and reality, the tree stands as if before the Last Judgment, without apology. It is what it is—chooses to be so even in its nakedness, let all the stars crackle as they will.

True, existence is mostly impurity, the will to live hardly innocent, and these last days rightly shed off austerities as the early days shed off enticings. Welcomely "disinfectant" is this song like a dentist's drill, satisfyingly "thin-honed." Put to rest by a tragic asceticism, conscience closes the black book it has kept against the rooting, branching, and leafing will to self-activation; closes it like the December night around the oak. The spectacular white world of death under its crackling "high brightness" might be a physically daunting father who has at last succeeded in exacting conformity to his puritanical laws.

But at least this conformity has not come too soon; besides, it is not all it seems, for the tree is not esoteric but sings of its own existence, its presence as a particular thing, a fate. Just as it spreads before us in the not-quite-trapping unrhymed couplets of the poem (a thin-honed stanza form), so it stands immense on its hill—"stands alone in a world of snowy whiteness," indelible under the full moon. It is a noble instance of what R. W. B. Lewis named "the central theme of American literature, . . . *the hero in space*"—a successor to Whitman's live-oak in Louisiana, which, even "without any companion," and because of it, uttered joyous leaves—a tragic aloneness that Whitman fled (without altogether escaping it), and that Warren, at least in imagination, pursues.

In the end, the (tragic) beauty of truth is its reliable utterness, its exquisite authority. What emerges, and is beautiful, is the bedrock discovery of selfhood within a bedrock universe—the joyous, freeing certainty that the self is not the world but, in a founding tautology, precisely itself. (Lukács remarked that the longing of man for selfhood, "the deepest longing of human existence," is the metaphysical root of tragedy.)

In "Unless," the truth is said to be "fanged, unforgiving":

> All will be in vain unless—unless what? Unless
> You realize that what you think is Truth is only
>
> A husk for something else. Which might,
> Shall we say, be called energy, as good a word as any. As when
>
> The rattlesnake, among desert rocks
> And Freudian cactus tall in moonlight,
>
> Scrapes off the old integument, and flows away,
> Clean and lethal and gleaming like water over moon-bright sand,
>
> Unhusked for its mission. Oh, *neo nato!* fanged, unforgiving,
> We worship you.

Slipping through the slender husks of the stanzas as it does, this fearful truth "might . . . be called energy," the only criterion for absoluteness "under the storm of the / Geometry of stars." The miracle of tragedy is that it places in perfect balance the vast, diffuse, if "fanged" energy of the cosmos and the concentrated energy of the self. This astonishing mutual deliverance is not a harmony; it is simultaneously an opposition and a consent, its atmosphere clear, cold, harsh. The joy of it is almost rasping. Still, "This is happiness":

> The mountains, in starlight, were black
> And black-toothed to define the enormous circle
>
> Of desert of which I was the center. This
> Is one way to approach the question.
>
> All is in vain unless you can, motionless, standing there,
> Breathe with the rhythm of stars.
>
> You cannot, of course, see your own face, but you know that it,
>
> Lifted, is stripped to white bone by starlight. This is happening,
>
> This is happiness.

The lethal X-ray of the stars exposes the resistance of an individual armature, a "Freudian" will as hot as any the stars have mustered behind their light. This presence stands up to the stars as what serves to meet them. Yet, even as he discovers himself opposite the world, the tragic man sees that "all will be in vain" unless, without for a moment confusing it with himself, he allows it to world him. Where else can he glut his appetite for the real? What other utterness or fullness is possible to him, tormentingly partial as this one form is? Where else is there any true splendor, even if fearfully scattered abroad in the night, as if made by the only particles still virulent enough with original energy to have escaped the gravitational snap of the black-toothed mountains? What makes a man comical, noted Kierkegaard, is that he would gain himself, be the absolute. The tragic man would gain himself by breathing with the absoluteness of the world.

The "question" of truth might well be approached, then, through this desert-plain and compass-true geometry, this experiment with center, circumference, total context, and relativism, with nowhere to hide in the great circle and the pointed foot fixed in the crumbling sand. In any case, the approach had best be physical, a "happening." For the body itself knows truth through its sixth sense, the knit of the other five. And the imagination had best add its own peculiar slant on reality, standing off but turned back to it as an excited spectator. The tragic man's "glory" is to picture his own face stripped to white bone by starlight, shining once in the undistinguishing, destructive starlight and again in the distinguishing rays of his own mind's eye—a seeing that is chorus to his tragic destiny. In the center of a vast and hungry circle, the prey at once of earthbound and stellar elements, in the face of this mania, the tragic hero triumphs over the impulse both to flee (hysteria) and to repine (melancholia). He bears the brunt of the light, and himself becomes part of the surrounding circle; his are the conscious, watching eyes within it; he is the discoverer of its wonder, and of his own in relation to it.

There is a mutuality implicit in this meeting of the upraised face and the scouring starlight. The light might be thought to rub and rub at the face till not only the vain impurities are gone but its fundamental reality is exposed (as with the stripped oak), even if in the process it approaches its mortal limits. On the other hand, what is the appearingness of even the finest of phenomena, light, if there is nothing sentient in all its fall and field, no one to whom it can appear?

Tragic happiness is a final reconciliation with the father, or Law, in an atmosphere of terrible beauty, the mother's legacy of a passionate attachment to the world's body, of the need to bask in the light. That the encircling mountains are "black-toothed," like mountains in a tale, or that they "seem abstract" in the morning light, like the old translucent skin of truth, does not make them less real. Here, the Dionysian is not belied by Appearance; there is only Appearance; the snake is now in this skin, now in a new one. Truth need not be enacted "only . . . in dream." Tragedy, as Nietzsche argued, reconciles energy with appearance. The face lifted to starlight is energy confronting energy and—because visualized by the one whose face it is—appearance at one with appearance. The dregs of nightmare remain inactive. Tragedy is the loving triumph of Appearance, even in the last alarm of energy.

HAROLD BLOOM

Sunset Hawk: Warren's Poetry and Tradition

The beginning is like a god which as long as it
dwells among men saves all things.

—PLATO, *Laws* 775

Where can an authentic poet begin again, when clearly the past has ceased to throw its illumination upon the future? Robert Penn Warren's poetry spans nearly sixty years, from "Pondy Woods" to his long poem upon Chief Joseph, against whom the United States fought its last serious Indian war. No final perspective is possible upon a strong poet whose own wars are far from over. I have been reading Warren's poetry for thirty years, since I first came to Yale, but only in the second half of that period have I read him with the deep absorption that his poetry demands and rewards. Before the publication of *Incarnations: Poems 1966–1968*, I would have based my judgment of Warren's aesthetic eminence primarily upon his most ambitious novels, *All the King's Men* and *World Enough and Time*. The poetry seemed distinguished, yet overshadowed by Eliot, and perhaps of less intrinsic interest than the best poems of Ransom and Tate. But from *Incarnations* on, without a break, Warren consciously has taken on his full power over language and the world of the senses. In his varied achievement, his poetry now asserts the highest claims upon us.

From *A Southern Renascence Man: Views of Robert Penn Warren*, edited by W. B. Edgar. Copyright © 1984 by Louisiana State University Press.

Incarnations is an extraordinary book, and so it may be arbitrary to single out just one poem, but I still remember the shock with which I first read its strongest poem, "The Leaf." Few moments in the varied history of the American Sublime match Warren's sudden capture of that mode:

Near the nesting place of the hawk, among
Snag-rock, high on the cliff, I have seen
The clutter of annual bones of hare, vole, bird, white
As chalk from sun and season, frail

As the dry grass stem. On that
High place of stone I have lain down, the sun
Beat, the small exacerbation
Of dry bones was what my back, shirtless and bare, knew. I saw

The hawk shudder in the high sky, he shudders
To hold position in the blazing wind, in relation to
The firmament, he shudders and the world is a metaphor, his eye
Sees, white, the flicker of hare-scut, the movement of vole.

It may be gratuitous, but I am tempted to find, just here, a textual point of crossing, the place Warren's poetry turned about, on his quest for an ultimate strength. Certainly his stance, style, and thematics are different, in and after this passage through to the Sublime. "This is the place," Warren had written earlier in the poem, adding: "To this spot I bring my grief." His grief, as we might expect from so experiential and dramatic a writer, doubtless presented itself to him as temporal guilt. But poetry is a mediated mode of expression, in which poems are mediated primarily by other poems. I will read Warren's guilt in "The Leaf" as a literary anxiety, appropriate to a poem's inescapable dilemma, which is that it must treat literal anguish as being figurative, in order to find appropriate figuration that would justify yet another poem. Warren actually may have lain down on that high place of stone, but the actuality matters only as another order or degree of trope. "The Leaf" is a crisis poem of a very traditional kind, and in that kind the crisis concerns the fate of poetic voice, in a very precise sense of voice. The sense is American, though the tradition of the crisis poem is biblical in its origins, and British in its major developments. Like his poetic father, Eliot, Warren rehearses the crisis poem's origins, but more even than Eliot, Warren develops an acutely American sense of poetic voice. "The Leaf" occupies a place in Warren's canon analogous to the place of *Ash Wednesday* in Eliot's work, but with an American difference necessarily more emphasized in Warren.

Rather than qualify that "necessarily" I would emphasize its double aspect: historical and personal. Both the historical necessity and the personal modification are agonistic. The agon, whether with tradition or with Eliot as tradition's contemporary representative, is ambivalent in Warren, but a loving struggle is not less a struggle. When Warren writes "my tongue / Was like a dry leaf in my mouth," he is writing Eliot's language, and so the tongue still is not quite his own. *Incarnations* has two epigraphs, the first being the opening of Nehemiah 5:5, when the people say to Nehemiah: "Yet now our flesh is as the flesh of our brethren." Warren omits the remainder of the verse, which concludes: "for other men have our lands and our vineyards." The context is the rebuilding of Jerusalem, after the return from exile in Babylon. *Incarnations*' other epigraph is the heroic defiance of John Henry in his ballad: "A man ain't nuthin but a man"—which of course is less an expression of limitation than an assertion of individuality against overwhelming force. The epigraphs point to the secret plot of *Incarnations*, culminating in "The Leaf." Let us call the plot "deferred originality," and with that calling return to everything problematic in the poem. Here is its extraordinary first section:

> Here the fig lets down the leaf, the leaf
> Of the fig five fingers has, the fingers
> Are broad, spatulate, stupid,
> Ill-formed, and innocent—but of a hand, and the hand,
>
> To hide me from the blaze of the wide world, drops,
> Shamefast, down. I am
> What is to be concealed. I lurk
> In the shadow of the fig. Stop.
> Go no further. This is the place.
>
> To this spot I bring my grief.
> Human grief is the obscenity to be hidden by the leaf.

Warren portrays himself as Adam just after the Fall, with partial reference to earlier lyrics about the fig in the first sequence of *Incarnations*, a sequence concluding in "The Leaf." Whether by intuition or by acquired knowledge, Warren seems to have a sense of the ancient Jewish tradition that identified the forbidden fruit with the fig rather than the grape or apple of paradise (*etrog*). Only the fig tree therefore granted Adam permission to take of its leaves when he sought to cover himself. Warren concentrates upon a single leaf, more an emblem or trope of voice than of sexuality. In the second lyric of the "Island of Summer" sequence that closes with the crucial poem called "The Leaf," Warren introduces the trope as a version of death:

> . . . a single
> Leaf the rest screens, but through it, light
> Burns, and for the fig's bliss
> The sun dies . . .

The image of the leaf resumes in the sardonic poem bearing the long and splendid title: "Paul Valéry Stood on the Cliff and Confronted the Furious Energies of Nature." Whether Warren triumphs over the formidable seer of the marine cemetery is perhaps questionable, but we are left with a vivid critique of a transcendental consciousness:

> He sways high against the blue sky,
> While in the bright intricacies
> Of wind, his mind, like a leaf,
> Turns. In the sun, it glitters.

Warren would say that this is a disincarnation, and to it he opposes a further lyric in his sequence:

> Where purples now the fig, flame in
> Its inmost flesh, a leaf hangs
> Down, and on it, gull-droppings, white
> As chalk, show, for the sun has

> Burned all white, for the sun, it would
> Burn our bones to chalk—yes, keep
> Them covered, oh flesh, oh sweet
> Integument, oh frail, depart not

> And leave me thus exposed, like Truth.

Fig, flame, flesh, leaf, and sun are drawn together here into the dark intricacy that is an incarnation, the truth that is the body of death. With this as prelude, we are ready to return to "The Leaf" as Warren's great poem of the threshold, of a crossing over into his own image of voice. To see how drastic a swerve into originality is made here from the start, we have to recall something of the fiction of the leaves in Western poetry. I've written about this extensively, in *A Map of Misreading* and the more recent *The Breaking of the Vessels*, and don't wish to repeat here the long train of transumptions that holds together the history of this conceptual image from Homer and the Bible through Virgil, Dante, Spenser, and Milton on to Shelley, Whitman, and Wallace Stevens. Warren's fiction of the leaf is a baroque figuration, in a very different tradition. Unlike the transumptive line, Warren does not seek an ellipsis of further figuration. Most simply, Stevens does; Stevens wants the readers of "The Rock" or "The Course of a Particular" to believe that the fiction of the leaves attains a completion in those poems. This is the Romantic and Emersonian credence that Warren refuses, in favor of a more Eliotic vision of tradition and the individual talent. Hence Warren's moral vocabulary of shame and guilt, or should we call it rather his moral refusal to acknowledge that poetry refuses the distinction between shame culture and guilt culture? To refuse that distinction is to attempt an individual closure to tradition; to accept it, as Warren does, is to affirm that one's role is to extend tradition, to hold it open for a community of others. Warren's fundamental postulates, however tempered by skepticism, are biblical and Classical, but his rhetoric and his poetic dilemmas are High Romantic. He thus repeats the fundamental conflicts of his precursor Eliot, whose actual rhetorical art stemmed from Whitman and Tennyson, and not from more baroque sensibilities. Warren's dilemmas in some ways are both simpler and harsher than Eliot's. A shamanistic intensity, a sense of the abruptness of poetic force more suitable to Yeats or Hart Crane than to Eliot, somehow has to be reconciled with a cultural sense that demands rational restraints and the personal acceptance of historical guilt.

The handlike leaf of the fig has fingers that are "broad, spatulate, stupid, / Ill-formed, and innocent," which is pretty well Warren's judgment upon the Adamic condition, a judgment not exactly Emersonian. On what basis are we to accept Warren's peculiarly harsh line: "Human grief is the obscenity to be hidden by the leaf," unless the grief indeed is merely the poet's, any poet's, anxious resentment *as poet* in regard to the almost organic sadness of poetic origins? I am not under the illusion that Warren would accept this reading, but I set aside here my personal reverence for the man and my critical worship of the poet in order to enter again that area of grief that no strong poet will acknowledge as a poet. As I keep discovering, this is not enchanted ground upon which I am driven, doubtless obsessively, to trespass. But I would cite here a touch of external evidence of the most persuasive because most developmental kind. In the decade 1943–1953, when he wrote his most accomplished novels, *All the King's Men* and *World Enough and Time*, Warren's poetry simply stopped. So fecund an imagination does not cease from poetry only because its energies are caught up by the novel. As with Stevens' silence between 1924 and 1934, we have a very problematic gap in a major poetic career, and later in this essay I intend to return to Warren's poetic silence.

In my circular way I have come back to the Sublime second section of "The Leaf," and to the shock of my personal conversion to Warren when I first read the poem in 1969. Ransom and Tate were poets of enormous talent, but not exactly visionaries who favored shamanistic symbolic acts in their work, despite Tate's troubled relation to the primal exuberance of Hart Crane's poetry. Any close reader of Warren's poetry in

1969 would have known that the flight of hawks meant a great deal to him, but even that was hardly adequate preparation for the hawk's shudder in "The Leaf." In Warren's earliest book, *Thirty-Six Poems* (1935), there is a remarkable sequence, "Kentucky Mountain Farm," which I continue to hope he will reprint entire in his next *Selected Poems*. Section VI, "Watershed," not now available in print, has a memorable and crucially prophetic image: "The sunset hawk now rides / The tall light up the climbing deep of air." While men sleep, the hawk flies on in the night, scanning a landscape of disappearances with "gold eyes" that make all shrivelings reappear. This sunset hawk, first a vision in boyhood, keeps returning in Warren's poems. In the still relatively early "To a Friend Parting," the inadequacy of "the said, the unsaid" is juxtaposed to seeing "The hawk tower, his wings the light take," an emblem of certainty in pride and honor. Perhaps it was the absence of such emblems in his confrontation of reality that stopped Warren's poetry in the decade 1943-1953.

Whatever the cause of his silence in verse, it seems significant that *Promises: Poems 1954-1956* opens with an address to the poet's infant daughter that culminates in a return of the hawk image. Viewing the isolated spot to which he has brought his daughter, Warren celebrates "the hawk-hung delight / Of distance unspoiled and bright space spilled." In *Tale of Time: Poems 1960-1966*, he explicitly compares "hawk shadow" with "that fugitive thought which I can find no word for," or what we might call the poetry that would begin anew when he wrote *Incarnations*. I quote again the central vision from the second section of "The Leaf," but extending the quotation now to the entire section:

We have undergone ourselves, therefore
What more is to be done for Truth's sake? I

Have watched the deployment of ants, I
Have conferred with the flaming mullet in a deep place.

Near the resting place of the hawk, among
Snag-rock, high on the cliff, I have seen
The clutter of annual bones, of hare, vole, bird, white
As chalk from sun and season, frail
As the dry grass stem. On that

High place of stone I have lain down, the sun
Beat, the small exacerbation
Of dry bones was what my back, shirtless and bare, knew. I saw

The hawk shudder in the high sky, he shudders
To hold position in the blazing wind, in relation to
The firmament, he shudders and the world is a metaphor, his eye
Sees, white, the flicker of hare-scut, the movement of vole.

Distance is nothing, there is no solution, I
Have opened my mouth to the wind of the world like wine, I wanted
To taste what the world is, wind dried up

The live saliva of my tongue, my tongue
Was like a dry leaf in my mouth.

Destiny is what you experience, that
Is its name and definition, and is your name, for

The wide world lets down the hand in shame:
Here is the human shadow, there, of the wide world, the flame.

The poet offers himself here not to the hawk but to the hawk's shudder and the hawk's vision, and so to what shudder and vision incarnate, a stance or holding of position. That stance casts out shame even as it accepts guilt. That Warren practices a private ritual is palpable, even though we could only guess at the ritual until he wrote and published the extraordinary long autobiographical "Red-Tail Hawk and Pyre of Youth" that is the glory of *Now and Then: Poems 1976–1978*. Although the later poem is finer even than "The Leaf," it is not as pivotal, because it focuses on the young Warren alone, and not on the agon with forebears. What "The Leaf" discovers, with a clarity not often matched in our poetry, is the necessity of mediation despite the poet's longing for an unmediated relation between his mouth and the wind of the world. Both these terms, as Warren well knows, are Shelley's, a poet not much to Warren's taste, and so his treatment of the terms submits them to the stylistic cosmos of Eliot: "wind dried up / The live saliva of my tongue, my tongue / Was like a dry leaf in my mouth." We recognize that this is the Waste Land, and not an Italy waiting for the Revolution. But the revelation that comes is not much more Eliotic than it is Shelleyan:

The world is fruitful. In this heat
The plum, black yet bough-bound, bursts, and the gold ooze is,
Of bees, joy, the gold ooze has striven
Outward, it wants again to be of
The goldness of air and—blessedly—innocent. The grape
Weakens at the juncture of the stem. The world

Is fruitful, and I, too,
In that I am the father
Of my father's father's father. I,
Of my father, have set the teeth on edge. But
By what grape? I have cried out in the night.

From a further garden, from the shade of another tree,
My father's voice, in the moment when the
   cicada
      ceases, has called to me.

"The moment when the cicada / ceases" deliberately alludes to Eliot's "not the cicada" in "What the Thunder Said"; but the prophetic trope, in its reversal, overcomes the rhetoric of *The Waste Land.* There is a curious ambiguity as to whose is the father's voice that calls out this ambivalent blessing:

> The voice blesses me for the only
> Gift I have given: *teeth set on edge.*
>
> In the momentary silence of the cicada,
> I can hear the appalling speed,
> In space beyond stars, of
> Light. It is
>
> A sound like wind.

It is Warren's gift, by the reversal of the influence process, that has set Eliot's teeth on edge. Which is to say, it is Warren's rhetorical strength to have converted the Eliotic trope of orthodoxy, the light, into the appalling speed that sounds the wind of time, for time is Warren's trope, the center of his poetics. The hawk shudders to hold position in the blazing wind of time, and so transforms the world into a temporal metaphor. Warren's merger of identity with the hawk's shudder affirms the pride of his own stance and theme, the unforgiving shudder of poetic time. I want to hold on to Warren's vision of the hawk in order to trace something of the development of his poetry from *Incarnations* on to this moment. If my procedure is arbitrary, I defend it by the persistence of this vision, or something near to it, throughout his work.

Warren's best volume, *Or Else—Poem/Poems 1968–1974,* ends with an extraordinary poem bearing the curious title, "A Problem of Spatial Composition." The first section composes the space, a sunset through a high window, an eternity that is always beyond, a Sublime from which we are detached, as is traditional. But this is Warren setting us up for his original power in the second section and the closure in a single line of his third:

> [2]
> While out of the green, up-shining ramshackle of leaf, set
> In the lower right foreground, the stub
> Of a great tree, gaunt-blasted and black, thrusts.
>
> A single
> Arm jags upward, higher goes, and in that perspective, higher
> Than even the dream-blue of distance that is
> The mountain.
>
> Then
> Stabs, black, at the infinite saffron of sky.

All is ready.

The hawk,
Entering the composition at the upper left frame
Of the window, glides,
In the pellucid ease of thought and at
His breathless angle,
Down.
 Breaks speed.

 Hangs with a slight lift and hover.

 Makes contact.

The hawk perches on the topmost, indicative tip of
The bough's sharp black and skinny jag skyward.

[3]
The hawk, in an eyeblink, is gone.

This a different kind of hawk's vision, and shall we not call it a deliberate and triumphant figuration for the poet's new style? "The hawk, / . . . glides, / In the pellucid ease of thought and at / His breathless angle, / Down." As the hawk breaks speed and hovers, he "makes contact," giving us a trope that stands, part for whole, for the tense power of Warren's mature art: "The hawk perches on the topmost, indicative tip of / The bough's sharp black and skinny jag skyward." The emphasis is upon the immanent thrust of the natural object, rather than its transcendent possibilities. Another emphasis, as characteristic of Warren, is the temporal swiftness of this fiction of duration, or poem—gone in an eyeblink.

In 1975, Warren wrote a group of poems to form the first section of his *Selected Poems: 1923–1975*. The second of these poems, "Evening Hawk," is surely one of his dozen or so lyric masterpieces, a culmination of forty years of his art:

From plane of light to plane, wings dipping through
Geometries and orchids that the sunset builds,
Out of the peak's black angularity of shadow, riding
The last tumultuous avalanche of
Light above pines and the guttural gorge,
The hawk comes.

 His wing
Scythes down another day, his motion
Is that of the honed steel-edge, we hear
The crashless fall of stalks of Time.

The head of each stalk is heavy with the gold of our error.

Look! look! he is climbing the last light

Who knows neither Time nor error, and under
Whose eye, unforgiving, the world, unforgiven, swings
Into shadow.

              Long now,
The last thrush is still, the last bat
Now cruises in his sharp hieroglyphics. His wisdom
Is ancient, too, and immense. The star
Is steady, like Plato, over the mountain.

If there were no wind we might, we think, hear
The earth grind on its axis, or history
Drip in darkness like a leaking pipe in the cellar.

The hawk's motion is that of a scythe reaping time, but Warren has learned more than his distance from the hawk's state of being. I know no single line in him grander than the beautifully oxymoronic "The head of each stalk is heavy with the gold of our error." What is being harvested is our fault, and yet that mistake appears as golden grain. When the poet sublimely cries "Look! look!" to us, I do not hear a Yeatsian exultation, but rather an acceptance of a vision that will forgive us nothing, and yet does not rejoice in that stance. Emerson, Warren once snapped in a now notorious poem, "had forgiven God everything," which is true enough, since Emerson sensibly had forgiven himself everything, and God was identical with what was oldest in Emerson himself. Warren goes on forgiving God, and himself, nothing, and implies this is the only way to love God or the self. One does not imagine Ralph Waldo Emerson invoking the flight of a hawk as an image of the truth, but the poets of his tradition—notably Whitman, Stevens, and Hart Crane—have their own way of coming to terms with such an image. But, to Emersonians, the hawk is firmly part of Nature, of the Not-Me. Warren's trespasses upon a near-identity with the hawk clearly are no part of *that* American tradition.

Warren is not interested in similitudes when he achieves a Sublime vision, but rather in identifying with some aspect of the truth, however severely he indicates his own distance from the truth. I am not much interested in rehearsing Warren's polemic against Emerson because I voted for Emerson a long time ago, and my love for Warren's poetry is therefore against the grain. As I wrote once, I read Warren's poetry with a shudder that is simultaneously spiritual revulsion and total aesthetic satisfaction, a shudder that only Yeats also evokes for me in this century.

Much in what is problematic in Warren's hawk poems was clarified permanently by "Red-Tail Hawk and Pyre of Youth" in *Now and Then*, the poem in which Warren himself seems to have arrived at a full awareness of his creative obsession. Yet the poem, perhaps at the price of so full a knowing, is in many ways at variance with Warren's other hawk visions. Beginning with the boy hunter's confrontation of the hawk's gaze ("Gold eyes, unforgiving, for they, like God, see all"), Warren moves rapidly past the miraculous shot to center upon his clay-burlap stuffed hawk, mounted in his room on a bookshelf of the poets and of Augustine, set over them as an emblem of the boy's own ambitions. Vividly as this is portrayed, it is less memorable than Warren's later return to the emblem, and his placing of the hawk upon a pyre:

8

Flame flared. Feathers first, and I flinched, then stood
As the steel wire warped red to defend
The shape designed godly for air. But
It fell with the mass, and I
Did not wait.

What left
To do but walk in the dark, and no stars?

What is not consumed is the ecstasy of confrontation, the memory of the encounter shared with the hawk:

9

Some dreams come true, some no.
But I've waked in the night to see
High in the late and uncurdled silver of summer
The pale vortex appear once again—and you come
And always the rifle swings up, though with
The weightlessness now of dream,
The old .30–30 that knows
How to bind us in air-blood and earth-blood together
In our commensurate fate,
Whose name is a name beyond joy.

The vortex is what matters, and part of the point is surely that the stuffed hawk was merely text, while the vortex was the truth, the fate beyond joy but also beyond language. Warren's insistence upon truth puts the value of any fiction, including the poem he is writing, perhaps too severely into question. It is hardly possible not to be moved by the final section of "Red-Tail Hawk and Pyre of Youth," and yet the reader needs an answer to the query as to just what flared up on that sacrificial pyre:

10

And I pray that in some last dream or delusion,
While hospital wheels creak beneath
And the nurse's soles make their *squeak-squeak* like mice,
I'll again see the first small silvery swirl

Spin outward and downward from sky-height
To bring me the truth in blood-marriage of earth and air—
And all will be as it was
In that paradox of unjoyful joyousness,
Till the dazzling moment when I, a last time, must flinch
From the regally feathered gasoline flare
Of youth's poor, angry, slapdash, and ignorant pyre.

The hawk spins outward and downward not to bring the truth *as* blood-marriage between boy and bird, but *in* that sacrament of slaughter. The killing is not the truth, but only an angry and youthful way to the truth. What can the truth be except solipsistic transport, the high and breaking light of the Sublime? If Warren were Stevens, he might have written, "Am I that imagine this hawk less satisfied?", but being Warren, he would deny that he had *imagined* the hawk. Warren longs to be what Stevens once termed "a hawk of life." Stevens said he wanted his poems "To meet that hawk's eye and to flinch / Not at the eye but at the joy of it." Such an ambition stops at similitudes, and shies away from identification. But Warren is about halfway between the shrewd Stevens and the fanatical Yeats, whose hawklike hero, Cuchulain, could confront death by crying out, "I make the truth." Like Whitman, Stevens chooses a fiction that knows itself to be a fiction. Warren, in his prose "Afterthought" to *Being Here: Poetry 1977–1980*, somberly ends by remarking that "our lives are our own supreme fiction." There is an implicit thrust here against Stevens, who would not have agreed. Yet Warren is a dramatic lyrist, whose boys and hawks are not fictive. Stevens, infinitely nuanced, would not have deigned to write a dramatic lyric. In Stevens, "the truth" sagely reduces to "the the," but Warren wants and needs the truth, and will risk placing all his own poems and stories upon the pyre if that will spur the truth to appear.

The risk is extended all through recent Warren, with necessarily mixed results. We are given a poetic art that dares constantly the root meaning of *hamartia*: to shoot wide of the mark. From the Sublime lyric, this very late Warren has passed to the tragic mode, which fails sometimes very badly in *Being Here*, and then suddenly gives us perfection, as in "Eagle Descending":

Beyond the last flamed escarpment of mountain cloud
The eagle rides air currents, switch and swell,
With spiral upward now, steady as God's will.

Beyond black peak and flaming cloud, he yet
Stares at the sun—invisible to us,
Who downward sink. Beyond new ranges, shark-

Toothed, saw-toothed, he stares at the plains afar
By ghostly shadows eastward combed, and crossed
By a stream, steel-bright, that seems to have lost its way.

No silly pride of Icarus his! All peril past,
He westward gazes, and down, where the sun will brush
The farthermost bulge of earth. How soon? How soon

Will the tangent of his sight now intersect
The latitudinal curvature where the sun
Soon crucial contact makes, to leave him in twilight,

Alone in glory? The twilight fades. One wing
Dips, slow. He leans.—And with that slightest shift,
Spiral on spiral, mile on mile, uncoils.

The wind to sing with joy of truth fulfilled.

This is parenthetically subtitled "To a dead friend," identified by
Warren as Allen Tate, and is an elegy worthy of its subject, with eagle
replacing the personal emblem of the hawk. Hovering throughout, there is
a sense of the precursor poem, the first section of Eliot's *Ash-Wednesday*, a
poem equally influential upon Tate and Warren. The despairing voice that
opens *Ash-Wednesday* has abandoned the agonistic intensities of poetic
tradition: "Desiring this man's gift and that man's scope / I no longer
strive to strive towards such things." Warren says of his eagle that it too
has given up the poetic quest if that quest is only a Sublime battle against
human limitations: "No silly pride of Icarus his!" This eagle's pride is
rather in persistence of sight; he goes on staring at the sun, at the plains of
Hades, at the westward sweep outwards and downwards of human speculation. And this gaze *is* instrumental, for unless it intersects the sunlight
there will not be a final vision "in twilight, / Alone in glory." That
Sublime will survive the fading of twilight, the survival being manifest in
the slow dip of wing with which the descending eagle makes its last
exercise of will. Echoing the *clinamen* of Lucretius, Warren celebrates "that
slightest shift" which is poetic and human freedom. Tradition becomes
the spiral on spiral, mile on mile, uncoiling of a singing wind whose
message is the fulfilled truth of the eagle's dying will. This does seem to
me a Lucretian rather than a Christian elegy, but so vexed is the issue of
Warren's unforgiving emphasis upon identity of truth and poetry that I
express my own judgment here with considerable qualms.

Warren in his current phase, exemplified by *Rumor Verified: Poems
1979–1980* and by *Chief Joseph*, still under revision, is in the midst of
undergoing yet another stylistic change, comparable in scope to the one
that ensued in *Incarnations* and *Audubon: A Vision*. Clearly he is not one
of the poets who unfold, like Stevens, but one of those who develop, like

Yeats. But the alteration in idiom shows no signs of modifying his obsession with the identity of poetic truth and the fierce but entropic freedom emblematic in the image of the hawk. I quote from *Chief Joseph* with a gingerly feeling, so revisionary is Warren, but there is a striking and relevant passage spoken by the chief as he leads his people's flight from their oppressors:

> Past lava, past schist, past desert and sand—
> A strange land we wandered to eastern horizons
> Where blueness of mountains swam in their blue—
> In blue beyond name. The hawk hung high.
> Gleamed white. A sign. It gleamed like a word in the sky.
> Cleanse hearts and pray. Pray to know what the Sky-Chief
> Would now lean to tell. To the pure heart, Truth speaks.

By now, then, a high-hanging hawk is for Warren not just a sign, but the inevitable sign of the truth. Nothing is more dangerous for a belated poetry (and as Americans we can have no other) than to establish a proper sign for the truth. I want to put Warren's poetry to the test by showing how much that danger both mutilates and enhances his achievement. As a final exemplary text, I give the final poem of *Now and Then*, "Heart of Autumn," primarily because I love it best of all Warren's poems:

> Wind finds the northwest gap, fall comes.
> Today, under gray cloud-scud and over gray
> Wind-flicker of forest, in perfect formation, wild geese
> Head for a land of warm water, the *boom*, the lead pellet.
>
> Some crumple in air, fall. Some stagger, recover control,
> Then take the last glide for a far glint of water. None
> Knows what has happened. Now, today, watching
> How tirelessly V upon V arrows the season's logic,
>
> Do I know my own story? At least, they know
> When the hour comes for the great wing-beat. Sky-strider,
> Star-rider—they rise, and the imperial utterance,
> Which cries out for distance, quivers in the wheeling sky.
>
> That much they know, and in their nature know
> The path of pathlessness, with all the joy
> Of destiny fulfilling its own name.
> I have known time and distance, but not why I am here.
>
> Path of logic, path of folly, all
> The same—and I stand, my face lifted now skyward,
> Hearing the high beat, my arms outstretched in the tingling
> Process of transformation, and soon tough legs,

With folded feet, trail in the sounding vacuum of passage,
And my heart is impacted with a fierce impulse
To unwordable utterance—
Toward sunset, at a great height.

This seems to me the essential Warren poem, as much his own invention as "The Course of a Particular" is Stevens' or "Repose of Rivers" is Hart Crane's. Eliot, prime precursor, is so repressed here that one might think more readily of Melville or Hardy—both Shelleyans—as closer to Warren's mode, though certainly not to his stance or vision. But how much have that stance and vision changed from the poetry of the young Warren? I quote pretty much at random from Warren's earliest verse, and what I hear is the purest Eliot:

What grief has the mind distilled?
The heart is unfulfilled
The hoarse pine stilled
I cannot pluck
Out of this land of pine and rock
Of red bud their season not yet gone
If I could pluck
(In drouth the lizard will blink on the hot limestone)
At the blind hour of unaimed grief,
Of addition and subtraction,
Of compromise,
Of the smoky lecher, the thief,
Of regretted action,
At the hour to close the eyes,
At the hour when lights go out in the houses—
Then wind rouses
The kildees from their sodden ground.
Their commentary is part of the wind's sound.
What is that other sound,
Surf or distant cannonade?

Both passages would fit well enough in "Gerontion" or *The Waste Land*, but that was Warren more than a half-century ago. In an older way of critical speaking, you might say that he had weathered Eliot's influence, while extending both Eliot's tradition and Eliot's sense of *the* tradition, the sense we associate with Cleanth Brooks, as with Warren. But I tend to a different kind of critical speaking, one which would emphasize Warren's passage into poetic strength as an agonistic process that the Eliot-Warren-Brooks tradition tends to deprecate, or even to deny. Does a poem like "Heart of Autumn" show Warren in a benign relation to tradition, and does Warren's desire to embody the truth find a place within Eliot's sense of the tradition?

Whitman began the final section of *Song of Myself* by juxtaposing himself to a spotted hawk, who swoops by and accuses the poet, complaining "of my gab and my loitering." For the Emersonian Whitman, identification took place not with the hawk, but between one's own empirical and ontological selves. In late Warren, the ontological self is identified with, and as, the flight of wild birds, and "the imperial utterance," crying out for distance, is beyond the human. The "high beat" transforms Warren himself, and he crosses the threshold of a wordless Sublime, as his heart identifies with the heart of autumn. Whatever such an identification is, its vitalism has broken the canons both of Whitman's American Romantic tradition and of Eliot's countertradition of neo-orthodoxy. Warren chooses an identification not available to poets like Whitman, Stevens, and Hart Crane, who know their estrangement from the universe of sense. But his choice of identification also brings to an end Eliot's firm separation between poetry and shamanism. For the tradition of Emerson, Warren feels a range of reaction that varies from genial contempt to puzzled respect. For Eliot's poetry, Warren has the agonistic and ambivalent love that always marks the family romance. A poem like "Heart of Autumn" possesses an extraordinary *ethos*, one that mixes memory and desire, where the memory is of a tradition that clearly could distinguish the path of logic from the path of folly, and the desire is to know the shamanistic path of pathlessness, since the traditional paths have proved to be all the same.

Warren, on this reading, is a sunset hawk at the end of a tradition. His usurpation of the Sublime has about it the aura of a solitary grandeur. "I thirst to know the power and nature of Time . . ." is the Augustinian epigraph of *Being Here*, to which Warren adds: "Time is the dimension in which God strives to define His own being." The epigraph is truer to Warren than the addition is, because the trope of a hawk's shuddering immanence is not wholly appropriate for the God of Abraham, the God of Isaac, the God of Jacob, the God of Jesus. Such a trope, whether in Hopkins or Warren, Yeats or Hart Crane, shows rather the poet's agonistic striving, not so much for the foremost place, but for the blessing of a time without boundaries. In *Audubon*, Warren found the inevitable trope for that time: "They fly / In air that glitters like fluent crystal / And is hard as perfectly transparent iron, they cleave it / With no effort." Such a trope is not an Eliotic baroque extension of tradition, but marks rather an ellipsis of further figuration. Warren stands, his face lifted now skyward, toward sunset, at a great height.

PAUL MARIANI

Robert Penn Warren

Since his *Selected Poems: New and Old, 1923–1966*, for which he was awarded the Bollingen, Warren has published three books of poetry: *Incarnations* (1968), the 380-line *Audubon: A Vision* (1969), and now, nearly seventy, he has published a new volume, a long sequence made up of discrete entries, ambiguously titled *Or Else: Poem/Poems 1968–1974*. That is three volumes in six years, years when Warren has also been busy writing fiction, a monograph on Theodore Dreiser, another on *Democracy and Poetry*, a time too when he was also editing an excellent two-volume college textbook-anthology of American literature for St. Martin's Press. Warren is a dean of American letters, distinguished not only as the anthologizer, but as one of those anthologized. He is also one of the very few who has managed to capture a Pulitzer for both fiction—*All the King's Men* (1946)—and poetry—*Promises* (1957). And there are other signs of recognition as well: the National Book Award, the National Medal for Literature.

And yet it is hard to gauge precisely the man's reputation in 1975, to say just where the poetry stands today. Over a glass of beer I ask one poet, a dozen years Warren's junior, what he thinks of Warren's latest volume; he is noncommittal, barely shrugging his shoulders, asking me what *I* think of it. Another colleague, a specialist in Southern fiction who regularly teaches *All the King's Men*, confesses that he has not kept up with Warren's poetry. And a young poet—in his late twenties—scratches his head, says, "Is he still around?" One thing is certain: Warren *is* still very much around; he is, in fact, something of a presence. But that is also one of the reasons it is so difficult to get one's metaphorical hands around him, to accurately take the man's measure. There are nine novels, now, a play, a book of short stories, the seminal critical essays, two studies on race relations, ten volumes of poetry, and more. The stiff, magisterial reality of a dictum like *ars longa, vita brevis* weighs heavily on one's shoulders (meaning I cannot read it all), and since the published criticism on Warren's poetry (what there is of it) seems with few exceptions inattentive to the man's real and underestimated importance, the critic is forced back on the poetry itself, a form of collapse this master of old-style New Criticism would very much enjoy.

A brief look at Warren's *Democracy and Poetry* can help to focus on his primary concerns in *Or Else*, for at bottom the concerns of the essays inform the poems themselves. This is a relatively modest but delightful book, a fleshing out, really, of the two Jefferson lectures Warren gave in 1974 as part of the National Endowment for the Humanities Program. The subject of these lectures, Warren tells us in his preface, is really the grid of interrelations formed by the trinity of democracy, poetry, and the self. For most of his life, Warren has been centrally concerned with the act of discovering himself as a man springing out of a specific place and a specific time. The kind of reflective overview such a man can offer us is invaluable, and I'd like to see this little book done in an inexpensive format for students of American literature; it provides one way into the central importance of the literary "documents" that are our heritage.

It is particularly important to remember the moment out of which these two essays were born. When Warren gave the Jefferson Lectures in early 1974, Nixon was still beseiged in the White House, still denying any central complicity in the whole Watergate mess. At one point in his essays, Warren quotes from the White House tapes; in this excerpt Nixon is discussing with Haldeman how his daughters should spend their time before the opening of the '72 Republican Convention:

> PRESIDENT: For example—now the worst thing (unintelligible) is to go to anything that has to do with the arts.
> HALDEMAN: Ya, see that—it was (unintelligible) Julie giving [given?] that time in the Museum in Jacksonville.
> PRESIDENT: The arts you know—they're Jews, they're left wing—in other words, stay away.

How are the arts to fare, then, in an America that has moved this far from the leadership afforded by a figure like Jefferson himself? The first essay serves as a review of our literature which Warren sees as a criticism— "often a corrosive criticism—of our actual achievements over the years in democracy." What Warren does with the brilliance and grace that over forty years of teaching has given him is to point to "the decay of the concept of self" which has occurred in the actual unfolding of our democratic experiment over the past two centuries.

In the second essay, Warren documents—at some length—what most of us already feel along our pulse: that the decay of the concept of a real self is related "to our present society and its ideals." This is the reading of a moralist, a conservative in the best tradition of Edmund Burke, and it leads to a discussion of poetry not as a diagnosis of our ills, but as a form of therapy, as a way of allowing all of us to realize our most central selves. Poetry, for Warren, has all along been his "central and obsessive concern." Far from being a superfluous avocation, it has provided him with what it can provide others: a way "to grasp reality and to grasp one's own life." It is the "Archimedean point from which we can . . . consider the world of technology, and indeed, of democracy. And . . . the world of the self." *Or Else* is the latest chapter in Warren's exploration of that self which he has inhabited now for seventy years, a self caught up in time, place, memory, and that other condition we call love.

Or Else, Warren tells us in a prefatory note, "is conceived as a single long poem composed of a number of shorter poems as sections or chapters. It is dated 1968–1974, but a few short pieces come from a period some ten years before, when I was working toward a similar long poem." Those few short pieces—seven of them—were first published as part of a ten-piece sequence at the beginning of the *Selected Poems* in the section called "Notes on a Life to be Lived." From *Incarnations*, as he reminds us, he has transposed the two-part "The True Nature of Time." But he has also borrowed his three-part "Homage to Theodore Dreiser" from his 1971 monograph of the same title. Together, these poems make up a quarter of the book's hundred pages. And most of the other pieces have appeared separately in a large number of wide-circulation magazines. I remember, for example, being stunned by the power and timeliness of "News Photo" when I first read it in a copy of the *Atlantic Monthly* in some doctor's office (although as I reread it now, it seems to have yellowed somewhat in a surprisingly short time).

What is new here, though, is the arrangement of the volume as sequence, forming a kind of trajectory like a comet seen at evening, the old poet singing vespers in a time of general drought. Warren suggests both the image of evensong and of parched wilderness in his epigraph to the entire collection, a passage taken from Psalms: "He clave the rocks in the wilderness, and gave them drink as out of the great depths." There are wasteland images everywhere in this book: landscapes (almost all of them American places) the poet remembers or through which he is now passing. Consider, for example, New York in the late sixties:

> Times Square, the season
> Late summer and the hour sunset, with fumes
> In throat and smog-glitter at sky-height, where
> A jet, silver and ectoplasmic, spooks through
> The sustaining light, which
> Is yellow as acid.

Times Square, where old men, coming out of "the hard-core movies" at that hour, stare at the sky, trying not to call attention to their drawers "drying stiff at the crotch." Another American image is Warren's recollection of the last lynching in Gupton (Guthrie?), Kentucky, circa 1915, when some "fool nigger" made the mistake of shooting a member of a posse out looking for him and was hanged by Warren's neighbors quickly if not cleanly:

> When the big
> bread truck they had him standing on
> drew out, he hung on with both feet
> as long as possible, then just
> keeled over, slow and head-down, in-
> to the rope, spilling his yell out. . . .

Vermont in a time of drouth shrinks to a handful of images; it is a time when

> The heel of the sun's foot smites horridly the hill,
> And the stalk of the beech leaf goes limp,
> And the bright brook goes gray among boulders.

And Warren's own childhood in Guthrie in blazing summer is remembered as a small white house, the pasture "brown-bright as brass," singing "like brass . . . with heat," a heat so bright it is "leprous." Or another remembered image—this time from "Rattlesnake Country," of an artificial oasis in mesquite country, where "wicker chairs, all day, / Follow the shimmering shade of the lone cottonwood," and where

> all day,
> The sky shivers white with heat, the lake,
> For its fifteen miles of distance, stretches
> Tight under the white sky. It is stretched
> Tight as a mystic drumhead. It glitters like neurosis.
> You think it may scream, but nothing
> Happens.

One of the most powerfully realized of these landscapes is the image of a black sharecropper's hovel remembered from the Depression. Here Warren slows down the image, freezing it, rendering it immovable, implacable, one of those secret images we carry with us into death, an image stripped of sociological significance, even of philosophical "meaning," and presented instead as the hard thing itself. The force of the image as it unfolds in "Forever O'Clock" demands that the entire poem be read slowly, meditatively, with attention to Warren's techniques for retarding the syntax, slowing the long falling lines until you too think you are in the world of no-time, where the minute hand on the old clock trembles, suspended between one stroke and the next:

> A little two-year old Negro girl-baby, with hair tied up in spindly
>   little tits with strings of red rag,
> Sits in the red dust. Except for some kind of rag around her middle,
>   she is naked, and black as a ripe plum in the sunshine.
>
> Behind the child is a gray board shack, and from the mud-chimney
>   a twist of blue smoke is motionless
>   against the blue sky.
> The fields go on forever, and whatever had been planted there is
>   not there now. The drouth does not see
>   fit to stop even now.

This reads like a Zen study in composition, and in fact many such visual meditations are scattered throughout the volume, as though the poet were composing (in both senses of that word) his world as parts of an extended indwelling on the mystery of being, moving logically and inexorably to the final poem, a composition without human figures, the ghost-poet looking out from his living room over the Connecticut countryside. He stares out onto a place of trees and blue hills where depth, as in Cézanne's landscapes, is both suggested and denied, where verbs of force suggest incessant motion, activity, the presence of a primitive, insistent life force, where, finally, a hawk, "Entering the composition at the upper left frame" perches and then, "in an eyeblink, is gone." That "is," suggesting being, presence, is the final verb in the entire sequence, but it is immediately negated by the last word, *gone*: "is gone"—presence moving inexorably into nonpresence.

It is this paradox, of a reality so much in flux that what is is always becoming was, that constitutes one of Penn Warren's most characteristic concerns, and that, for me at any rate, is both a strength and a weakness in the poetry, at least when I measure it against the sense of immediacy, of present-action, that I find in long sections of Pound's *Cantos* or something like Williams's *Desert Music* or some of the younger poets working in that tradition (and even in some of the old Objectivists). You do not have to read very much of Warren's work in whatever genre to see that he has been preoccupied for most of his life with the nature of time and with one of its principle corollaries: history. Consider for a moment the gradual education of Jack Burden in *All the King's Men*, digging into the epic loam for so many Southern writers—the glory and human tragedy of the Civil War—to reconstruct the shadowy figure of Cass Mastern, adulterer, penitent, Christlike noble soldier, romantic icon, dead in an Army field hospital outside Atlanta, defending a society from which he is morally alienated. Or consider the posthumous education of Thomas Jefferson in the commanding *Brother to Dragons* (1953), the paragon of Enlightenment principles coming at last to accept his blood affinity with his own sister's son, Lilburn, who one night in December 1811 systematically meat-cleavered a sixteen-year-old black slave named George, throwing the bloody pieces into a fire.

Warren's ability to reconstruct our past, to flesh it out into a meaning, is for him, as he says at the end of "Rattlesnake Country," "The compulsion to try to convert what now is *was* / Back into what was *is*." And one of the most compelling attempts comes in the central image of his recent *Audubon: A Vision*, in the long second section called "The Dream He Never Knew the End Of," which takes up fully half the poem. That whole section derives from a single incident in Audubon's *Ornithological Biography* (1839), which Warren has included in Volume I of his *American Literature: The Makers and the Making*. In this episode, Audubon quite matter of factly describes a night of terror spent in a wilderness cabin watched by a one-eyed Indian, while a prairie woman and her two drunken sons prepare to kill him (and the Indian) for his watch, but who are stopped by the chance appearance of some frontiersmen. I quote at length from Audubon and Warren because we can see here Warren's characteristic concern for translating dead history into living drama. Audubon, watching his "hosts" carefully as he pretends to sleep in a corner of the cabin with his dog, speaks:

> I turned, cocked my gun-locks silently, touched my faithful companion, and lay ready to start up and shoot the first who might attempt my life. The moment was fast approaching, and that night might have been my last in this world, had not Providence made preparations for my rescue. All was ready. The infernal hag was advancing slowly, probably contemplating the best way of despatching me, whilst her sons should be engaged with the Indian. I was several times on the eve of rising and shooting her on the spot:—but she was not to be punished thus. The door was suddenly opened, and there entered two [RPW has three] stout

travelers, each with a long rifle on his shoulder. . . . The tale was told in a minute. The drunken sons were secured, and the woman, in spite of her defence and vociferations, shared the same fate. . . . Day came, fair and rosy, and with it the punishment of our captives.

They were now quite sobered. Their feet were unbound, but their arms were still securely tied. We marched them into the woods off the road, and having used them as Regulators were wont to use such delinquents [a euphemism for lynching], we set fire to the cabin, gave all the skins and implements to the young Indian warrior, and proceeded, well pleased, towards the settlements.

During upwards of twenty-five years, when my wanderings extended to all parts of our country, this was the only time at which my life was in danger from my fellow creatures.

How to recapture that moment, to dig under the prose stratum covering that event, and, like an alchemist, transmute dusty *was* into electric *now*, another of Warren's lexical and ontological signatures? For at the moment the woman moves toward him, Audubon suddenly ceases to be the observer-narrator and becomes a character in the unfolding of the narration, the event itself partaking of fairy tale and nightmare:

> With no sound, she rises. She holds it in her hand.
> Behind her the sons rise like shadow. The Indian
> Snores.
>   He thinks: "Now."
>   And knows
> He has entered the tale, knows
> He has entered the dark hovel
>
> In the forest where trees have eyes, knows it is the tale
>
> They told him when he was a child, knows it
> Is the dream he had in childhood but never
> Knew the end of, only
> The Scream.
>
> But no scream now, and under his hand
> The dog lies taut, waiting. And he, too, knows
> What he must do, do soon, and therefore
>
> Does not understand why now a lassitude
> Sweetens his limbs, or why, even in this moment
> Of fear—or is it fear?—the saliva
> In his mouth tastes sweet.
>
> "Now, now!" the voice in his head cries out, but
> Everything seems far away, and small.

But the "event" is interrupted, the mother and sons "trussed up" to await the morning. Where Audubon is devoid of any but the most summary kind of reflection, however, Warren is preoccupied with the artist and some-time portrait-painter instinct in his protagonist. What, really, was the *meaning* of that event for Audubon? The woman, Warren's Audubon comes to realize, will complete the dream which he has all his life been dreaming: the dream of learning how to die. Warren as well as Audubon is spellbound, in fact sexually aroused, by the woman's cold acceptance of her fate:

> Under
> the tumbled darkness of hair, the face
> Is white. Out of that whiteness
> The dark eyes stare at nothing, or at
> The nothingness that the gray sky, like Time, is, for
> There is no Time, and the face
> Is, he suddenly sees, beautiful as stone, and
> So becomes aware that he is in the manly state.

The execution scene itself, hurried past by Audubon, is told with charac-teristic precision by Warren, who knows how to enact the violent event which is so much a part of our history. "The affair was not tidy," Warren offers with typical understatement:

> bough low, no drop, with the clients
> Simply hung up, feet not much clear of the ground, but not
> Quite close enough to permit any dancing.
> The affair was not quick: both sons long jerking and
> farting, but she,
> From the first, without motion, frozen
> In rage of will, an ecstacy of iron, as though
> This was the dream that, lifelong, she had dreamed
> toward. The face
> Eyes a-glare, jaws clenched, now glowing black with congestion
> Like a plum, had achieved,
> It seemed to him, a new dimension of beauty.

That kind of clarity and moral insight into the human condition in my reading places Warren in some very good company: Hawthorne, Melville, Mark Twain, Faulkner, Flannery O'Connor. But also with Theodore Dreiser, whose gift, in Warren's phrasing, was

> to enact
> All that his deepest self abhors,
> And learn, in his self-contemptive distress,
> The secret worth
> Of all our human worthlessness.

It ties him too with young Flaubert in Egypt, capable of screwing the local dancing girls with a vengeance ("That night three *coups*, and once / performs cunnilingus"), and even of buggering a bathboy, "in a clinical spirit and as / a tribute to the host country," carrying home with him the "trophy" of syphilis. And yet here too is someone capable of praising God that he can observe with precision "the motion of three wave-crests that, / in unison, bowed beneath the wind. . . ."

Time is an obsession with Warren, here as in his other work: the sense of time running out, with its attempts, usually fumbled, to order one's priorities, to somehow grasp the mystery of its passing. Approaching his own end, though in no hurry to do so, Warren keeps swinging back to his own beginnings. Many of these poems are about his own youth, half a century and more gone. In "Time as Hypnosis," he harks back to a snow storm in Kentucky during his twelfth winter, when he walked all day in the strange whiteness: "I looked back, saw / my own tracks march at me. / Mercilessly, / They came at me and did not stop." A childhood Christmas is reenacted in bold surrealistic strokes in a scene where Warren tries to reenter the irrecoverable past to discover his dead, rotting parents waiting for him in "I am Dreaming of a White Christmas." It is a haunting argument that, indeed, we cannot go home again. Several poems, notably "Ballad of Mister Dutcher," "Small White House," and "Forever O'Clock," evoke his lost Southern youth. There is, too, the "mesquite, wolf-waiting," "Rattlesnake Country," remembered images of France, and other landscapes transfigured by lust, anger, love, terror, small deaths. Warren recalls a drunken romp in New Orleans as a young man with two nameless friends when they looked up into the raw face of God in all of their splendid drunkenness and, unlike Housman's Terence, "mouthed out our Milton for magnificence." Now one of those men is dead while the other spends his retirement deep-sea fishing, sometimes coming "back in with no line wet." In these pages Warren remembers the pain he felt at his mother's death, when he stood by her hospital bedside and wondered if he too would, like her, someday have to wear false teeth:

> She is lying on her back, and God, is she ugly, and
> With gum-flabby lips and each word a special problem,
>   she is asking if it is a new suit that you are
>   wearing.
> You say yes and hate her uremic guts, for she has no
>   right to make you hurt the way that question
>   hurts.
> You do not know why that question makes your heart hurt
>   like a kick in the scrotum,

> For you do not yet know that the question, in its
> murderous triviality, is the last thing she
> will ever say to you. . . .

There is too the recollection of his father's terrible virtue, an old man with "blanket / Over knees, woolly gray bathrobe over shoulders, hand-kerchief / On great bald skull spread, glasses / Low on big nose" reading Hume's *History of England,* or Roosevelt's *Winning of the West,* or Freud on dreams, or Coke or Blackstone. How to explain his father's going, his disappearance into the past, that "unnameable and de-timed beast" which lifts its brachycephalic head with its dumb, "magisterial gaze" looking into the distance?

And how to redeem the time, to understand the fact of being, to learn to live well so that one can at least die well? These are very old questions, shared by all, or at least most, of us. One thing the poet can try to do is to keep the past—which annihilates but also preserves—from slipping away. And this Warren does by blooding that past with his words. The other thing, tied to this evocation, is to celebrate the redemptive presence of love. There are few explicit love poems in this volume, although of course many of these poems are poems of concern, for one's parents, one's children, one's place. But two poems in particular are centrally concerned with the man's love for his wife: the exquisitely lyrical "Vision Under the October Mountain," with its vision of a floating mountain, gold in the golden autumn air, and its mode of address, all the more powerful for its slight self-consciousness and indirection:

> I want to understand the miracle
> of your presence here by my side, your
> gaze on the mountain. I want
> to hear the whole story of how
> you came here, with
> particular emphasis on the development of
> the human scheme of values.

But the poem that I find particularly attractive is "Birth of Love," with Warren watching his wife, her body "marked by his use, and Time's," rise at the lake's edge one summer evening after sunset to dry herself. The title refers, of course, to the image of Venus Anadyomene, and this husband and lover, still, out in the darkening lake, sees his wife frozen for a moment in an attitude resembling the goddess's. That moment, he knows,

> is non-sequential and absolute, and admits
> Of no definition, for it
> Subsumes all other, and sequential, moments, by which
> Definition might be possible.

That is the hard-won moment, when meaning falls away and the woman simply *is*, is before she climbs up through the path and is gone. All he can do, the poet realizes, in that gathering gloom, is to cry out from the heart in silence that some star may protect her. In a sense, his own tenuous presence in the poem becomes a problem in spatial composition, for time alone is enough to radically alter one's location: the poet sings and then, in an eyeblink, like the hawk, is gone.

I could quarrel with certain things in Warren I find alien to my own sense of poetics: a sometimes loose, rambling line, a nostalgia verging on obsession, a veering toward philosophical attitudinizing, the mask of the redneck that out-rednecks the redneck. But I would rather leave such critical caveats for others. There is enough here to praise, and I have been given to drink from a spring clear and deep.

1975

Coda: January 1984

When I first wrote this review of Warren, exactly ten years ago this month, Warren was approaching seventy and I was thirty-three. I now feel compelled—it is Warren's achievement over the past decade which itself compels me—to make far greater claims for him than I was able to make then. Like Harold Bloom, I am a late convert to Warren; like him, I believe that Warren's late poetry—by which I mean the poetry he has written since he reached seventy—makes him the foremost poet writing today in the American Romantic tradition. Warren's vision is troubled, cantankerous, the vision of a man who has eaten bitter fruit all his life and who knows that everything he utters will be uttered through clenched teeth. The image, from Jeremiah, is his own for himself. By extension, we his readers cannot have escaped tasting that same grittiness of the fallen self that has so shaped Warren's poetic voice. "I am gall, I am heartburn. God's most deep decree / Bitter would have me taste: my taste was me." So Hopkins, and so, with a vengeance, Robert Penn Warren.

A friend who knows Warren personally tells me that Warren keeps Hardy's *Collected Poems* by his bedside. Whether or not that is the case, it should be. For Warren is clearly paralleling Hardy's poetic example in its most rigorous outlines. Warren's poetry radically changed somewhere around 1960, that is, when he was in his fifties. For his part Hardy turned his attention almost exclusively to poetry at the same age, that is, after reeling from the critical reception of *Jude the Obscure*. True, Warren has been publishing poetry since the beginning of a career that is now sixty years old, and for a long time it looked as if he would be remembered as a novelist (*All the King's Men*) who also wrote some very good poetry. Now it is clear that, like Hardy, Warren is foremost a poet. And it is precisely the work of the past ten years that has convinced me of his greatness.

Since my review was published, Warren has proceeded to publish, along with several other books, five more volumes of poetry. *Selected Poems: 1923–1975* (his *third* selected poems!) appeared in 1976, and contained a new sequence as well as a reordering of priorities to favor his later work. Two years later *Now and Then: Poems 1976–1978* was published. Two more years and another volume, *Being Here: Poetry 1977–1980*, followed the next year by yet another volume, *Rumor Verified: Poems 1979–1980*. And then, in 1983 came his book-length poem in the *Audubon* mode, *Chief Joseph of the Nez Perce*. Together, these volumes—along with the very good work appearing recently in such places as the *New Yorker* ("New Dawn," one of the best antinuclear poems so far written, which appeared there in mid-November 1983, is but one example)—demonstrate that Warren is one of those poets whose late poems are not a falling off or even a stasis, but rather an extraordinary late flowering. In this Warren joins that select group of poets who continued to write and write well right up to the last: Stevens, Williams, Yeats, and Hardy. That is heady company for any poet to be classed with, but I believe that in the final assessment Warren must be numbered among these voices.

I say this, as aware of Warren's shortcomings as I am of Hardy's with whom I would compare him in stature. I know what the anti-Warren critics say: that he has published far too much in these last years, that he is garrulous, that his diction is old-fashioned, harking back to an earlier high-Romantic mode, or—conversely—too crabbed, too mannered in the style of Hopkins, that he keeps replaying the same tunes of self, history, and time on the old gramophone, that he is often vulgar, that his portrayal of Joseph, the great chief of the Nimipu, is an embarrassment in which Joseph is made to speak Indian Ugh-talk, that Warren is given attention today primarily because of his venerable stature as encroaching octogenarian and elder statesman of American letters. But if we make the best case for all of these negative assessments, Warren, no less than Hardy, rises above them to take his solitary position of eminence above any other American poet who would attempt the high style of the Romantic sublime today.

Like Bloom, I too do not often feel comfortable with Warren. Not because I am a Gnostic—I do not think I am, though I have been so charged in print—but because I feel uncomfortable with the radical and perhaps not even secular Calvinism underlying Warren's vision. Warren reminds me sometimes of that old Confederate Stonewall Jackson sitting on a pine-rail fence sucking on a lemon, waiting, planning out his strategies. And though he has seen more of the world than most of us will ever see, and has lived and taught in Yankee Connecticut for many years, he was shaped by the old South and, when the chips are down, when he is exasperated by his search for the consolations of philosophy, he will suddenly shift back into the world and language of the poor Southern white. He is looking for correspondences, for some sort of sign of God's presence, asking with the insistence of a redneck shit-kicker (I say this with grudging admiration, a New York City boy recognizing in the Guthrie boy an even greater toughness) if the final sign he has spent his life looking for won't be something like the image memory has dredged up from his childhood.

> Tinfoil wrappers of chocolate, popcorn, nut shells, and poorly
> Cleared up, the last elephant turd on the lot where the circus had been.

One aspect of Warren's Southern heritage is the strong, rhetorical and narrative tradition of Southern writing which has informed his poetry for the past quarter century. It has taken me a long time—and much reading of Faulkner, Dickey, and Smith—to appreciate this literary tradition which after all flies in the face of all I was taught to admire in my Modernist masters: brevity, lack of connectives, eschewal of narrative line, the ability to let the image talk (Eliot's objective correlative, so to speak) rather than rely on a poetry of statement. And I still think that some of Warren's poems—like Hardy's—suffer at times from too many philosophical and theological abstractions. But what I have come to see is that Warren has set up a strategy (not unlike late Stevens and Eliot in *Four Quartets*) between meaning and being. That is, Warren allows himself to ask the large philosophical questions so that we may see, finally, after having knocked our heads against the wall for sixty or seventy years, just how unanswerable those large questions are. And then he gives us something else: the consolation of what it *means* to *be* here. So the repetitiveness of the philosophical questioning is most likely part of Warren's final strategy. I have tried and tried, he seems to say. I have listened and I have watched for any sign, no less than Edward Taylor did three hundred years ago, no less than Emerson himself did, but I cannot read the signs, if they *are* after all signs. Coming late in the Romantic tradition, Warren sees himself as a poet singing at evening, like some thrush, perhaps, who

> knows the hour past song
> Has come, [when] the westward height yet
> Stays sallow, and bats scribble
> The sky in miniscule murder, which,

From one perspective, is beauty, too.
Time will slip in silence past, like God's breath.

If the bats in their search for prey can be said to "scribble," they write their message on the twilight in a language for which the poet has no key (other than the primitive one of survival). Try as he may, he cannot interpret nature's signs in any finally optimistic sense, and he will not manufacture his answers to console us or himself. At least with Hardy there was a residual nostalgia, the vestiges of a liberal humanitarianism, an old man projecting himself onto his readers as in "Afterwards," seeing himself as one who thought of such natural sights and was at home there. Warren's stance in these late poems is more like Larkin's in "Aubade," an old man staring at the ceiling of his bedroom in the dark, waiting for the light of predawn to enter the room so that he can witness at least one more precious day. He is afraid, though he does his best to cover that fear over for his family's sake. But the darkness is so very deep and no past glory, no past memory of love or anger or even of violence can sustain him for long. He wants the feel of reality, not of dream, and that reality takes the same shape that it took for Dr. Johnson: the plash of cold water, stroke on stroke, the sharp zing of a tooth cracking, the incessant drip drip of a Vermont thaw signaling the coming of another season. In his own poem, "Afterward," clearly modeled on Hardy's, Warren, having looked at the cold options of glacier and night desert open to him, chooses instead the warmth of company where, after a time at least, some sort of trust and mutual comfort is possible. Even the great poet is, after all, a human being like the rest of us. At the close, then, not more light, but more warmth.

And yet Warren has come to understand that the past need not be only a burden, for it too—as Eliot saw—can sometimes redeem the present emptiness. Increasingly as Warren has grown older, images of his childhood and his youth crowd on him, becoming more vivid than most of the present. So, in "October Picnic Long Ago," the poem that opens *Being Here*, Warren remembers a picnic with his family which took place seventy years ago. He himself was six, then, and he recalls his father talking about the future, as men will, when his ship would finally come in. But his mother knows better. She knows that if she is to have happiness, it will have to be in the present, in what she now possesses. Even then, of course, this time-obsessed poet knows, the future was lying in wait, for the moment only chained up like some mad dog, while the mother—happy in the October day and in her family—sang. Now of course his mother and father and most of his friends are dead, as Warren's other poems tell us, and the poet is—willy-nilly—the late solitary singer singing of what is as night comes on.

It is instructive to consider the poem that closes this volume, for Warren has deliberately and subtly juxtaposed that past image of childhood innocence and lyrical blessedness with the image of the poet now, alone, walking in the New England woods at night. He has been walking a long time, thinking of a warm hearth and of someone to receive him, though he has been out so long now that he is not sure that there even is such a thing as a destination any more. He passes someone in the dark and wishes him well, though that other is probably—and eerily—none other than himself. The final sounds in this poem belong not to the poet or to his mother but to nature itself, and if we do not know what they mean, it is probably just as well. For what, if anything, are we to make of the "crack of bough burdened with snow" and the dubious benediction of the owl, one of Warren's predators—like the hunter God he often invokes. The world has grown more and more present to Warren with time, so much so that not only have the animals and birds become more prominent, but the weather itself, and the trees and the very rocks, which soon he knows he must join forever. Warren has an image of his father, reading philosophy as he sits wrapped up against the cold. And he is his father's son, one of those in search of meaning and scanning the text of the world for signs. But even more so, in these late poems, he has come to appreciate what it was his mother taught him early, to sing while there was still time to sing.

It would take a monograph to say what needs to be said about Warren's achievement, his honesty of diction, his uncanny ability to flesh out in precise imagery such concepts as time and history and self, his range of language, from a language very much in the demotic American grain (in Williams's sense) and moving up to the sublime, and finally, his ease and surety in employing a panoply of poetic forms. And this note is only intended as the coda to an earlier essay review. But I want to end by looking at one of the great poems of our time and one that embodies, incarnates, the native sublime for us. It is a poem that Bloom has already singled out for praise: the poem that concludes the volume, *Now and Then:* "Heart of Autumn." It is fall and the great geese are heading for warmer waters, though some of them—thanks to the hunters—will never reach that destination. Death comes unexpectedly; the wounded geese do not even know what has happened to them. Unbeknown to them, the poet suddenly realizes with a shudder, they are enacting his own story. For they have risen into the autumn skies to cry out with their "imperial utterance," calling out the joy of their nameless tragic destiny. In this, the poet has come to understand, they seem to know more perhaps than the poet knows about himself. And if it is the path of some inner logic, this pull to the south, or merely the path of folly, where the hunter lies in wait, what matter finally? What does matter is the great wing beat across the heavens. Wing beat, high beat, the poet hears and for a moment imagines himself transformed and following in their wake. And now his heart

> is impacted with a fierce impulse
> To unwordable utterance—
> Toward sunset, at a great height.

Only a great poet could have uttered these lines, a cry beyond the human while yet partaking of our humanity. Approaching eighty and his own sunset, Warren has mastered a great height.

JOHN BURT

The Self-Subversion of Value in Warren's "World Enough and Time"

How ones reads *World Enough and Time* is largely a matter of how one judges its principal character. It is traditional to treat the book as a critique of romantic idealism which uses Beaumont as a case in point and as a negative definition of better or at least less dangerous standards of value. But nobody knows Beaumont's vulnerability to criticism better than he does himself, and his self-knowledge is acute not only in the bitter and rueful moments of his final recognition but also at the height of his error; in fact, what most goads him to behave as he does is not, say, his quixotic idealism, but his sense that his motivations may be suspect. He acts not because he is unaware of the irony of history but because he is nettled by it and turns to desperate means to escape it. Beaumont's book is not a critique of romantic idealism—as if "realism" and "romantic idealism" were ever capable of being measured against some common standard—but an examination of the destructive consequences of value itself, not only those values in whose name Beaumont suffers and murders, but all values which seek to ground themselves in transcendence, which is to say, all values whatsoever.

What moves Beaumont to his crimes, his murder of Cassius Fort and his domination of Rachel Jordan, is not "blind idealism" but a keen appreciation of the dangers of blind idealism. He is someone who has already learned too well the lessons we expect the novel to teach. Because

Beaumont anticipates the charges we might bring against him, indeed, because it is the effort to respond to those charges that undoes him, we cannot view his history merely as the consequence of his motivating error. Nor can we use that error to define, as a counter-principle, the novel's central affirmation, for Beaumont precedes us in our search for some principle capable of redeeming the tendency of principle to become unravelled in action, and his failure demonstrates the inevitability of our own. We will not be able to uncover even a negatively defined affirmation, for Beaumont's deepest error seems to be his desire to discover such an affirmation. What leads him astray, that is, is not that he stands for the wrong things but that he stands for anything at all.

The only alternative to Jeremiah Beaumont, then, seems to be what he, with justifiable contempt, calls the "world," for it is easy to see that any claim to value beyond mere expedience inevitably leads in this novel to bloodshed and the betrayal of that value, and that the only safety is in renunciation of values. Even if Beaumont turns to his ideal on account of his personal emptiness (as Jack Burden had turned to Willie Stark in *All the King's Men* or as Munn had turned to the Association in *Night Rider*) this does not mean that it is only his emptiness which causes those ideals to be destructive; his emptiness may make him vulnerable to the claims of the ideal, but the destructiveness he embraces is the destructiveness of the ideal itself. It is easy enough to carp at him, but perhaps doing so puts us in the unhappy company of Wilkie Barron and Sugg Lancaster and other representatives of the all too wise world, people who have a keen enough eye on their own interests to take their claims to ideals lightly. And perhaps, as we prepare to reflect on Beaumont's errors, we would do well to wonder how it might be possible to criticize Jack Burden's breezy cynicism and Jeremiah Beaumont's "idealism" in the same breath, how we might denigrate the latter without sounding rather like the former.

The historian-narrator's account is equivocal. On one hand, he ruthlessly points out Beaumont's vanity and error. He shows us how Beaumont engineers a high drama for himself in order to satisfy his idea of himself. In the service of this idea he commandeers the destiny of Rachel Jordan, and, having forced her to demand the murder of his own benefactor Cassius Fort, who had seduced her years earlier, he carries out what he convinces himself is their mutual desire. The narrator sees Beaumont, and Beaumont, after Rachel's final accusation of him, sees himself, as one capable of the most serious violation of the integrity of others, as one capable of forcing another not only to do as he wishes, not only to profess as he professes, but also to believe that she is doing so on her own account. He masters Rachel as every romantic suitor masters his beloved, by presenting himself as her servant; he usurps her personality by acting as though she has usurped his. But he does so more thoroughly and more radically than any other suitor, for he masters not only her body and her affections but also her sense of herself. He is the natural brother of Hawthorne's Aylmer, who like Beaumont is so maddened by the fact of human imperfection that he overbears and drives to death the woman dearest to him, all the while convinced that he is doing her bidding and all the while so swamping her that she in fact demands what he wishes her to demand.

It is the deepest irony—although perhaps in love a not altogether unfamiliar one—that Beaumont does this in all honesty, that he is himself perfectly convinced that he fulfills Rachel's wishes when it is clear that Rachel wishes as she does primarily because he has bullied her into doing so. He is not so dull that in the months preceding his murder of Fort he fails to be dimly and bitterly aware that his wife is not altogether of his counsel, but it is characteristic of his egotism (an egotism that seems to transcend self and reappear as a queer sort of humility) that in forcing her to demand Fort's death a second time he feels not that he is coercing her but that he is bringing her back to herself, preventing her from betraying herself (and betraying him). He is not blind, but even when he sees he deprives Rachel of her own mind; and doing so he deprives himself of his own mind also, for he knows and values himself only as the servant of Rachel.

Even as the narrator criticizes Beaumont he honors him for his crime, not only because it is the product of an all-consuming hunger for the right, but also because it is a crime only available to those capable of grandeur, a crime which we who read his story are not likely to commit because we are built on a smaller scale and are capable only of petty vices and pettier virtues. Beaumont has greatness, if only the greatness of one who takes his world greatly. Brooding over his story, the narrator (like the commentator of *The Ballad of Billie Potts*) feels small beside him, despite his superior wisdom:

> Puzzling over what is left, we are like the scientist bumbling with a tooth and thigh bone to reconstruct for a museum some great, stupid beast extinct with the ice age. Or we are like the louse-bit nomad who finds, in a fold of land between his desert and the mountains, the ruins of parapets and courts, and marvels what kind of men had held the world before him.

Now perhaps all of Beaumont's commitments are no more than bloody vanities, the arias he sings upon a high secret stage where truth is only a prop but where the knives are sharp and the blood is real. Like Jack Burden of *All the King's Men* the narrator likes to undermine "drama" and speaks of Beaumont's story as a piece of stagecraft, "grand, with noble gestures and swelling periods, serious as blood." What effect this drama is capable of having it has despite itself; it has the pathos of failure, not the pathos of tragedy, the pathos of *Godot* rather than of *Hamlet*:

> But the actors were not well trained. At times it all was only a farce, though a bloody farce, which, with its comic parody of greatness, struck a desperate doubt into his soul. To us, at this distance, with the blood all dried to powder, it is sometimes the most serious speeches and grand effects which give the farce. And by the same token, we may find the pathos only in those moments when the big speeches are fluffed or the gestures forgotten, when the actor improvises like a lout, when he suffers nakedly from the giggles and the inimical eyes, or flees from the stage. We find the pathos then, for that is the kind of suffering with which we are most fully acquainted. It is not, however, the effect Jeremiah Beaumont had labored to prepare.

The joke, however, seems to be as much at our expense as at Beaumont's, for the fact that the only pathos we find is in his botching tells against us more than it does against him, demonstrates that we could not have had his tragedy because we could not have taken his values, or any values for that matter, with the requisite seriousness. Beaumont prepares an ambiguous drama which seems both to affirm and to deny life, yet for all its fluffed effects and self-consciousness, Beaumont, who lives a drama, is a larger figure than we are, who are wiser and who thus live nothing:

> It may have been the drama Jeremiah Beaumont had to prepare in order to live at all, or in order, living, to be human. And it may be that a man cannot live unless he prepares a drama, at least cannot live as a human being against the ruck of the world.

Learned as we are in the wisdom of wrong, we can condescend to pity Beaumont's mistakes; having deflated him entirely we offer him that sympathy which is more abasing than any ridicule. Yet even this seems to count more against us than it does against him. Of our attempt to recover pity for Beaumont, the narrator remarks:

> That idea would have struck him as ridiculous, as worse than ridiculous, for it would rob him of the last shred of pride as the author of his own ruin and leave him alone without identity, staring into the blank face of suffering. The idea would have been ridiculous to him, for in the end he did not ask for pity, at least not human pity. But piy at the price of his self-respect is what we are most ready to give him. For with us pity for others is the price we are anxious to pay for the privilege of our self-pity.

The narrator continually undermines Beaumont, and in doing so he does only what the world has done already, for the plot of the novel demonstrates nothing except the entanglements to which principle is subject. But he does not take the satisfaction most natural to underminers, that feeling of superiority available even to the thoroughgoing nihilist; if he behaves as the world behaves, then he is, alas, merely a part of the world. Beaumont in his effort is larger than the narrator in his truth, and the narrator's debunking has an edge to it, the edge of his hunger for the sanction even of delusory or self-repealing principle. The narrator, in other words, is someone who is doing his best to resist both the natural tendency of his own rhetorical resources and the natural conclusions to which the facts at hand lend themselves, and therefore every time he undermines Beaumont he undermines himself yet more severely, attempting to recover value from the general wreck of value by jeering at his own destructiveness, creating tragedies out of what he himself reduces to farce. There is no superior standpoint from which Beaumont may be judged, no way that we can look down upon him without betraying our own emptiness, no affirmation we can make except the deadly affirmation Beaumont makes himself.

We cannot criticize Beaumont, then, as a way of defining a counter-principle to which his novel leads us. For the alternatives the novel gives us are limited: we can believe something, with Beaumont, and pay the price of that belief; or we can believe nothing, with Wilkie Barron, and suffer the emptiness which eventually drives him to suicide; or we can, with the narrator, neither believe nor be comfortable in unbelief, and remain in a state of longing, hungry for principles which we know already are poisonous, but afraid to take the poison.

Beaumont's error is the belief that he can take personal responsibility for his world, that he can act on the transcendental warrant of absolute right, that he can shape or transform the world in the fire of an idea. He is a sort of Catharist, with private access to an otherworldly (but not quite religious) power which frees him from and refutes the claim of the world. Linked to his desire to reject the world as a moral guide (prudence being no substitute for right) in his desire to reject sexuality in favor of a sexual purity sometimes hard to distinguish from a highly refined perversion. His Catharist metaphysics matches a Catharist erotics which he holds in common with other nervous idealists (Faulkner's Quentin Compson chief among them) and which Denis de Rougemont has taught us is the basis of our modern ideas about love. The consequence of Beaumont's error is that he suffers the reversals inherent in every intent. His desire to seek the sanction of a law beyond law naturally leads him, by logical steps, to lawlessness. His fascinated recoil from sexuality is itself a kind of prurience which banishes sexuality to the darkness where it proliferates into ever more exotic forms, until, with the identification between repression and license which seems common to Catharist sensibilities, the pure Rachel and the gross half-breed Beaumont copulates with after his conversion in McClardy's meadow grow to resemble one another.

Beaumont is not the only character in *World Enough and Time* who abases himself by means of the gigantic egotism of the idea. Indeed, he is outdone by Percival Skrogg, whose abstract passion for justice easily transforms itself into the chill precision of his skill as a duellist, a skill he uses to demonstrate to himself the unreality of other people (until he himself, belatedly convinced of the reality of his own body, learns fear and loses his life). Skrogg, like Professor Ball of *Night Rider* (whose extremism he shares) is a caricature, not fully a character, and he serves to define the desiccated terrible thing one becomes when the ideal both displaces and inflates the self. He demonstrates not only the willing sacrifice of his own humanity which Beaumont always flirts with, but also how the ruthlessness of abstract devotion becomes indistinguishable from simple amorality, how Skrogg, the pure man of the idea, comes to resemble Wilkie Barron, the pure man of the world.

There is a fine line which separates Skrogg from Beaumont. Skrogg is Beaumont without self-doubt, without those hesitations and scruples which allow one to differentiate between will and program. Skrogg is fully abstract and thus fully inhuman. Beaumont, even at his most terrible, is fully human, always a man wrestling with the bosom serpent and not the serpent itself. Skrogg is a man who has become his idea, Beaumont a man who longs to do the same, doubts his ability to do so, and therefore is capable, as Skrogg is not, of experience, of suffering, and of grandeur.

Beaumont's project is to remake the world to answer the moral imperative he feels small before and which he—unlike Skrogg—does not feel that even he himself is capable of embodying. He is—and this is his virtue as much as his problem—still a part of his world, although a part under the pressure of transcendental demands.

The imperative with which he labors is at the same time political, moral, and sexual. The political problem faced by all the characters in *World Enough and Time* is the familiar contradiction of law and need. The panic of 1819 bankrupted much of the populace of Kentucky, and also nearly bankrupted the Bank of Kentucky, which, heavily in debt to the Bank of the United States, began to issue its own nearly worthless notes. The legislature, dominated by men of the Relief party, passed a replevin bill calling for a two year moratorium on the collection of debts. When the state Supreme Court struck down the replevin bill as unconstitutional, the legislature appointed a new Court, made up of Relief partisans, to replace the old Court. The two Courts existed side by side, with New Court and Old Court supporters engaging in a near civil war, until New Court and Relief were defeated in the 1826 elections, which close the novel. Old Court and New, flesh and spirit, obligation and need, law as master and law as servant, legalism and higher law, both sides are motivated by what Warren calls "a crazy dream of justice." Both are fatal, necessary, and irreconcilable, except to Cassius Fort, who died before he could reveal his solution.

Beaumont, as a man of the idea, is naturally enough a partisan of the New Court (although Jeroboam Beauchamp, his real-life counterpart in the "Kentucky tragedy" on which the novel is based, was a partisan of the Old Court). But Beaumont's politics, unlike his historical counterpart's, are far from fanatical. He inclines toward Relief, but he takes part in the election-day fight at Lumton not because of his political beliefs but because he cannot stand to see the anti-Relief thugs beat up Skrogg— which is to say that his first political act is not the result of possession by an abstract idea but the result of generous anger at a very concrete outrage. Beaumont responds exactly the same way when he sees the Relief riff-raff at Tupper's Tavern preparing to beat the obese and elderly Squire MacFerson. He is, then, not at all a political fanatic, not at all even an ideologue. His convictions are—until self-doubt stampedes him—rather like those of Cassius Fort, sympathetic to Relief but skeptical of the New Court and the attempt to undermine law which the New Court represents.

It is characteristic of Warren's political writings no less than of his novels that even Beaumont's moderate convictions only create confusion about his loyalties, that Squire MacFerson believes Beaumont has attacked him, while the crowd is ready to damn Beaumont as an anti-Reliefer. It is also characteristic that the most potent stimulus to political action is self-doubt, the suspicion that scruple is weakness and rationalized interest. That it is the attack on Skrogg, rather than principle, that moved Beaumont to act in the cause of Relief, for example, is for Beaumont himself grounds for continual self-reproach. What moves Beaumont to run for the Legislature on the New Court ticket is not deep devotion to the cause of Relief, but his inability to be certain of his own reply when Wilkie Barron, whose devotion to principle Beaumont at the same time admires and suspects, implies that he is slack in his devotion to relief because his marriage to Rachel and collaboration with the speculator and anti-Relief activist Parham make it all too easy to be so.

Wilkie Barron's reproaches spur Beaumont's private commitments just as they do his public ones, for what first leads Beaumont to Rachel is not inner compulsion but the guilt he feels when Wilkie attacks him for not sharing his generous rage over Fort's seduction of her and hints that Beaumont's coolness is the result of his professional relationship with Fort. Beaumont's moral and sexual imperatives are identical—and perhaps this has to be so, since our only deeply-felt standard of morality (as Fiedler has argued) has for many years been our standard of sexual conduct. Beaumont's attachment to Rachel, and the murder of the seducer that attachment seems to him to imply, allow him to play out the old drama in which revenge upon a seducer enables the revenger at once to be sure of his rectitude while committing a crime and to possess the sexual object while denying his own vulnerability to sexual desire. But what Beaumont wants is not simply the satisfaction of the revenger—violence and sex without guilt—for he is aware of the vulgarity and dishonesty of that desire. What he wants is a sanction which justifies him in being himself and marks him off as different in kind from other men.

When, at the end of chapter III, Rachel demands that he kill Fort, Beaumont experiences a shock of terror and joy which he likens (using imagery to which Warren reverts repeatedly—most tellingly at the end of "Tale of Time" and in the recent "Twice Born") to a bolt of lightning striking a summer tree. Her demand surprises him not because he has not been expecting it, for clearly he has been forcing this demand from her for the last fifty pages, but because he had not been aware that that was what he had been expecting. Only when he has forced her to demand that he fulfill his wish (a wish that she, under pressure, claims is her own) does he discover what it is that he has been wishing for from the beginning. It is the logical conclusion of his earlier discovery that "all our freedom is in the necessity within us." We cannot say whether he discovers or creates this compulsion (although our moral assessment of him hangs upon this distinction) for this compulsion is the originating condition of his selfhood. Whatever choice he may have exercised in the matter was prior to his existence as a fully constituted subject, and is therefore not relevant in deciding the question. If he did not desire to kill Cassius Fort, he could not be Jeremiah Beaumont, nor could he point to any transcendental warrant to account for his own being. His compulsion is partly self-willed, as if he could make himself by his own *fiat*, and partly the work of a transcendental other, an injunction laid upon him from above, a purpose beyond mere self-satisfaction. On one hand, he cannot be himself without his compulsion, and he chooses it in order to become himself. On the other hand, without the compulsion he can only be himself; he is limited to himself and has no transcendental purpose which dedicates him to something beyond self. It is a strange moment, in which, like a poet invoking a muse (while at the same time dictating to the muse who dictates to him) he both finds and escapes himself.

The alternative to compulsion is emptiness, and for this reason we should hesitate to judge it. Beaumont does by will what Jack Burden finally does by accident, and had he not done so he would have been nothing:

> So she had said it, and had laid on him the obligation. Or we may say more accurately that he had at last succeeded in laying the obligation on her and thereby on himself, for the obligation sprang from the depth of his nature, from the "midnight pulse." But the promptings of the midnight pulse must find their shape in the world, must find the word and the deed, for otherwise they are nothing. Jeremiah Beaumont had to create his world or be the victim of a world he did not create. Out of his emptiness, which he could not satisfy with any fullness of the world, he had to bring forth whatever fullness might be his. And in the end must not every man, even the most committed and adjusted worldling, do the same? If he is to live past the first gilded promise of youth and the first flush of appetite?

He does not seek to do what justifies him in the sight of the world but rather to do what places him beyond the world. He chooses not to marry Rachel until after he has killed Fort—a choice he turns out not to be able to realize—because to marry Rachel first would be to give the color of worldly justification to his act, an act which he wishes to be "gratuitous" and "pure." He no more wants to be a "revenger" than he wants to be a seducer; what he wants is to be absolutely other, to be someone who not only escapes from every snare of the world but who also rejects and transcends every role the world provides. To murder the seducer of his wife would be not only to play a worldly role but to act in self-interest. The self his gratuitous act is to serve is a self beyond himself, a self so shadowy and abstract that it does not seem to be a self at all, a self which is only known through denials and which is distinguishable only in terms of what it refuses to be. And chief among the things he refuses to be—although his pity and envy for old Mr. Barron's love for his wife seems to him to show the reverse—is an ordinary, sexually mature man. As he leaves to make his first attempt on Fort, Rachel denies him her hand to kiss, and this denial suits him exactly:

> Further conversation or endearments such as lovers commonly use would but distract us, and even the touch of my lips to her hand, which she had denied on parting, would stain the moment of our resolve and make what we hoped to be not better than any bumkin Jack and Jill.

Beaumont's next question, "What had I done as yet to make me worthy?" demonstrates the "otherness," as it were, of the purity he seeks. The idea is always larger than the self, and even the most monstrous inflation of the self moved by the idea will for this reason always look like self-abasement. The transcendental warrant always troubles and escapes the self it justifies. The idea is like the romance beloved, who is forbidden not by, say, the law against adultery, but by the fact that the beloved must be a sexual object beyond sexuality, someone whom even the purest love would defile because she must always differ in kind from the lover. She at the same time makes clear our abasement, the necessity for sublimation or repression of sex, and the impossibility of doing so. She leaves us, as the narrator remarks, with irony characteristically directed more at himself than at Beaumont, discontent with the flesh, and unable to become spirit:

> For who is Hecuba, who is she, that all the swains adore her? She is whatever we must adore. Or if we adore nothing, she is what we must act as if we adored. And if we adore her, we must do so, not because we know her, but because we do not know her. If before we go out on our great design we lean to kiss her hand, she will always withdraw it and we must ride away to leave her brooding on a winter lawn. Or to regard the matter in a different light, we can never leave Hecuba. She is what we must carry in the breast, though we can never know her. She is our folly and our glory and despair. And if we do not adore her, we can adore nothing or only Silly Sal, who was found tasty in Bowling Green by the hot boys of the town.

The difference between the drifter and the fanatic, those two repeated character types in Warren, is only a difference in time; it is not a difference in kind. The fanatic is what the drifter becomes when he discovers what he has been hungry for. The drifter drifts, is empty, because he claims no inward authority, no transcendental warrant. The fanatic kills because he makes that claim; murder is his way of proving his possession to himself. But since what moves him is a hunger for transcendentals, and since transcendentals necessarily escape him, it is only intensity which distinguishes his situation from that of the drifter, as it is only an article which distinguishes a void from the void, a nothing that is there from the nothing that is there. To reduce this proposition to psychology, to claim that the fanatic grasps fanaticism because he has nothing else to sustain him (not having the healthy-mindedness we lovers of Silly Sal have), is to miss its force. For the point is not that the values of the fanatic are a reflection of his sickness but that all value is itself a kind of sickness (and that, by the same token, to abandon the sphinx-question of value is not a kind of health but a kind of death).

He who has the idea can spurn the world, and having spurned it, can play the immoralist since he can no longer be measured by a worldly standard. The narrator remarks of Beaumont's behavior during his election campaign (the campaign in which the accusations against Fort of bastardy and against Rachel of miscegnation appear):

> He felt that he had stumbled on a great and comic secret: if you knew that the hurly-burly of the world was a mock-show, and a flight from another more dire mock-show, then you could play your part the better to win applause from all.

It is the old claim, common to Hogg's justified sinner, the Antinomians, and the wilder varieties of gnostic, that the redeemed is redeemed from the law as much as from the world, and can break the law in favor of the higher law.

But if the world is no judge, then the world provides no standard either, and with infinite warrant for action goes infinite self-doubt also. There is no unit of measure by which one's distance from one's ideal can be gauged, and therefore every time the fanatic does what he is compelled to do he cannot tell whether he is fulfilling his destiny or betraying it. This is why Beaumont is, for all his separation from the world, inordinately sensitive to public opinion, why his huge egotism is at the same time huge self-disgust.

Beaumont is driven to his crimes on one hand by the necessity of taking responsibility for his world, and on the other by the fear that he is not capable of doing so. He looks continuously for the one act which will prove to himself that his motives are pure, or which will redeem the impurity of his motives, and since it is in the nature of transcendental demands that such proof is never available, necessarily his attempts to find that proof become more and more extravagant. He is sensitive to the accusations of the world—the jeerer at Tupper's Tavern's accusation that he married Rachel out of desire for her land, Wilkie's insinuations about his private and public laxity—because his commitment necessarily cannot provide him with evidence to meet those accusations. It even deprives him of that sense of self-worth which might bear him silently through these accusations, for it is also the nature of his commitment to turn him against the self as much as to turn him against the world, and it is the need for self-transcendence, not just weakness of character, which accounts for his vulnerability and self-contempt.

The belief that the idea redeems the world cannot stand before the rush of the doubt that one has adopted the idea simply for the sake of convenience and interest. The idea does not redeem the world because the idea never allows one to rest secure in one's claim to the warrant of the idea. This is what Beaumont means when he says, at the moment he decides to murder Fort, that he must renounce the notion that the idea redeems the world, and embrace instead the notion that the world must redeem the idea:

> He had known the world as a trap. He had known that all his life, and he never would have taken its bait had he not taken the sweeter bait of another trap more cunningly concealed, concealed in the "dark run and footway" of his own heart. And that trap was the "idea"—the idea itself and pure.
>
> It was perfectly clear. He had lived so long with the idea that that alone had seemed real. The world had seemed nothing. And because the world had seemed nothing, he had lived in the way of the world, feeling safe because he held the idea, pure, complete, abstract, and self-fulfilling. He had thought that he was redeemed by the idea, that sooner or later the idea would redeem his world.
>
> But now he knew: the world must redeem the idea. He knew now that the idea must take on flesh and fact, not to redeem, but to be redeemed.

Beaumont's desire for inward justification by the idea introduces an instability into the structure of thought about justification which causes it to fall catastrophically upon the heads of all the characters. To justify, the idea must be beyond him, but if the idea is beyond him, he can never know whether it justifies, and, in his doubt, must turn to acts which place justification that much the further out of reach. The act is an act in blindness, for if he could see the purpose it served, he would not need to commit it. He murders Fort not because justice demands it but because that is the only way he can discover whether the compulsion he feels within him is the compulsion of justice. The murder is not an act moved by the delusion of mastery, but a desperate and disillusioned gamble intended to reveal whether mastery was ever in question:

> I had seen before [Beaumont writes] that the idea as but idea had been a vanity, too, and a deceit I practiced, and that it had to be redeemed by the world. But how could the world redeem the idea but by the flesh and way of the natural world? And the world was but the world, and its way crooked and dark. Then I put the last question. If the idea could not wear the dark flesh and could not keep its foot firm in the crooked track, what was it worth, after all? I knew that that was the last hazard, and like the bold gamester I staked all on a card. I would submit the idea to the way of the world.

The intractability of Beaumont's central compulsion is mirrored in the intractability of the novel's central images. Beaumont describes his childhood fascination with an illustration in Foxe's *Book of Martyrs* which depicts, with delicious sadism, a young woman tied cruelly to a post "so that the bonds seemed to crush her sweet flesh and her face lifted up while the flames rose about her." Beaumont's three mutually exclusive but equally compelling responses to this picture prefigure his complex relation with Rachel:

> Sometimes the strange fancy took me that I might seize her from the flame and escape with her from all the people who crowded about for her death. At other times it seemed that I might throw myself into the fire to perish with her for the very joy. And again, my heart leaping suddenly like a fish and my muscles tight as at the moment when you wait to start a race, I saw her standing there bound, with no fire set, and I myself flung the first flaming faggot and could not wait to see her twist and strive against the tight bond in the great heat and toss her head with the hair falling loose to utter a cry for the first agony.

The image of the young woman at the stake, and Beaumont's ambiguous response, recurs early in Beaumont's courtship of Rachel—at the moment of his first proposal of marriage—and it serves to make us uncertain whether the cruelty of Beaumont's courtship, his attempt to force Rachel to confess what happened to her and to demand the murder of Fort, is the cruelty of the physician or the cruelty of the voluptuary. Beaumont himself shares this uncertainty:

> But in my joy at the thought of victory was a kind of sadness at the necessary way, for I could not say to her that I would conquer her country only to love in the end its queen more dearly, as Theseus took the Amazon Hippolyta, and that I would expiate all ravage by becoming not her master but her most devoted slave.

The picture is transfixing not only because it depicts the central action of the story but because it captures the unsolvable problem of that story. The apprehension of the picture—like Hawthorne's apprehension of the Scarlet Letter in "The Custom House"—is an experience of meaningfulness which calls for the development of a narrative in order to examine what that experience meant. But the narrative can only develop further the contradiction already implicit in the static picture, and its purpose is to depict that contradiction, that crux of feeling, as bluntly as possible.

There are two possible ways of reducing the contradiction to order, but both are ruled out. The picture can be described as a classical symbol which, by capturing the paradox within its referent, demonstrates the reconciliation of its opposing terms in a higher unity as, say, love reconciles pleasure and pain in the oxymoron of courtly cliché, or reconciles the spiritual and the animal in the synthesis of sentiment. Or we can argue that the picture attacks the idea it appears at first to depict, and that its effort is to undo the "higher synthesis" of symbolism by showing that what appears to be romantic heroism is only sensual cruelty. But neither the "idealist" view of the picture nor the "disillusioned" view really conveys its force, any more than a "pro-Beaumont" or an "anti-Beaumont" view of *World Enough and Time* conveys the force of the book. For the picture, no less than the book, has the force neither of paradoxical unity nor of ironical deflation; it has the force of a crux which we must, and yet cannot ever, resolve. It is of great importance to us to disentangle what the picture tangles so inextricably, to show Beaumont, for all his perverseness, as the true servant of truth, or to show him as diabolically self-deluded and sadistic. But neither version satisfies, and what we are left with is the act of holding two contradictory propositions in our minds which we can neither decide between nor reconcile. The symbol does not direct the action but tears it apart, and the confusion in which it leaves us, the tormenting doubt which does not quite issue in disillusion, is not very different from Beaumont's own confusion; reading the book intensely is a way of experiencing first-hand the predicament which undoes its main character.

The other controlling images of the novel have the same character. The keelboat which Beaumont describes (in a lyrical passage) drifting west to music, an image which surfaces in his mind whenever he thinks of making a "new start" on the frontier, is upset but not entirely replaced by the fetid keelboat in which he and Rachel make their journey to the western anti-Paradise of the Gran Boz's camp. The cave in which the boy Beaumont loses himself is repeated but not undone by the underground cell in which he is confined in Frankfort. The earlier cave seems to be a sublime revision of Plato's cave, for it is not a place of illusion but of as it were deep truth, more fundamental than the truth of the daylight outside. Standing in the darkness of his cell, which is shortly to become a place of delusion and lust, Beaumont likens it to the cave:

> Then he remembered how, when he was a boy, he had explored some of those sinks and caves that riddled tortuously the soft stone beneath the land of his home section, and how once he had crawled back a long way, through winding, cranky gullets that constricted breath, how he had come to great chambers and stood (he knew their size despite the blackness because when he shouted his voice bounded back from high unseen ceilings and farther walls), how he had felt along the wall, inch by inch, to another aperture, how he had crawled again, deeper, deeper and narrower, and had come at last to a place where he could crawl no

more, it was so close. "So I lay there, and breathed the limey, cool, inward smell of the earth's bowels, which is not like any smell common to the superficies, though in spots dank and unvisited by the sun. It is a smell cleanly and rich, not dead and foul but pregnant with secret life, as though you breathed the dark and the dark were about to pulse. And while I lay there, I thought how I might not be able to return, but would lie there forever, and I saw how my father might at that moment be standing in a field full of sun to call my name wildly and might run to all my common haunts to no avail. I felt a sad pity for him, and for all who ran about thus seeking in the sun and shade. But I felt no terror. It was like a dream of terror with the terror drained away, and the dark was loving kindness."

Perhaps we do not need the cave's undoing in the prison cell, for the language in which the cave itself is described at once conveys the idea and its contradiction. It is not simply that it is at once the hiding place of the vanished Indian gods and Plato's cave of illusions, at once a generous womb and a destructive gullet, at once cathedral and hell, but that the very feeling of exaltation Beaumont savors there, his very lack of terror, is in its way terrible, since it marks his transcendence, his passage beyond or beneath the humanity he pictures in the figure of his desperately worried and pitiable father. This cave is like the cave Warren's characters confront in *The Cave* (which is likewise a place of lonely exaltation and sexual excess); it is even more like the cave of Warren's recent poem "Speleology," in which the elderly narrator remembers how, caving as a youth (a youth of Beaumont's age when he too wandered in caves), he lay in the deep pulsating dark and felt the same delicious and deadly self-transcendence Beaumont describes. Like all ultimate truths in Warren, the truth of the cave is mortal, but what is more chilling than its mortal cost is the fact that it transforms what it kills into something drained of the human, something horrifyingly beyond the human.

The weird calm of the endangered caver—both in *World Enough and Time* and in "Speleology"—is perhaps related to the weird calm of Wordsworth's description, in the "Intimations" ode, of the grave as

> A lonely bed
> Without the sense or sight
> Of day or the warm light,
> A place of thought where we in waiting lie.

Wordsworth presented this description without irony, but Coleridge clearly perceived its horrifying quality. Wordsworth's grave, like Warren's cave, has the preternatural stillness of the presence of the inhuman ideal, the "Fallings from us, vanishings," the "Blank misgivings of a Creature/

Moving about in worlds not realized" which do not show us any fact, even the transcendental fact of spiritual immortality, but which detach us from facts and leave us lost in what Wordsworth (in his famous note to the ode) called "the abyss of idealism."

Wordsworth's attitude to such moments is dual: he may seek them in the ode, but he fears them in the notes, where he describes himself reaching for walls or trees (or—as in the last few lines of "Tintern Abbey"—for other people) to "recall himself to reality." So in the passage on Mont Blanc in Book VI of *The Prelude* Wordsworth moves from the physical presence of the mountain, which does not answer his imaginative expectations, to the blank shock of the pure imagination itself, to the tamer and more humane physical landscape of the pastoral lowlands, a landscape which "reconciled us to realities." To stand unreconciled to realities, in the blank misgivings and vanishings which swamp the mind whether it lie in grave or cave, is a highly dangerous if highly thrilling act, for it is hard to tell whether that thrill is the thrill of a positive transcendence or of a perfect and terrible alienation.

Wordsworth's act of grasping a tree to recall himself from the abyss of idealism is also, no less than his quiet in the grave, repeated by Jeremiah Beaumont, who, as a child on the verge of a religious ecstasy, walked out into a glittering frozen landscape (a landscape like that Warren describes in "Time as Hypnosis") and, touching an icicle on a beech tree, felt his own strength

> pass through my fingers into the very tree. I seemed to become the tree, and knew how it was to be rooted in the deep dark of earth and bear with my boughs the weight of glittering ice like joy. Then my substance seemed to pass beyond the tree and into all the land around that spread in the sunlight, and into the sunlight itself.

The moment is the opposite of the Wordsworthian moment—Wordsworth touches the tree to cure himself of the very visions Beaumont triggers by the same act. But even Wordsworth's attempt to break the power of the ideal is a way of confirming that power—most people don't have to grasp trees in order to reassure themselves of their own reality—and it is hard to know whether the act is more cure or symptom. Warren reads the Wordsworthian moment in both ways in his recent poem "Rather Like a Dream," in which the act of touching a tree—and he specifically refers to Wordsworth's act—confirms the dark and self-swamping idealism it is intended to reject. The same act is repeated later, and more ominously, in *World Enough and Time* itself. As the childhood cave, "pregnant with secret life" repeats itself in the prison cell where Jeremiah and Rachel indulge in all manner of sexual excess, so the childhood tree repeats itself in Beaumont's thoughts immediately before he stabs Fort. Standing in the lilacs under Fort's window, he has

> the fancy that he was growing into the ground, was setting root like the plants of the thicket, was one of them groping deeper and deeper into the cold, damp earth with the fingers of root and tentacles of hair.

The memory of the early fancy, how he had felt "his being flow into the shining tree" and "down the trunk into the secret earth" confirms him in the crime he is preparing to commit; it seems "to verify him, to say that all his past was one thing, and not rags and patches, and that all had moved to this moment." Once again, we cannot tell whether to give greater credence to the original image or to its dark repetition.

A fourth repeated figure which is compromised but not replaced by its opposite is that of the ideal woman. We have seen the duality which troubles this figure already partly embodied in the picture of the female martyr Beaumont alternately wishes to save and to burn. On one hand, she is Plato's Diotima, whom Beaumont first reads about early in his courtship of Rachel when, having surprised her in her arbor reading the *Symposium*, he takes the book from her hand and reads what she had been reading

> I began to read [he says] in the middle of a sentence at the top of the left-hand page, and I read of love, and how a man of high soul may use the beauties of earth as a ladder by which he mounts for the sake of higher beauties, resting at last in the single Idea of the absolute Beauty in that life which above all others a man should live to be fully man, the contemplation of the Beauty Absolute.

On the other hand she is the half-breed with whom, stirred into ecstasy by Corinthian McClardy's preaching, Beaumont copulates in the woods. The point is not simply that the woman has two forms, nor even that those forms are ultimately identified with each other, as the birth-marked Rachel eventually grows to resemble her half-breed opposite. The point is that the exaltation with which Beaumont would follow Diotima and the exaltation which leads him into the arms of the half-breed are impossible to distinguish. And it is because Beaumont is all too aware of this that his courtship takes on an edge at once of desperation and cruelty, so that, having suddenly had a vision of Fort and Rachel in a carnal embrace, he proceeds to torture her (by reading from Fort's copy of Byron) into making the ideal demand upon him he so hungers for.

Immediately after Rachel announces her pregnancy, Beaumont has a dream. Rachel's pregnancy has placed Beaumont in a difficult position.

On one hand, it allows him to avoid running, as Wilkie and Madison have been urging him to do, for the legislature, and it allows him to put off his revenge upon Fort. On the other hand, these very effects seem to him to be the ends for which the pregnancy is all too conveniently designed, and he cannot answer the accusation he brings against himself that he uses the pretext of Rachel's pregnancy to evade his duty. Rachel, opposed to his entering into the political career which she feels will take him away from her, and also opposed to his plans to murder Fort, has accused her husband of having forced her to hate Fort, and her accusation sharpens Beaumont's predicament still further. Beaumont cannot decide whether to see this accusation as a sign that he is indeed the victim of self-delusion, or as a sign that Rachel has in some deep way betrayed both herself and him, leaving him alone to answer the claims of the ideal. That evening, Beaumont has a dream which reveals the deep connection between the transfixing ideal and the sexuality it appears to spurn:

> He dreamed that he stood at the edge of a big woods, a forest, toward night, and the forest was full of shadow. It was fall or winter, for the trees were nearly bare. He seemed to recognize the place as some place he had seen in the West. . . .
>
> Then he saw the form on the ground before him. He saw it with no surprise because at the moment of perception he knew that he had already known it there. It was a strong man's form, naked, lying on the back, and bleeding from a wound in the chest. He could not make out the face, no matter how hard he tried, but he knew that it was the face of Cassius Fort. He knew that if he could only make out the face, he would feel the great joy that all had been done for, but when he looked, there was only a patch of grayness that swam in his sight and made him think of the gray growth on the eyes of the blind and made him fear that it was coming on his own. So he would look quickly away to be confirmed in his vision.
>
> Looking up thus, he saw Rachel, more beautiful than in life. She was kneeling on the ground, beyond the head of the bleeding form, and was staring at him with horror and reproach. He was compelled to speak to her, to justify himself, and tell her that now they could be happy. But the words would not come, though he thought he would strangle with the effort of speech.
>
> Then, as he looked, he saw that her face was changing. The brown spot on her cheek was enormous and each instant was larger and more devouring. It was Rachel's face and was not Rachel's face. It was Rachel's face but was also the face of the old woman, her mother, peering at him, spying from the shadows. Then it was all discolored, but still Rachel's face and the mother's face but was another face as well, and he knew its name, but like the names of the trees it would not come to him.

Then she lifted her hands to her face, where the horror was increased by the fact that he saw Rachel's white bosom beneath. She said, staring above her hands, to him, "Look, what you have done to me."

One might think that had Beaumont sufficiently examined his dream he might have behaved differently. But in fact, it is because Beaumont has understood from the beginning the cruelty of his idealization of Rachel that he does what he does. It is the rebuke of the dream which stings him, in his effort to escape the truth he already knows too well, into behaving in the way which makes the dream's realization inevitable. Having had this dream, in other words, makes him vulnerable to the insinuations of Wilkie Barron, who visits the next morning and convinces Beaumont, by playing on his self-contempt, to run for the legislature, setting in motion the chain of events which brings about the deaths of Fort, of Rachel, and of Beaumont himself.

What Beaumont's story reveals is what the major images of the book reveal; they reveal how those best instincts which make one worthy to have been one's self lead inevitably into self-repeal and self-destruction. We must distinguish, however, between self-repeal and disillusionment, for the latter refers to the consequences of some original error, but what concerns us in this novel is not some mistake of Beaumont's but the deadly ironies into which his truths lead him. In other words, what the novel demonstrates is not the wrongheadedness of the romance temper which governs the main character and shapes the novel, but the inevitability with which romance undoes itself, not the delusion which we erect in place of value, but how value itself, if we take it seriously, inevitably reduces itself to delusion.

World Enough and Time's concern is with the fatality of romance, how that freedom, that claim to inward justification which is the central fact about romance, subjects those who make it to bondage, repetition, and self-emptying. When in Warren's earlier novels the romance temper emerged out of the work's realistic or naturalistic structure, it demonstrated the possibility of an inward integrity available to the characters (even if it was fully grasped only by Jack Burden). Out of the confined story of interest and corruption emerged a larger story in which characters earn themselves a right to honor. But in *World Enough and Time* that very honor casts us back into the discrediting world.

World Enough and Time, no less than *All the King's Men*, is shaped by something which the principal character does not recognize until the end. But where Jack discovers that his world is governed after all by principle, and that every act connects every part of that world through a chain of consequences of scarcely imaginable complexity, Beaumont discovers only that he has been self-deluded, and, worse, the tool of political manipulators. Some divinity, although perhaps a gnostic one, shapes Jack Burden's ends. But Jeremiah Beaumont's ends are shaped by Wilkie Barron, who forged the handbill from Fort accusing Rachel of miscegnation and caused that miscarriage which triggered Beaumont's assassination of Fort. If Burden discovers himself to be a part of a world larger than the one he had imagined, Beaumont discovers himself a part of a world infinitely smaller than that in which he thought he had lived.

If ultimately we put Beaumont not in the company of Faust or Ahab but instead in the company of John Marcher and Pierre Glendinning, it is not because he is merely a fool or an egotist. For Beaumont's crime is Jack Burden's lesson—the latter gains a self, but the former discovers that self to be the source of wrong. If the self is—as Beaumont says on the last page of the confession he is bringing back to Frankfort with him when he is murdered by Wilkie's agents (a confession preserved, perhaps out of that unrecognized self-doubt which leads to his final suicide, by Wilkie himself) —the deepest crime, it is a crime in which the good have as large a share as the bad. It is perhaps that crime, and not some mythology about how crimes are reckoned to the account of the descendents of the criminal, which accounts for the universality of Original Sin, for the crime of self is the one crime which one cannot avoid committing, and it is also a crime which compromises every later attempt at righteous behavior.

Despite those compromises, we cannot wholly damn Beaumont even where he is most wrong. If Beaumont does recover his dignity at the last moment, and it is hard to read his last words without thinking so, he does so chiefly because he abandons the effort to vindicate himself, that effort which has confirmed him in wrong again and again. He has learned the terrible logic of life, and he has also learned that he cannot have redemption. As he returns to Frankfort to suffer and to lay down his life, his hope is that that knowledge is a kind of redemption, that all the lies, his own among them, "will at last speak together is a great chorus of truth in many voices." It is only a pious hope, but it is no inconsiderable hope at that. We cannot answer his final anguished question—was all for naught?—and the author, by repeating it in his own voice, makes it his own question as much as Beaumont's. But it must have been for something, even if it is in the nature of things that we cannot say for what.

Chronology

1905	Born April 24 in Guthrie, Kentucky, to Robert Franklin Warren, a banker, and Anna Ruth Penn Warren, a schoolteacher.
1920	Accidentally blinded in one eye by stone thrown by his brother.
1921–25	Attends Vanderbilt University, where he studies poetry under John Crowe Ransom and Donald Davidson. Publishes poems in college magazines. Graduates *summa cum laude*.
1925–27	Does graduate work in English at the University of California, Berkeley, where he receives M.A.
1927–28	Does graduate work at Yale University.
1928–30	Attends Oxford on a Rhodes Scholarship. While there, publishes first book, *John Brown: The Making of a Martyr*. Receives B.Litt. from Oxford. Marries Emma Brescia.
1930–34	Begins academic profession—holds appointments at various southern universities. Publishes first fiction, and writes two novels which are rejected by publishers.
1935	*Thirty-Six Poems*. Founds journal *Southern Review* with Cleanth Brooks, Charles W. Pipkin and Albert Erskine.
1936	Receives Houghton Mifflin Literary Fellowship Award. Edits first of many books with Cleanth Brooks, *An Approach to Literature* (also edited by John T. Purser).
1939	*Night Rider*. Travels to Italy on first Guggenheim Fellowship. Writes unpublished verse play, "Proud Flesh," whose hero is prototype of Willie Stark of *All the King's Men*.
1942	Becomes Professor of English at the University of Minnesota. *Eleven Poems on the Same Theme*.
1943	*At Heaven's Gate*.
1944	*Selected Poems: 1923–1943*.
1946	*All the King's Men*, which receives both the Pulitzer Prize and the National Book Award.
1947	*The Circus in the Attic, and Other Stories*.
1950	*World Enough and Time: A Romantic Novel*. Divorced from Emma Brescia.

1952   Marries author Eleanor Clark, by whom he has two children, Rosanna and Gabriel.

1953   *Brother to Dragons: A Tale in Verse and Voices.*

1955   *Band of Angels.* Father dies.

1956   *Segregation: The Inner Conflict in the South.*

1957   *Promises: Poems 1954–1956,* which also receives both the Pulitzer Prize and the National Book Award, as well as the Edna St. Vincent Millay Prize of the Poetry Society of America.

1958   *Selected Essays.*

1959   *The Cave.*

1960   *You, Emperors and Others: Poems 1957–1960.*

1961   *Wilderness: A Tale of the Civil War* and *The Legacy of the Civil War: Meditations on the Centennial.* Appointed Professor of English at Yale University.

1964   *Flood: A Romance of Our Time.*

1966   *Selected Poems: New and Old 1923–1966,* which is awarded Bollingen Prize in poetry from Yale University.

1968   *Incarnations: Poems 1966–1968.*

1969   *Audubon: A Vision,* which receives both the Van Wyck Brooks Award and the National Medal for Literature in 1970.

1974   *Or Else: Poem/Poems 1968–1974.* Delivers third Annual Jefferson Lecture in the Humanities for the National Endowment for the Humanities.

1975   Receives the Emerson-Thoreau Award of the American Academy of Arts and Sciences.

1977   *A Place to Come To.*

1978   *Now and Then: Poems 1976–1978,* which receives the Pulitzer Prize.

1979   Revision of *Brother to Dragons: A Tale in Verse and Voices.*

1980   *Being Here: Poetry 1977–1980.* Awarded the Presidential Medal of Freedom.

1983   *Chief Joseph of the Nez Perce.*

1985   *New and Selected Poems: 1923–1985.*

Contributors

HAROLD BLOOM, Sterling Professor of the Humanities at Yale University, is the author of *The Anxiety of Influence, Poetry and Repression*, and many other volumes of literary criticism. His forthcoming study, *Freud: Transference and Authority*, attempts a full-scale reading of all of Freud's major writings. He is the general editor of *The Chelsea House Library of Literary Criticism*.

W. M. FROHOCK, Professor Emeritus of Romance Languages at Harvard University, is the author of the novel, *Of Violence in America*.

CLEANTH BROOKS, Gray Professor Emeritus of Rhetoric at Yale University, is the author of *The Well-Wrought Urn, Modern Poetry and the Tradition, The Hidden God*, and three critical studies of William Faulkner.

JOSEPH FRANK, Professor of Comparative Literature at Princeton University, is the author of *The Widening Gyre*, and of the definitive biography of Dostoevsky.

JONATHAN BAUMBACH teaches in the English Department of Brooklyn College and is the author of *The Landscape of Nightmare* and several works of short fiction.

ARTHUR MIZENER, Professor Emeritus of English at Cornell University, is the author of biographical studies of F. Scott Fitzgerald and Ford Madox Ford.

WALTER SULLIVAN, Professor of English at Vanderbilt University, is the author of *Black Holes, Death by Melancholy: Essays on Modern Southern Fiction* and *Landprints: On the Magnificent American Landscape*.

ALLEN SHEPHERD is Professor of English at the University of Vermont.

DANIEL AARON, Professor Emeritus of American Literature at Harvard University, is the author of *Writers on the Left, Men of Good Hope*, and *The Unwritten War: American Writers and the Civil War*.

RICHARD HOWARD, poet and translator, is the author of *Alone with America*, a study of contemporary American poetry. His own poetry includes *Untitled Subjects* and *Findings*.

RICHARD LAW, Associate Professor of English at Washington State University, has published articles on Robert Penn Warren in *American Literature, The Southern Literary Journal* and *Studies in American Fiction*.

DAVID WYATT teaches English at the University of Virginia and is the author of *Prodigal Sons*.

T. R. HUMMER is a Professor of English at Oklahoma State University and is the author of *The Angelic Orders: Poems* and *The Passion of the Right Angled Man*.

CALVIN BEDIENT has written critical studies of Warren's poetry and of contemporary British poetry.

PAUL MARIANI is Professor of English at the University of Massachusetts, Amherst. His books include a biography of William Carlos Williams, a commentary on Gerard Manley Hopkins and two volumes of poetry: *Timing Devices: Poems* and *Crossing Cocytus: Poems*.

JOHN BURT is Assistant Professor of English at Brandeis University. His forthcoming books include critical studies of Warren, and of the romance genre in America.

Bibliography

Bedient, Calvin. "Greatness and Robert Penn Warren." *Sewanee Review* 3, vol. 89 (1981): 332–46.

——. *In The Heart's Last Kingdom*. Cambridge, Mass.: Harvard University Press, 1984.

Beebe, Maurice, and Field, L. A., eds. *Robert Penn Warren's "All the King's Men": A Critical Handbook*. Belmont, Cal.: Wadsworth Publishing Co., Inc., 1966.

Beiner, Robert. "The Required Past: *World Enough and Time*." *Modern Fiction Studies* 6 (1960): 55–64.

Bohner, Charles H. *Robert Penn Warren*. New York: Twayne Publishers, Inc., 1964.

Callander, Marilyn Berg. "Robert Penn Warren's *Chief Joseph of the Nez Perce*: A Story of Deep Delight." *The Southern Literary Journal* 2, vol. 16 (1982): 24–33.

Chambers, Robert H., ed. *Twentieth Century Interpretations of "All the King's Men": A Collection of Critical Essays*. Englewood Cliffs, N.J.: Prentice-Hall, Inc., 1977.

Clements, A. L. "Theme and Reality in 'At Heaven's Gate' and 'All the King's Men'." *Criticism* 1, vol. 5 (1963): 27–44.

Core, George. "In the Heart's Ambiguity: Robert Penn Warren as Poet." *The Mississippi Quarterly: The Journal of Southern Culture* 22 (1969): 313–26.

Davison, Richard Allan. "Robert Penn Warren's 'Dialectical Configuration' and *The Cave*." *CLA Journal* 4, vol. 10 (1967): 349–57.

Edgar, Walter B., ed. *A Southern Renascence Man: Views of Robert Penn Warren*. Baton Rouge and London: Louisiana State University Press, 1984.

Fiedler, Leslie A. "Three Notes of Robert Penn Warren," In *No! In Thunder: Essays on Myth and Literature*. Boston: Beacon Press, 1960.

Gray, Richard. *The Literature of Memory*. Baltimore: The Johns Hopkins University Press, 1977.

——. *Robert Penn Warren: A Collection of Critical Essays*. Englewood Cliffs, N.J.: Prentice-Hall, Inc., 1980.

Grimshaw, James A., Jr. *Robert Penn Warren: A Descriptive Bibliography 1917–1978* Charlottesville: University Press of Virginia, 1982.

——. "Robert Penn Warren's *Annus Mirabilis*." *The Southern Review* 2, vol. 10 (new series) (1974): 504–16.

——, ed. *Robert Penn Warren's "Brother to Dragons": A Discussion*. Baton Rouge and London: Louisiana State University Press, 1983.

Guttenberg, Barnett. *Web of Being*. Nashville: Vanderbilt University Press, 1975.

Justus, James H. *The Achievement of Robert Penn Warren*. Baton Rouge and London: Louisiana State University Press, 1981.

Kaplan, Charles. "Jack Burden: Modern Ishmael." *College English* 1, vol. 22 (1960): 19–24.

King, Richard H. *A Southern Renascence: The Cultural Awakening of the American South, 1930–1955*. New York and Oxford: Oxford University Press, 1980.

Law, Richard G. "*Brother to Dragons*: The Fact of Violence vs. The Possibility of Love." *American Literature* 4, vol. 49 (1978): 560–79.

Lieberman, Laurence. "The Glacier's Offspring: A Reading of Robert Penn Warren's New Poetry." *The American Poetry Review* 2, vol. 10 (1981): 6–8.

Longley, John L., Jr. *Robert Penn Warren*. Austin, Texas: Steck-Vaughn Co., 1969.

———, ed. *Robert Penn Warren: A Collection of Critical Essays*. New York: New York University Press, 1965.

Moore, John Rees. "Robert Penn Warren: You Must Go Home Again." *The Southern Review* 2, vol. 4 (new series) (1968): 320–32.

Moore, L. Hugh, Jr. *Robert Penn Warren and History: The "Big Myth We Live."* The Hague: Mouton and Co., 1970.

Rotella, Guy, "Evil, Goodness and Grace in Warren's *Audubon: A Vision*." *Notre Dame English Journal* 11 (1978): 15–32.

———. " 'One Flesh': Robert Penn Warren's *Incarnations*." *Renascence* 1, vol. 31 (1978): 25–42.

Shepherd, Allen. "Robert Penn Warren as a Philosophical Novelist." *The Western Humanities Review* 2, vol. 24 (1970): 157–68.

Snipes, Katherine. *Robert Penn Warren*. New York: Frederick Ungar Publishing Co., 1983.

Spiegelman, Willard. "The Poetic Achievement of Robert Penn Warren." *Southwest Review* 4, vol. 62 (1977): vi–vii, 411–15.

Strandberg, Victor. *The Poetic Vision of Robert Penn Warren*. Lexington: The University Press of Kentucky, 1977.

Tjanos, William. "The Poetry of Robert Penn Warren: The Art to Transfigure." *The Southern Literary Journal* 1, vol. 9 (1976): 3–12.

Walker, Marshall. *Robert Penn Warren: A Vision Earned*. Glasgow: Robert MacLehose and Co., Ltd., 1979. (In the U.S.: Barnes and Noble Import Division of Harper and Row).

Wilcox, Earl J. " 'A Cause for Laughter, A Thing for Tears': Humor in *All the King's Men*." *The Southern Literary Journal* 1, vol. 12 (1979): 27–35.

Acknowledgments

"Mr. Warren's Albatross" by W. M. Frohock from *The Novel of Violence in America* by W. M. Frohock, copyright © 1950, 1957 by W. M. Frohock. Reprinted by permission.

"R. P. Warren: Experience Redeemed in Knowledge" by Cleanth Brooks from *The Hidden God: Studies in Hemingway, Faulkner, Yeats, Eliot and Warren* by Cleanth Brooks, copyright © 1963 by Yale University Press. Reprinted by permission.

"Romanticism and Reality in Robert Penn Warren" by Joseph Frank from *The Widening Gyre* by Joseph Frank, copyright © 1963 by Rutgers University Press. Reprinted by permission.

"The Metaphysics of Demagoguery: *All the King's Men*" by Jonathan Baumbach from *The Landscape of Nightmare* by Jonathan Baumbach, copyright © 1965 by New York University Press. Reprinted by permission.

"Robert Penn Warren: *All the King's Men*" by Arthur Mizener from *The Southern Review* 3, (1967), copyright © 1967 by *The Southern Review*. Reprinted by permission.

"The Historical Novelist and the Existential Peril: Robert Penn Warren's *Band of Angels*" by Walter Sullivan from *The Southern Literary Journal* 2, vol. 2 (Spring 1970), copyright © 1970 by the Department of English, University of North Carolina, Chapel Hill. Reprinted by permission.

"The Poles of Fiction: Warren's *At Heaven's Gate*" by Allen Shepherd from *Texas Studies in Literature and Language* 4, vol. 12 (Winter 1971), copyright © 1971 by University of Texas Press. Reprinted by permission.

"The Meditations of Robert Penn Warren" by Daniel Aaron from *The Unwritten War: American Writers and the Civil War* by Daniel Aaron, copyright © 1973 by Daniel Aaron. Reprinted by permission.

"Dreadful Alternatives: A Note on Robert Penn Warren" by Richard Howard from *Georgia Review* 1, vol. 29 (Spring 1975), copyright © 1975 by University of Georgia. Reprinted by permission.

"Warren's *Night Rider* and the Issue of Naturalism: The 'Nightmare' of Our Age" by Richard Law from *The Southern Literary Journal* 2, vol. 8 (Spring 1976), copyright © 1976 by the Department of English, University of North Carolina, Chapel Hill. Reprinted by permission.

"*Brother to Dragons*" by Harold Bloom from *The New Republic* (September 1 & 8, 1979), copyright © 1979 by *The New Republic*. Reprinted by permission.

"The Critic as Artist" by David Wyatt from *Prodigal Sons: A Study in Authorship and Authority* by David Wyatt, copyright © 1980 by Johns Hopkins University Press. Reprinted by permission.

"*Audubon* and the Moral Center" by T. R. Hummer from *The Southern Review* 4, vol. 16 (October 1980), copyright © 1980 by Louisiana State University. Reprinted by permission.

" 'Truth's Glare-Glory' " by Calvin Bedient from *In the Heart's Last Kingdom* by Calvin Bedient, copyright © 1984 by the President and Fellows of Harvard College. Reprinted by permission.

"Sunset Hawk: Warren's Poetry and Tradition" by Harold Bloom from *A Southern Renascence Man: Views of Robert Penn Warren* edited by W. B. Edgar, copyright © 1984 by Louisiana State University Press. Reprinted by permission.

"Robert Penn Warren" by Paul Mariani from *A Usable Past: Essays on Modern and Contemporary Poetry* by Paul Mariani, copyright © 1984 by University of Massachusetts Press. Reprinted by permission.

"The Self-Subversion of Value in Warren's *World Enough and Time*" by John Burt. First published in this volume. Copyright © 1985 by John Burt.

Index